Ecological Education in Action

Ecological Education in Action

On Weaving Education, Culture, and the Environment

edited by
Gregory A. Smith
and Dilafruz R. Williams

STATE UNIVERSITY OF NEW YORK PRESS

Figure 1.1, p.26 is reproduced with permission of Food Works, Montpelier, Vermont

Published by
State University of New York Press

Printed in the United States of America

For information, address the State University of New York Press, State University Plaza, Albany, NY 12246

Marketing by Nancy Farrell
Production by Bernadine Dawes

Library of Congress Cataloging-in-Publication Data

Ecological education in action : on weaving education, culture, and the environment / edited by Gregory A. Smith and Dilafruz R. Williams.

p. cm.

Includes bibliographical references and index.

ISBN 0-7914-3985-2 (alk. paper. — ISBN 0-7914-3986-0 (pbk. : alk. paper)

1. Environmental education. 2. Environmental sciences—Study and teaching. I. Smith, Gregory A., 1948– . II. Williams Dilafruz R., 1949– .

GE70.E26 1999

363.7'0071—dc21 98-7525

CIP

1 2 3 4 5 6 7 8 9 10

CONTENTS

PART II: HIGHER EDUCATION AND NONFORMAL SETTINGS

ACKNOWLEDGMENTS

This book emerged from the interactions and discussions we had with each other about ways in which we were "greening" our curriculum and pedagogy in higher education and the responses we were getting from our students. Through these conversations both of us gained strength from each other to continue to bring ecology to the forefront of our mainstream educational courses. We invited students to give us feedback on the impact our courses were having on their own professional and personal lives. We are immensely grateful to those countless students who have taken the issues of environment to the practice of possibility. We are also thankful to our author-colleagues and community members and practitioners mentioned in this book from whom we continue to gain inspiration.

Special thanks go to James Wallace for his editorial assistance; his detailed scrutiny required us to work with the authors in this book for accuracy. His sense of humor kept us going even as we wrote and rewrote the manuscript. To Nel Noddings and Denis Phillips a special thank you from Williams for the offer of a visiting scholar's position at Stanford University during her sabbatical leave. And, to the State University of New York Press's Priscilla Ross and Jennie Doling, we are grateful for encouragement and prompt responses.

And, finally, we want to thank our families: Becky, for her kind patience; and our children—Eliot, Ethan, James, and Paul—in whose innocence, energy, and enthusiasm, we find a renewed sense of hope.

Introduction

Re-engaging Culture and Ecology

Gregory A. Smith and Dilafruz R. Williams

Much of the conventional writing about the environment in newspapers, magazines, popular books, and scholarly publications centers on information related to environmental problems that affect our lives in one form or another. A review of two weeks of Portland's daily paper, *The Oregonian,* in April 1997, revealed sixty-nine stories about environmental topics ranging from the outbreak of pfisteria in South Carolina to controversies over protective measures aimed at restoring coho salmon and bull trout in the Pacific Northwest, to the difficulties PCBs now pose for the cleanup of nuclear wastes at the closed Hanford Nuclear Reactor facilities. In raising awareness of these issues, such information can evoke cynicism and fear that prevent people from addressing the very problems that are described. We deliberately take a different approach in this book.

We encourage readers to challenge taken-for-granted cultural assumptions about our relationship with nature, and to take action toward crafting an ecologically sustainable form of living through education. Action is seldom possible in isolation. This book is about the efforts of people who have broken the spell of stasis and are taking steps to shape a culture that is more responsive to the needs of human beings and the requirements of natural systems. When we refer to "culture" in this way, we are not suggesting a single set of responses that must be identically adopted by all people; such a culture may well be multifaceted in its manifestations.

At its heart, sustainability is about the relationship between human beings and the world; it is about morality. Indian physicist and ecofeminist Vandana Shiva explains that the term "sustainability" is derived from "sustain" which means "to support, bear weight of, hold up, enable to last out, give strength to, endure without giving way" (Shiva 1992, 191). Sustaining economies, such as those encountered in many nonindustrialized societies, recognize natural limits and derive an understanding of sustenance directly from nature. Edward Goldsmith

(1992), editor of *The Ecologist,* calls for a turn away from the practices of industrial growth societies to a culture premised on the sustenance of healthy natural systems. For Goldsmith and a growing number of international commentators and activists, the creation of such a culture must involve a recognition that the welfare of human societies is contingent on our ability to conform to ecological principles that appear to govern activities of nonhuman communities. Wes Jackson (1994), a soil scientist who has spent the past two decades developing a "natural systems agriculture," argues that this will happen only when we consult with nature rather than imposing our will upon her.

Wendell Berry (1990), in his book *What Are People For?* calls into question the way human energies in recent history have been bent to the purposes of an extractive economy determined to dominate nature and increase the material wealth and security of our own species. Berry suggests that human welfare and meaning are located not in the values of the marketplace but in the relationships that can emerge among people and landscapes where care and continuity rather than commercial success are the central aims. The economic and social implications of such a shift in human purposes are far reaching, linked as they are to the restoration of noncommercial virtues such as restraint, thrift, and generosity. The maintenance of relationships also requires a reevaluation of the preoccupation with individual choice and possibility that has become a dominant theme in modern societies. Rather than seeing individual identity as embedded in communal contexts, many people in industrial growth societies have sought to liberate themselves from such ties. We recognize that individuals must be granted the opportunity to criticize oppressive relations and the freedom to leave community, but we also believe that if people were to seek security and satisfaction through collective effort instead of individual striving, we might have less need to turn to the market and the attractions of consumerism. By choosing such a course, we could create ways of living that minimize humanity's impact on other species and the nonanimate world while at the same time providing for our own material and spiritual welfare. One way of seeing this issue, writes Shiva (1992), is to turn to the wisdom of a Native American elder: "Only when you have felled the last tree, caught the last fish, and polluted the last river, will you realize that you can't eat money." Both as debtors and as beneficiaries, we need to craft an ethic that reengages culture and ecology by challenging the *status quo* of Western notions of progress and promoting genuine multiculturalism.

Except in small measure, the field of environmental education has not as yet embraced such concerns. Marginalized when offered, classes in environmental education focus on scientific analysis and social policy—not cultural change. They approach issues related to the degradation of the environment as problems capable of being solved through the collection of better data, the framing of regulatory legislation, or the development of institutional procedures aimed at reducing waste. Children are exposed to information regarding environmental problems and explore such topics as endangered species, the logging of tropical rainforests, or the monitoring of water quality in local streams and rivers. Some adopt manatees or whales, or raise funds to purchase a small piece of forest in Costa Rica or Brazil. Others create school-wide recycling programs to encourage their classmates to become more thoughtful about resource use. A few move into the legislative domain and participate in writing legislation to regulate the disposal of toxic wastes (Lewis 1991). These efforts are without question commendable in that they develop awareness for and an understanding of real-life environmental issues (Elliott 1991; OECD 1991; OECD 1995). Missing in most of these efforts, however, is a recognition of the deeper cultural transformations that must accompany the shift to more ecologically sustainable ways of life.

We have chosen to entitle this book *Ecological Education in Action: On Weaving Education, Culture, and the Environment* in an effort to distinguish the efforts described here from more common forms of environmental education. For us, ecological education connotes an emphasis on the inescapable embeddedness of human beings in natural systems. Rather than seeing nature as other—a set of phenomena capable of being manipulated like parts of a machine—the practice of ecological education requires viewing human beings as one part of the natural world and human cultures as an outgrowth of interactions between our species and particular places. From this standpoint, arguments over a human-centered or an earth-centered orientation toward the environment miss the point. There is no way to disentangle human beings from the earth, and as long as our species exists, no way to separate the earth from humans. Kat Anderson and Gary Nabhan's (1996) investigation of the relationship between people and local ecosystems in North America points to the degree to which the apparent wilderness of this continent had been shaped by human intentions prior to the arrival of European settlers.

The reverse of this process is also true; human cultures have arisen in response to the demands and opportunities of particular ecosystems. Technologies associated with the construction of dwellings; hunting, gathering, and agricultural practices; cooking; clothing; and defense are all closely tied into the resources available in specific places

(Kroeber 1939). Behind the extraordinary variability of human cultures is this adaptive principle. Stories, religious and moral systems, and even language are intimately connected to place, as well (Basso 1990). We are place-based creatures as much as the animals Darwin encountered on the Galapagos Islands, but instead of producing distinctive plumage or beaks or extravagant flowers, we have created different forms of cultural interaction appropriate for varying biotic communities and natural conditions.

What environmental education has tended to forget and ecological education attempts to remember is this ineluctable relationship between specific biosystems and cultures, and that cultures that have demonstrated their sustainability have often developed highly specific practices well suited to the characteristics of their particular region. One of the central problems with the culture associated with industrial growth societies is its lack of relationship to particular places and the way it is being imposed on the rest of the world from industrial and postindustrial centers. Helena Norberg-Hodge has described what happens when a finely tuned indigenous culture is disrupted by the process of modernization. Her exposition provides a useful example of issues that need to be placed in the foreground if students are to comprehend the relationship between human behaviors and beliefs and the health of the natural systems in which we live.

In her book, *Ancient Futures: Learning from Ladakh* (1991), Norberg-Hodge describes a Himalayan culture she initially encountered in the 1970s. People in Ladakh during this time continued to live much as they had during earlier centuries. They grew crops well suited to the short and dry growing season of the Tibetan plateau, constructed their own substantial and comfortable clay-brick homes, maintained irrigation systems built by their ancestors, governed their own affairs primarily through small village councils, and supported Buddhist monasteries whose religious ceremonies were closely linked to the lives and values of the lay community. Extended families and neighbors provided the forms of mutual support and care so often encountered in premodern societies where security is synonymous with the maintenance of human relationships and patterns of obligation. Children were educated through their constant observation of and participation in adult life. Struck by the material security and contentment of the residents of Ladakh, Norberg-Hodge asked a young man if there were any poor people in a village she was studying at the time. The man replied, "No, there are no poor people here."

The advent of a paved road to the south, modern consumer goods, tourists, and government-subsidized food has begun to end all that.

Eight years later, she overheard the same man beseeching a group of Westerners to "help us poor Ladakhis." During this time, one set of expectations about the appropriate ends of human life had been replaced by another. And with this change has come a change in the relationship of Ladakhis to their land and to one another. Traditional agricultural practices that had been sustained for generations are being replaced with the use of fertilizers and machines. As young men and women, attracted to the amenities and baubles of consumer society, seek wage-paying jobs in the region's capital city Leh, extended families are giving way to nuclear families. The resource of shared and nonmonetized labor—both within the family and the neighborhood—has become a rarity as children are drawn to school and adults are absorbed by the market economy. More and more people now live in cramped apartments rather than in commodious homes. A landscape that had featured pure air and water has been fouled with exhaust from internal-combustion engines, sewage, and litter. Most important, individuals are now expected to provide for their own support rather than relying on the support of their communities. Within a generation, the definition of security and satisfaction formerly shared by the residents of Ladakh and the social and environmental practices that had once contributed to the ecological sustainability of Ladakhi culture, have been fundamentally altered.

The microcosm of Ladakh demonstrates in miniature the global phenomena that lie at the heart of the environmental crisis. Moving away from this crisis will require a fundamental transformation of the way we perceive the world and one another as well as the nature of our membership in both the human community and the community of all beings. Such a transformation is not likely to occur as a result of taking courses in environmental studies that are primarily driven by conventional academic concerns. As educators, we need to teach in a manner that aims to transform the way our students interact with the world and one another. As the children of Ladakh have been inducted into a process of formal education aimed at replacing a vision of the world premised on local relationships and knowledge with one that celebrates participation in a global economy, we need to find ways to induct our own children into an educational process that reaffirms what is being lost in Ladakh. This is not to say that we should uncritically seek to restore the lifeways of more egalitarian, local, small-scale land-based societies. What may be required of us, however, is a careful reexamination rather than discounting of lessons learned by our ancestors over the millennia about the forms of human interaction with the natural world that are likely to enable our communities to persist over time. Rather than seeking purely technological or legal solutions to the environmental disruptions that are now gaining prominence in the daily news, we need to revisit cultural traditions that have proven their sustainability and examine our own behaviors and beliefs in their light.

As we enter the closing years of the twentieth century, the ability of our own societies to persist is in question. Human beings are now expropriating for their own purposes approximately forty percent of the land-based primary productivity of photosynthesis (Vitousek et al. 1986). If our numbers continue to increase at their current rate, the human population will double sometime in the middle of the next century. What will it require to acknowledge the implications of these data and appropriately adjust our cultures? If we take as our touchstone the argument laid out earlier in this introduction that human culture necessarily emerges out of our species' relationship to particular places, there can be no single answer to this question. A multiplicity of responses will be required. Underlying these responses, however, may be a common set of principles that point to our fundamental interdependence with natural systems and our need for one another. It is toward the discovery of these principles and their implementation in the classroom that we and other authors in this volume are directing our efforts.

PRINCIPLES OF ECOLOGICAL EDUCATION

In our own work, the following principles of ecological education have become dominant and currently guide the shaping of our courses and work with other educators. In designing this book, we have sought out authors knowledgeable about formal and nonformal educational efforts for all ages of students and citizens that embody one or more of these principles.

- Development of personal affinity with the earth through practical experiences out-of-doors and through the practice of an ethic of care
- Grounding learning in a sense of place through the study of knowledge possessed by local elders and the investigation of surrounding natural and human communities
- Induction of students into an experience of community that counters the press toward individualism that is dominant in contemporary social and economic experiences
- Acquisition of practical skills needed to regenerate human and natural environments

- Introduction to occupational alternatives that contribute to the preservation of local cultures and the natural environment
- Preparation for work as activists able to negotiate local, regional, and national governmental structures in an effort to adopt policies that support social justice and ecological sustainability
- Critique of cultural assumptions upon which modern industrial civilization has been built, exploring in particular how they have contributed to the exploitation of the natural world and human populations

Educational experiments across the curriculum and across age groups have much to teach us about possible directions we might pursue in our attempt to engender a more ecologically sustainable culture.

Development of personal affinity with the earth through practical experiences out-of- doors and through the practice of an ethic of care

Stephen J. Gould (1991) has argued that human beings are unlikely to protect what they do not love, and that we cannot love what we do not know. Similarly, David Orr (1996) suggests that the simple possession of data regarding resource depletion or pollution is no guarantee that people will make decisions favorable to other species and the planet. One of the great hazards of modern life is that the close connection people once shared with the natural world has been disrupted as an increasing proportion of human activities has been channeled into the built environment. Recent studies (Nabhan and St. Antoine 1993) suggest that over the course of their lives most people spend only four to five percent of their time out-of-doors. Contrast this with the experience of hunters and gatherers or our own ancestors three to four generations back—most of whom were farmers—and it becomes clear that the basis for forming a relationship with the natural world no longer exists in the way it once did. Within the context of cities and suburbs it becomes easier to forget nature and to believe that human beings and our economy are able to exist outside the requirements of the ecosystems we have covered with our highways and shopping malls and skyscrapers. That relationship must be reestablished.

Adults need to consciously redirect themselves to the kinds of renewal and reconnection that can occur through outdoor work and recreation. For many children, educational settings may provide some of the few places where this relationship can be initially engendered. By situating learning beyond the confines of the classroom, teachers can help rectify this situation. Schoolyards can be turned into laboratories where gardens and small ecological field stations along with textbooks and videotapes serve as sources of student learning. Local parks can become the sites of nature studies, play, and quiet reflection. Children, as well as adults, need to be encouraged to learn how to look and listen and smell and feel without the mediating influence of electronic screens or digitized sound. Developing a sense of affinity with the land, students of all ages may come to recognize its beauty and then take the steps needed to guard its integrity. The moral underpinnings of such embedded and contextualized understanding can be found in an ethic of care (Noddings 1995).

Grounding learning in a sense of place through the study of local knowledge and the investigation of surrounding natural and human communities

Within the context of the society as a whole, little exists to draw youngsters or adults into a sense of membership in their own place. With the coming of modernity, face-to-face interaction is replaced with relations between "absent" others, fostered through a variety of technologies (Giddens 1990). The mobility of families, the media, and the way automobiles isolate all of us from nature and our neighbors make it imperative for educators to construct learning experiences aimed at helping students encounter the forms of knowledge and personal interaction that in the past would have entered their lives in a more natural manner. In their development of curriculum, teachers need to seek out local resources, focus on local issues, and help students learn how to ask and answer questions about the phenomena and events that surround them. By relocating the curriculum in the local in this way, educators may be able to further the regeneration of the unique responses to particular places that have contributed to the development of the diverse cultures now being subsumed in the global monoculture purveyed by the market and the media. Such a project is necessarily one of affirmation of cultural and biological diversity and in no way precludes critical thinking about the condition of human and biotic communities.

Induction of students into an experience of community that counters the press toward individualism that is dominant in contemporary social and economic experiences

Some social psychologists believe that one of the central contributors to the perpetuation of today's market society is the growing social isolation of individuals and individual families. Paul Wachtel (1989), for example, has argued that Americans' preoccupation with affluence stems from the declining strength and importance of communal institutions that once provided for the material and emotional welfare of people. In the past, such institutions were necessary if people were to survive in challenging natural conditions. One of the benefits of the scientific revolution is that we have been able to reduce the negative consequences of the vagaries of nature. The downside of this process is that the forms of sharing and obligation that once offered security have become vestigial. Now that security rests upon our ability to provide for ourselves and our immediate loved ones as individuals rather than as members of interactive and supportive communities. The result is a society-wide drive to compete for the jobs, salaries, and goods that promise to guard us from harm and to forget forms of cooperation that do not require the individual acquisition of wealth to ward off the unknown.

Although transcending the press to acquire and consume will not be easy, formal and nonformal educators can at least introduce students to the potential of community. Teachers, for example, can be assigned to work with a single class for two or more years. The creation of smaller schools that incorporate opportunities for informal interaction and joint projects outside the classroom can also contribute to the development of a sense of social membership among students (Smith 1993). Efforts to bridge the gap between school and the broader community such as those described in the two preceding principles could also help children develop an awareness of their ties to others and the forms of obligation, responsibility, and support associated with those relationships. Adult learners can also benefit from community building and support.

Acquisition of practical skills needed to regenerate human and natural environments

People's sense of connection to their community is likely to be further enhanced if they believe that they can contribute to the welfare of others. One way to engender the experience of connection is to invite children and adults to participate in projects aimed at restoring damaged ecosystems or improving the lives of others in their community. Central to the experience of alienation and isolation of people in contemporary society is the absence of regular opportunities to serve others. Without such opportunities, it is easy for individuals to believe that they have little value in themselves. Current efforts in schools to include community service reflect an understanding of the important role that this kind of labor can play in helping young people become members of the adult world. These efforts are likely to be most powerful if they are coupled with the teaching of practical skills. Young people who learn how to renovate deteriorated homes, replant damaged riparian zones with appropriate species, grow food, create parks, or set up businesses that meet previously unfulfilled community needs discover their own capacity to contribute to beneficial projects. Adults who participate in such projects can encounter a similar form of affirmation. The creation of a sustainable culture will necessarily take place on the ground as well as in our minds and hearts and will involve the ability to do as well as think and feel.

Introduction to occupational alternatives that contribute to the preservation of local cultures and the natural environment

One of the most distinctive characteristics of industrial growth societies can be found in the way that people of varying ages live separate lives. A consequence of this fact is that youngsters have little direct contact with the vocational experience of adults. When it comes time to choose their own occupations, they are then at a loss about which direction to pursue. The current glut of doctors and lawyers in the United States is indicative of the lack of imagination young adults are able to bring to the task of choosing their life work; they remain restricted to the most obvious categories in the *Dictionary of Occupational Titles*. Young people, furthermore, have little sense of the way that the labor of adults contributes to the welfare of the broader community. Work is primarily seen as a vehicle for achieving personal security and status rather than as a way to give back to others. Service learning opportunities such as those described above, especially if they occur in situations where adults and children are involved in some common project, can begin to mitigate this problem. The creation of multiple internship opportunities for young people could also help them begin to grasp the possibility of pursuing socially and ecologically beneficial callings.

Youngsters, for example, could be introduced to what it means to practice sustainable forestry, run a community-supported farm, maintain a credit union that makes low-interest loans available to local residents, educate children in ways that lead them to love and respect the natural environment, design and/or construct energy-efficient and low-polluting buildings, or assist low-income people to organize to improve the quality of their lives. From such experiences could emerge a generation of adults willing to use their energy, intelligence, and good will to craft institutions and technologies aimed at fostering the long-term health of the human and natural communities in which they dwell.

Preparation for work as activists able to negotiate local, regional, and national governmental structures in an effort to adopt policies that support social justice and ecological sustainability

The creation of viable community and regional governments, responsive to the needs and viewpoints of all citizens will necessitate inducting the young, and reeducating their elders, into the give and take of political life. The building of such skills can begin in the classroom where students can be asked to shape classroom rules and expectations and to participate in the development of curriculum and learning activities; this process can be extended into the community of adults through the creation of organizations, such as watershed councils, that bring citizens together to grapple with serious local issues often overlooked by other governmental agencies. Schools, too, can draw much more heavily than they do on student participation in important institutional decisions. This does not mean that teachers and administrators should abrogate their responsibilities, but that the voices of children and young adults be given significant weight in decisions that affect their lives. In a handful of innovative public high schools across the United States, students and adults have developed strategies to share the governance of their institutions in an effective manner (Purpel 1987; Gregory and Sweeney 1993); their experiments bear careful consideration and replication. Young people can also be given the opportunity through their coursework to participate in research that has bearing on local problems or controversies. There are instances in which such activity has prodded adults to rectify problems identified by the children of their communities (Lewis 1991).

Critique of cultural assumptions upon which modern industrial civilization has been built, exploring in particular how they have contributed to the exploitation of the natural world and human populations

Undergirding the enactment of all of the preceding principles must be a recognition of the fundamental relationship that exists between human activities and the natural world. Rather than seeing the economy as separate from natural systems, for example, it is imperative that people begin to understand that the human economy is a subset of the ecology of particular places and the planet as a whole (Daly 1996). If human economic activities threaten the well-being of these natural systems, our own well-being must eventually be threatened. We must further come to understand that a way of life based on the celebration of human inclinations of greed and avarice must eventually come to injure ourselves and the communities in which we live. From an ecological understanding of the way in which our lives are ineluctably tied to the lives of other people and other nonhuman beings—as well as to the welfare of rivers and mountains and sky—must emerge an evaluation of the appropriateness of human possibilities and actions. For example, the pursuit of self-interest without an awareness of our broader relationships will then be seen for what it is—a tear in the fabric of human and natural communities. Ecological education must call into question these understandings and urge teachers and their students to thoughtfully consider aspects of our lives that either contribute to or detract from the creation of an ecologically sustainable culture.

The chapters in this volume provide an opportunity to explore different facets of emerging forms of educational practice that implicitly recognize the close relationship that exists between human cultures and the environment. Although all of the authors may not subscribe to the preceding analysis in its entirety, their work or the work of people they describe demonstrates a similar form of understanding. Together the chapters create an image of what an ecologically grounded form of education for our own era could look like. It is imperative that models of the possible be placed in the hands of educational practitioners throughout our society in an effort to encourage further investigation as well as hope. The vast and many-sided nature of the environmental crisis can become immobilizing. It is difficult to know where to begin or what action is likely to stimulate movement in the right direction. Stasis in our current situation, however, will only allow for the continued deterioration of the natural and social communities essential to our well-being. We have chosen to include examples of work across the educational spectrum because we believe that what is required is a society-wide effort to transform peoples' thinking about the aims of human life and the social and ecological consequences of a continued reliance on the institutions that dominate industrial growth societies. We also believe that students of all ages have much to learn from one another. The arbitrary boundaries we have associated with different age groups often obscure our commonalities more than they illuminate our needs as learners and as people.

THE ORGANIZATION OF CHAPTERS

The first six chapters of this volume describe educational efforts in grade K–12 schools throughout the North American continent from

Alaska to Mexico, Oregon to Vermont. The next six chapters consider the work of people in higher education and nonformal educational settings and their attempts to instill an ecological perspective into the learning of college students and adult community members.

In chapter 1 of part I, Joseph Kiefer and Martin Kemple tell the story of the nonprofit Common Roots program in Vermont, a school restructuring project that has involved the implementation of a grade K–6 curriculum built around agricultural and ecological themes. Born out of a concern regarding hunger in Vermont and the declining ability of people to feed themselves in a state that is still largely rural, Common Roots has served to bring together schools and communities to educate children about their agricultural heritage and the skills and knowledge associated with growing food. In chapter 2, Paul Krapfel describes his efforts to develop an approach to the teaching of natural science that is aimed at cultivating in children a sense of continuity with the world around them. Like Kiefer and Kemple, Krapfel works outside the public school system but strives to influence educational practice there by developing curriculum units and modelling a form of science teaching grounded in close observation, inquiry, and discovery. Madhu Prakash and Hedy Richardson in chapter 3 recount the story of an effort to develop a similar kind of understanding among children and community members in a small city in central Mexico. Together with Mexican journalist and social activist Gustavo Esteva, Prakash worked with middle school students in an impoverished community to the south of Mexico City on a project aimed at developing ecological literacy. They sought to stimulate this understanding by involving students in a study of alternatives to modern sewage treatment systems. Turning their learning into practical action, students in association with other community members acquired the ability to construct and install dry latrines. Through this project they encountered important lessons in what it means to design technologies that work with natural systems in a manner that safely recycles waste rather than simply transporting it to some other location. This project models the combination of critical analysis, imaginative design, and practical action required by communities if they are to create technologies and social practices that are sustainable rather than environmentally destructive.

Chapter 4, by Dilafruz Williams and Sarah Taylor, tells about the efforts of other middle school educators to make the environment a central focus of the school experience of young adolescents, this time in the United States. Started in the fall of 1995 in Portland, Oregon, the Environmental Middle School places the environment at the heart of the curriculum. From this focus have emerged school-wide projects on rivers and mountains that orient students to an exploration of local watersheds and geologic phenomena and provide ample opportunities for field work and community service activities. Elaine Schwartz in the following chapter builds a case for the development of ecofeminist literacy, a way of reading both the word and the world (Freire 1991) that elicits an awareness of the triple oppressions of women, the cultures of nondominant groups, and the natural world. For Schwartz, as for many ecofeminists, the exploitation of the earth arises from the same disregard and carelessness as the exploitation of people. At issue for her is nurturing in children an experience of interconnectedness so powerful that they choose to act in a manner that supports and respects the lives of the beings around them. In the final chapter of part I of this book, Oscar Kawagley and Ray Barnhardt of the University of Alaska-Fairbanks describe their efforts to integrate Western science and the grounded knowledge of people who have lived for generations in particular places. As a Yupik Eskimo and a former science teacher, Oscar Kawagley straddles both worlds. He and Barnhardt argue that the teaching of science needs to incorporate multiple perspectives rather than simply assuming the superiority of an approach based on reductionism, the fragmentation of scientific disciplines, and the failure to consider complex variables that frequently arises from these tendencies. As an alternative, they describe a form of science education that links understandings developed over generations in Alaska Native communities to the understandings of Western science, exploring the relationship between observed phenomena and indigenous technologies (e.g., food preservation practices, population estimates of fish and game, weather prediction) and the principles and theories presented in science textbooks.

The chapters in part II of this volume explore efforts among people in colleges and universities as well as nonformal educational settings to impart new perspectives about the environment to older students. Chapter 7, by Stephanie Kaza, provides details about the content and teaching approaches she uses in four courses offered in the Environmental Studies Department at the University of Vermont. Kaza, with academic training in ecology as well as ethics, draws on science, social science, and humanities perspectives in a set of courses aimed at transforming the understanding and social practices of her students. In her work, she strives to help undergraduates confront the facts of the environmental crisis but does so in a way that enables them to move beyond despair to an understanding of their own capacity to effect change.

C. A. Bowers in chapter 8 presents an account of recent efforts at

Portland State University to create a model of teacher education that embodies an ecological perspective. At the heart of Bowers's work is his belief that the cultural changes required to avert environmental disaster necessitate a careful examination of the linguistic roots of contemporary thinking as it relates to our definitions of self, intelligence, creativity, knowledge, and progress, among others. He challenges the common tendency in schools of education to segregate environmental education into science methods courses and argues that teacher educators concerned about these issues must find ways to integrate ecological concerns and understandings across the curriculum. As a teacher in small liberal arts colleges over the last fifteen years, Peter Corcoran has been working to achieve similar ends with undergraduate education majors; Corcoran, however, comes at this process from a different direction. In chapter 9, he describes the way he has sought to uncover vital affective connections to the earth among the students who have participated in his classes during this time. Although the environmental courses he teaches incorporate a strong intellectual component, Corcoran concentrates on restoring to students their own memories of experiences in the natural world, experiences that will ideally inform their development of curriculum and future work with children.

Gregory Cajete, in chapter 10, discusses the characteristics of cultures in which the maintenance of right relations between humans and the earth was of paramount importance. A Tewa Indian who has written extensively about indigenous education, Cajete creates a multifaceted description of the way that the sentiment of biophilia—love for nature and nonhuman beings (Wilson 1992)—has influenced the cultures of peoples who once lived, and in some cases continue to live, close to the land. Chapter 11, by Gregory Smith, offers a description of two nonprofit organizations, the Mattole Restoration Council and the Northwest Earth Institute, that are attempting to build comparable forms of understanding among people in the Pacific Northwest and northern California. Each of these organizations works with adults in nonformal educational settings in an effort to develop a deeper understanding among the general population of ecological principles and their cultural and economic implications. The final chapter, by David Orr, describes the process by which the building that will house Oberlin College's Environmental Studies Department was designed, incorporating the input of students and community members. This building project has given students at Oberlin the opportunity to grasp how they can translate their idealism into practical action through the process of designing one aspect of a more ecologically beneficent culture.

EPILOGUE

The ideas and models presented in this volume offer ways to reconceptualize not only the relationship between education and the environment, but the purpose of education itself. In the late twentieth century, education in its multiple forms has come to be viewed primarily as a vehicle by which individuals are able to gain a foothold in an increasingly competitive global market. Neglected in this shift in educational purpose is the role that acculturation and socialization once played in the maintenance of the health of the broader community. In earlier societies, that community often included nonhumans as well as people and a profound sense of relatedness to the land. Individuals were not educated for themselves alone but for what their education would mean to the welfare of the whole.

We recognize that the development of such an educational process is likely to be controversial. Even environmental education as currently practiced is eliciting reactions from those who have a stake in the maintenance of the status quo of market economics (Sanera and Shaw 1996). Under the rubric of being "conservative," these political attacks on environmental education have left the field vulnerable to being coopted. All education, however, inevitably takes some moral point of view—whether it is promoting the values of the market and technology or values premised on the maintenance of caring relationships with other people and the earth. Educators must strive to design curriculum and implement it through a balanced perspective, exposing students to all sides of controversial issues. This could include bringing ecological interdependence and an ethic of care in from the margin to the center of the debate.

In reengaging culture and ecology, the educational efforts described in this volume demonstrate what it means to craft an ethic of sustainability, an ethic anchored in a recognition of interdependence. Learners in these formal and nonformal educational settings grasp important skills and insights that they are able to direct to the benefit of others. They are able to grow and share food, participate in the eradication of nonnative species, model the meaning of voluntary simplicity, contribute to the restoration of watersheds, encourage awareness of a broader ecosystem perspective, help with the design of technologies that are more earth-friendly, and act out of an understanding of their fundamental relatedness to all things. This is only a partial list of the gifts people who have had these ecologically based educational experiences will possess, but it points to ways that education can help to ground local cultures and communities in an understanding of the particularities of place. Only from the sensibilities and efforts of people in thousands of such communities will cultures characterized by ecological sustainability and social justice be able to emerge.

References

Basso, Keith. (1990). *Western Apache language and culture: Essays in linguistic anthropology.* Tucson: University of Arizona Press.

Berry, Wendell. (1990). *What are people for?* San Francisco: North Point Press.

Daly, Herman. (1996). Sustainable growth? No thank you. In Jerry Mander and Edward Goldsmith (ed.), *The case against the global economy and for a turn toward the local,* pp. 192–196. San Francisco: Sierra Club Books.

Elliott, John. (1991). Environmental education in Europe: Innovation, marginalization or assimilation. In Organization of Economic Cooperation and Development. *Environment, schools, and active learning,* pp. 19–38. Paris, France: OECD.

Freire, Paulo. (1991). The importance of the act of reading. In Candace Mitchell and Kathleen Weiler (eds.), *Rewriting literacy: Culture and the discourse of the other.* Granby, Massachusetts: Bergin and Garvey.

Giddens, Anthony. (1990). *The consequences of modernity.* Stanford, California: Stanford University Press.

Gould, Stephen Jay. (1991). Enchanted evening. *Natural History* (September), p. 14.

Gregory, Tom, and Mary Ellen Sweeney. (1993). Building a community by involving students in the governance of the school. In Gregory A. Smith (ed.), *Public schools that work: Creating community,* pp. 101–128. New York: Routledge.

Jackson, Wes. (1994). *Becoming native to this place.* Lexington, Kentucky: The University Press of Kentucky.

Lewis, Barbara. (1991). *A kid's guide to social action: How to solve problems you choose—and turn creative thinking into positive action.* Minneapolis: Free Spirit Publishing.

Nabhan, Gary Paul, and Sara St. Antoine. (1993). The loss of floral and faunal story: The extinction of experience. In S. R. Kellert and E. O. Wilson (eds.), *The biophilia hypothesis,* pp. 229–250. Washington, D.C.: Island Press.

Norberg-Hodge, Helena. (1991). *Ancient futures: Learning from Ladakh.* San Francisco: Sierra Club Books.

Noddings, Nel. (1995). *Philosophy of education.* Boulder, Colorado: Westview Press.

Organization for Economic Cooperation and Development. (1991). *Environment, schools and active learning.* Paris, France: Author.

Organization for Economic Cooperation and Development. (1995). *Environmental learning for the 21st century.* Paris, France: Author.

Orr, David. (1996). Reconnecting the pieces: Ecological design and education in the 21st century. Keynote address at the Ecological Education Institute, Lewis & Clark College, Portland, Oregon, August 21, 1996.

Purpel, David. (1989). *The moral and spiritual crisis in education: A curriculum for justice and compassion in education.* Granby, Massachusetts: Bergin and Garvey.

Sanera, Michael, and Jane S. Shaw. (1996). *Facts not fear: A parent's guide about environmental education.* New York: Regnery Publishing.

Shiva, Vandana. (1992). Recovering the real meaning of sustainability. In David Cooper and Joy Palmer (eds.), *The environment question: Ethics and global issues,* pp. 187–193. London: Routledge.

Smith, Gregory A. (1993). *Public schools that work: Creating community.* New York: Routledge.

Snyder, Gary. (1992). Coming in to the watershed. In Scott Walker (ed.), *Changing community,* pp. 261–276. Saint Paul, Minnesota: Graywolf Press.

Vitousek, Peter M., Paul R. Ehrlich, Anne H. Ehrlich, and Pamela A. Matson. (1986). Human appropriation of the products of photosynthesis. *Bioscience* 37(6): 368–373.

Wachtel, Paul. (1989). *The poverty of affluence: A psychological portrait of the American way of life.* Philadelphia: New Society.

Wilson, Edward O. (1992). *The diversity of life.* Cambridge, Massachusetts: Harvard University Press.

Part One
K–12 Settings

1 Stories from Our Common Roots

Strategies for Building an Ecologically Sustainable Way of Learning

Joseph Kiefer and
Martin Kemple

Common Roots is a comprehensive school development process designed to reconnect public elementary schools with the traditional knowledge and natural heritage of their local communities. In the 1996–97 school year alone, teachers from dozens of elementary schools in Vermont and across the country participated in graduate courses, workshops, and presentations on adapting various aspects of the Common Roots process to fit the unique needs of their communities. These teachers are pioneering a growing movement to transform schools into local centers for food and ecological research demonstrating practical methods for learning "the basics" founded on sound natural principles. This ongoing story reflects an extraordinary awakening of educators, indeed of people from virtually all walks of life, to an expanding ecological consciousness which recognizes humans' capacity to understand nature as both teacher and curriculum.

In the midst of putting together notes and anecdotes on our work in public schools, one of us recalled a brief encounter with a former student which is a useful starting point for introducing the "pedagogy of place" we call Common Roots:

It was on a slightly overcast September day a number of years ago that I was walking with a friend through a crowd of people at the Church Street marketplace in Burlington.

Suddenly, I heard someone yell my name.

"Joseph, Joseph Kiefer," a low-pitched voice called out.

I turned to find a young man of about nineteen, with a broad smile and deep blue eyes.

"It's Ben," he said excitedly, pumping my hand. "Ben Rifkin. You remember?"

I had to admit I was drawing a blank on the name. A quick search of my mental Rolodex brought nothing up.

"From the Main Street Middle School in Montpelier. You helped us build the garden behind the school."

Of course, I knew those school grounds like my own backyard. That was one of our first experiences turning a school lawn into a food garden. Now to sort through all of those bright young faces of so many years ago and fast-forward to this young man standing before me. Gradually, it started to come back. He had been one of the quiet, hard-working types.

"And we used to bring the harvest down to the food shelf," he said. "That was the year our class created the Montpelier Food Policy."

Those were the early years of a hunger education garden science program that soon blossomed into a community-wide "foodscaping" effort around the school, at local churches and—we hoped—in the hearts and minds of the students. In 1987–88, the sixth-grade class worked all year to create the first food policy in the state of Vermont, detailing a comprehensive vision and plan for making the capital city food self-sufficient.

Ben continued to clutch my hand. "I want to thank you for doing that garden with us. That experience really stayed with me all these years."

Naturally, I was touched. Gratified that he had made the extra effort to stop and share this memory with me, I asked what he was doing now.

Ben released my hand and straightened his shoulders. "I'm a student here at the University of Vermont. Environmental Studies major. I feel like I'm really following up on so many of the things we were doing in the gardening program."

There you go, I thought, now doubly impressed. Today, Environmental Studies; tomorrow, the world. You never know what yield will come from seeds planted so many seasons past.

But why should such an experience be so surprising? Why is it that we teachers are so often startled to learn that our students have simply stayed true to their essential instincts, cultivating the same natural curiosity we had seen so clearly in them as children? Why do we so readily assume that the demands of "the real world" will eventually prevail and that their innate sensitivity to the earth will be abandoned, or at least put aside, in pursuit of a career, or fortune, or material security?

This is the story of how whole communities are struggling with these kinds of questions; and how they are trying to answer them by creating ways of learning that honor the fundamental intuition of children, of all of us, to realign ourselves in harmony and balance with the natural world. And because this involves real people dealing with real problems—family stress, economic insecurity, community breakdown, and environmental decay, to name a few—this is a story in progress.

FOOD WORKS

By the mid-1980s, awareness of the quiet crisis of childhood hunger in Vermont and across the country had finally surfaced in the public mind. In the midst of the dramatic famine in the Horn of Africa in 1985, the Harvard School of Public Health published a shocking study, "Hunger in America," stating unequivocally that "with the cuts in federal assistance programs over the past six years, hunger has reached epidemic proportions in the United States." Shortly thereafter, the Governor's Task Force on Hunger in Vermont issued a report revealing that "hunger exists in every corner of the state."

In the wake of these troubling findings, a small group of us founded the Vermont Food Bank, a statewide clearinghouse dispatching surplus foods to emergency food shelves, soup kitchens, battered women's shelters, and mental health programs throughout the state's fourteen counties. In the Food Bank's early years, demand continually outstripped the supply of food items donated each month. Today the Vermont Food Bank is an unfortunate success story.

In north-central Vermont, we formed a community task force against hunger to conduct systematic research into the extent and causes of local hunger and undernutrition. Our goal was to develop practical strategies for providing short- and long-term relief. One of the many outcomes that emerged from this task force was a Hunger Education Garden Science Program. This initiative integrated the themes of local hunger, food growing, and community service into the existing science curriculum at the Main Street Middle School in Montpelier.

At the Main Street School we started our first garden demonstration site for building local food security. Students conducted their own research on local, hardy, adaptable foods to grow. Working in teams, fifth- and sixth-grade students cultivated edible varieties of herbs, fruits, and vegetables. One team built a three-bin compost system to demonstrate how to recycle nutrients for improving soil quality. Others worked side by side with elders who shared stories and lessons they had learned from farming and gardening over the generations. Students sold food at the Saturday Montpelier Farmer's Market and conducted monthly food drives of nonperishable foods. In season, classes donated fresh garden produce to the Montpelier Emergency Food Pantry.

To culminate their study, the sixth graders researched, wrote, published, and presented to the public "The Montpelier Food Policy," which the Chair of the Senate Agriculture Committee, Patrick Leahy, called "one of the clearest and simplest reports on hunger I've ever read." Simultaneously, a small video production company out of New York City contacted us about creating a short documentary on innovative approaches to addressing hunger in America. What emerged was a twenty-eight-minute video, "Small Steps," detailing this student-centered, interdisciplinary approach to hunger.

From this small food and hunger awareness project at the Main Street Middle School grew the realization that schools can use gardens to create grade-by-grade curriculum that addresses real community issues. Specifically, this experience convinced us of the critical need for empowering children with the preventive skills of food growing as the first step in addressing the root causes of childhood hunger.

In order to broaden our work to include public schools across the state, we founded an educational nonprofit organization called Food Works. Having discovered what a powerful teaching tool food can be as part of our daily life, we set out to work with teachers and students designing food gardens in order to teach the food growing cycle from field to table. Our reasoning was simple: If children were allowed to grapple with the problem of local hunger and undernutrition from a broader, more holistic standpoint based on their own experiences, then they would be empowered to address the root causes of the issue and take effective action themselves.

Shortly after the release of "The Montpelier Food Policy," a parent from another nearby school contacted us to set up a meeting between Food Works and her local school board. Following our presentation, which included the "Small Steps" video, the Board agreed to support a comprehensive gardening/hunger awareness project as part of their school restructuring process.

The lessons we learned from this first schoolwide attempt at incorporating gardens across the curriculum were many. First, the tremendous commitment and participation by parents and community members demonstrated that people were clearly searching for deeper meaning and value in their children's education. An eighty-six-year-old farmer, Delmar Story, plowed and disked a series of historic theme gardens for each grade around the perimeter of the school building. Over the course of a week, parents and community members volunteered to build a grades K–2 Three Sisters Garden, a grades 3–4 Community Heritage Garden, and a grades 5–6 Raised Bed Sustainable Garden.

From a series of public meetings facilitated by Food Works, the school hosted a number of community events. Delmar Story and his wife Edna began joining students for school lunches, often bringing elderly friends from the community. Others came into the school to teach bread making and butter making to students and their families. On a community-wide work day, indoor gardens were built for each classroom along with earthworm farms for composting. Most successful of all were the Spring Planting and Fall Harvest ceremonies held at the school, which were attended by more community members than any school event in recent memory.

The local press, naturally, loved the innovative school/community linkages being fostered and covered our activities extensively. From across the state, education officials and politicians visited the small primary school to praise this modest experiment in schoolwide outdoor education which linked food gardening with the pressing local issue of childhood hunger. Vermont's Commissioner of Education, Richard Mills (now New York State's Education Commissioner), told a reporter: "It's obvious that the children own these gardens. This is an outstanding example of the new thought needed in school. There is a lot of science, writing, and thinking being snuck in under the guise of gardening."

Although the community participation in this school gardening/hunger awareness project was extremely powerful and effective, the long-term curricular changes created by the gardens were far less so. By the end of the first full year of experimenting with gardening across the curriculum, few if any outdoor learning activities had been fully integrated into traditional subject areas. Essentially, we did not provide teachers with the guidance necessary for creating garden-based lesson plans to cover subject areas already being taught.

As the project unfolded, we did offer a series of impromptu workshops with teachers reviewing the basics of gardening and hunger awareness, but we failed to make explicit connections to the existing district and state guidelines for each grade. While teachers drew up seasonal curriculum plans exploring various themes for the school gardens, which included focused discussions about the different subjects that could be taught through the garden, no unifying, grade-by-grade thematic areas were identified from which to develop a consistent framework of practical activities.

In order to assist teachers in this process of deeper curriculum integration, we created interdisciplinary activity and content webs. These webs have a theme question at the center—for example, "What can be discovered in the Three Sisters Garden?" Lines extend outward to a series of boxes representing each of the traditional subjects such as social studies, science, language arts (see figure 1.1). With the activity webs, teachers develop lesson plans in the garden corresponding to the sub-

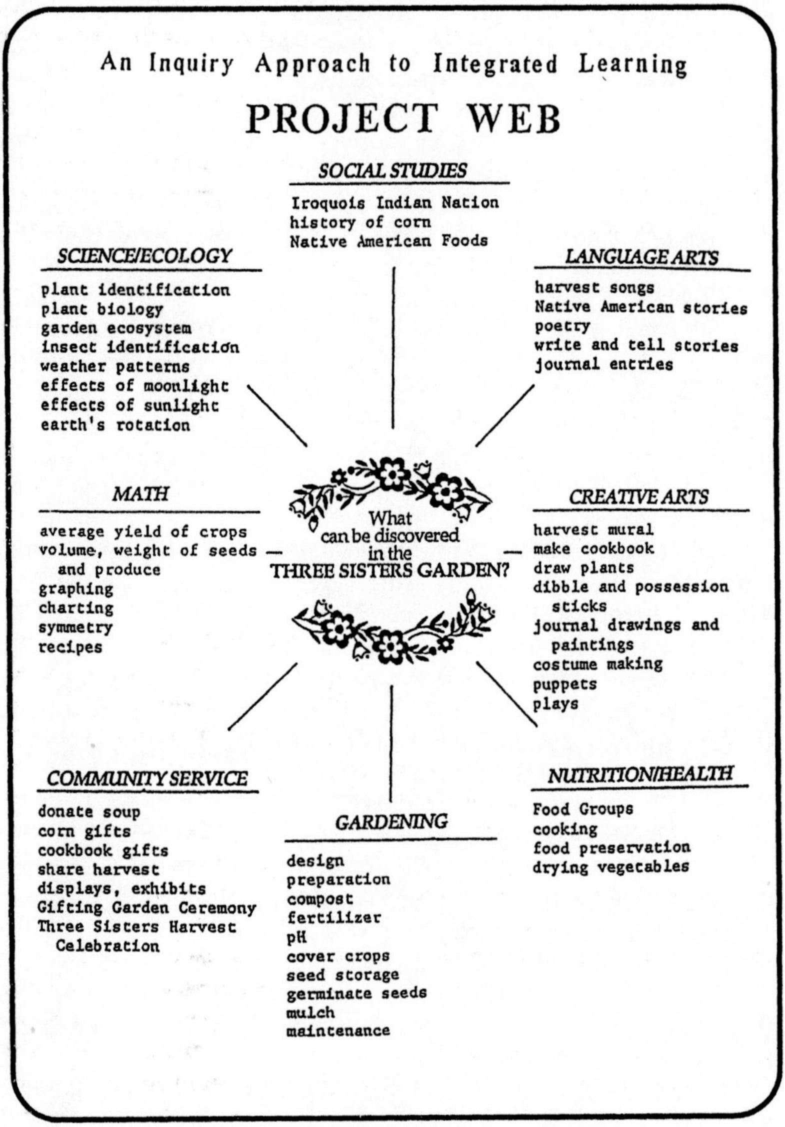

Figure 1.1. The Common Roots Curriculum Centered on Gardens. Source: JoAnne Dennee, Jack Peduzzi, and Julia Hand (1995), *In The Three Sisters Garden*. Montpelier, Vermont: Food Works.

ject areas based on the central question. They then cross-reference these new lessons to the district and state curriculum they specify in their content web.

In anticipation of the garden harvest that first fall, we passed out the webs to teachers, somehow hoping that they would intuitively understand (and have the extra time to figure out) how to connect the theme questions to their own curriculum without any further guidance. This component of our own on-the-job training, it turned out, was our greatest lesson: Without engaging teachers in a comprehensive process to reflect on, critique, envision, and implement new curriculum tools and methods, all of our best effort would become add-on activities, soon relegated to the back burner. Alas, by simply creating another "extra" which teachers had to work into their already overfilled schedules, we had managed to become part of the problem we were trying to address!

We learned that for any innovation to work, all components of the process must be firmly in place: the theory, the curriculum ideas, the webs, the activities, the methods, the assessment, and the time for teachers to develop and implement them together. Equally important, we discovered how vital it is to create opportunities and guidance for integration: integration of subjects around unifying themes; integration of grades through a consistent schoolwide framework from year to year; integration of teachers as the main catalysts in the school change process; and integration of what is being learned in class with what is happening in the outside world.

In order to create consistency and unity out of typically disjointed subject areas and seemingly fragmented curriculum requirements from grade to grade, we learned that teachers must have ample freedom and assistance to communicate and explore together the curriculum strategies and activities for integration. Further, in order to ensure that this curricular integration remains a dynamic and holistic process, there must be an ongoing dialogue about the deeper pedagogical and cultural issues this fragmentation in schools raises. In fact, we have come to find that the depth and creativity of any school change process depends largely on whether there is built into the system an ongoing dialogue about the social, economic, political, and ecological causes and effects of current and evolving educational practices. Integrated learning means more than just tying together disconnected subject areas and creating a consistent continuum through the grades. It also means integrating the learning that happens in school with issues and concerns in the community and in the wider world.

The goal of this first schoolwide gardening experiment was to empower children to take back control of their own diets by restoring their ancient ties to the land. We discovered that this was not going to happen magically with the appearance of a schoolwide food gardening project, even if it caught on in every school in the state. The roots of the problem extend far deeper than that: they go right to the heart of the fragmented, isolated way we learn about the world in school.

Linking Modern Education and the Environment

The way we learn about the world both reflects and recreates that world. We have come to believe that our disjointed, piecemeal approach to dealing with endemic social and ecological problems in the wider society is both cause and consequence of our splintered educational system. Fragmented subject areas taught in schools engender segmented, disconnected knowledge without an organic understanding of our connection to nature and to one another. In our case, without allowing teachers the opportunity to embrace a holistic context for teaching real-life experiences across the curriculum, all of our best efforts to address in schools the root causes of local problems become reduced to an add-on, mere tinkering.

School reform movements sweep the country every ten or fifteen years or so, purportedly to address perennial questions about the relevance and accountability of our educational system. From years of working in public schools, we have become convinced that most contemporary school restructuring efforts—be they called "systemic school change" or "standards-based education"—are essentially programs for retooling students to become more efficient workers, designed to make children more competitive in the national economy or, more recently, in the emerging global economy. Absent from the debates nationally and locally about our educational system has been critical discourse on the responsibility of schools to the communities that support them and to the planet's life-support systems that sustain us all.

The litany of planetary ecological deterioration is now common currency in popular culture and hardly needs to be elaborated here beyond a few simple facts: the rate of extinction of mammals in this century alone, for example, is forty times what it was millions of years ago, and the earth loses seventy-two square miles of arable land per day to encroaching desert. In 1995, world population grew by 100 million, the largest yearly increase ever. Add to this weekly accounts of increased chlorofluorocarbons in the atmosphere, rapid ozone depletion, and rampant overfishing and increasing toxicity of the earth's oceans and we can see clearly that, ultimately, it is the planet's life systems of air, water, and soil which are in grave jeopardy (Orr 1994).

What does this dramatic transformation of our biosphere have to do with our educational system? We can address this problem on many levels. First, there is a growing feeling that schools have become disconnected from the "real world." Increasingly, parents and concerned citizens are voicing alarm that children are not learning "the basics" which they need to function in the wider society. What immediately leaps to the mind of an educator, then, is: Do we all collectively agree on what we mean by "the basics" and the "real world"? What are the most fundamental values, skills, and fields of knowledge children should learn in school? If teachers, administrators, and parents fully recognized the consequences of the unmistakable deterioration of our natural environment, for example, then how would they change the structure, content, and methodologies of our modern industrial schools?

Further, we can ask: How do schools reflect the values, attitudes, ways of thinking, and social structures that have fostered the economic, social, and political systems responsible for our current ecological predicament? As David Orr points out in his pathbreaking book, *Earth in Mind*:

> The disordering of ecological systems and of the great bio-geochemical cycles of the earth reflects a prior disorder in the thought, perception, imagination, intellectual priorities and loyalties inherent in the industrial mind. Ultimately, the ecological crisis concerns how we think and the institutions that purport to shape and refine the capacity to think. (1994, 2)

The history of the American school system reflects the ongoing national conflict over our notions of progress and our attitudes toward the natural environment. From our own experience in public schools and from the vast literature on the history of American education, focusing especially on this latest wave of school restructuring nationally, we feel that as a society we have been asking the wrong questions about what the role of schools in our society should be. Rather than ask, *How do we help our children learn better, more, faster?*, we should instead ask: *What is it that children should be learning in the first place, and how do we teach that?*

Gradually around the country and particularly throughout Vermont, many public schools have been responding to these broader educational and ecological concerns in essentially three ways: through isolated, one-shot activities such as nature awareness exercises or the occasional environmental education field trip; by implementing individual seasonal units with an environmental theme such as gardening, nature trails, and recycling; or by undergoing comprehensive, community-driven curriculum transformation, integrating practical, hands-on projects and activities involving local natural and cultural history, community service, food growing, the arts, and global environmental issues.

In school after school, we have seen how this third approach is consistently the most powerful strategy both for teaching basic skills and for preparing the child to meet the social, economic, and ecological challenges of the twenty-first century. The need to enact this agenda in schools across the country is more urgent than ever. Vice President Al Gore's book, *Earth in the Balance,* says: "We must make the rescuing of the environment the central organizing principle for civilization" (1992, 2).

We have come to believe that teachers and curriculum are not the problem with our educational system because we are not facing an educational crisis, we are facing a cultural crisis. If we do not squarely address the very essence of our social and cultural problems by coming to terms with the ecological realities of our age, then we will be perpetually tinkering with the segmented, industrial mindset in schools, at work, and at home, thereby reinforcing that fragmented way of thinking and being. Increasingly, the most promising literature from advanced educational scholars is recognizing the necessary link between contemporary school reform efforts and the state of the environment. C.A. Bowers, for example, has observed:

> (I)f the thinking that guides educational reform does not take account of how the cultural beliefs and practices passed on through schooling relate to the deepening ecological crisis, then these efforts may actually strengthen the cultural orientation that is undermining the sustaining capacities of natural systems upon which all life depends. (1993, 1)

Central to any fundamental school change process must be a guiding vision that recognizes the imperative of learning how to live in a more ecologically sustainable way. Further, in order to make this vision real, there must be a meaningful local context for transforming schools into true centers for community learning that teach and demonstrate local food and ecological security.

If there is, as we believe, a growing readiness for this emerging ecological approach to living and learning, then the question becomes: How do we begin transitioning schools from training children to perpetuate an unsustainable consumer-oriented, technologically-fixated society to nurturing the inborn curiosity, natural wonder, and creative passion of all children in finding their own niche in the ecological web?

COMMON ROOTS: A COMMUNITY-BASED STRATEGY

We at Food Works responded to this problem by initiating a program we call Common Roots, a holistic, comprehensive curriculum development process based in the community and driven by teachers.

On the heels of our first schoolwide project involving gardening came a phone call from Jeff Teitelbaum, the principal of a grade K–8 elementary school in Barnet, Vermont. Located in the Connecticut River watershed on the New Hampshire border, Barnet is on the eastern edge of Vermont's so-called Northeast Kingdom, the poorest and most rural agricultural region of the state.

Jeff needed assistance in writing a grant for school restructuring to be funded by Vermont's State Department of Education along with a consortium of corporate sponsors. Through a series of meetings, interviews with staff, and site visits to the ninety-plus acres of the school grounds, a vision gradually emerged of a school that would draw its curriculum from the natural and cultural heritage of this unique community. We proposed to base the school's curriculum on the human settlement patterns and natural environment of the Barnet community. In the late fall of 1990, we were overjoyed to receive word that the proposal to fund Common Roots had been approved.

Our first step was to design a three-credit hour Common Roots graduate course for the entire faculty. This fifteen-week class turned out to be the forerunner for all of our subsequent work in schools around the state, and now increasingly around the country. We learned from prior experience the critical need for schoolwide professional development coursework for teachers that reaches far beyond many of the isolated teacher-training courses offered under the guise of "school restructuring." Importantly, this coursework must be focused on the deeper cultural causes of curriculum segmentation and its implications for schools, for the communities that support them, and for the wider world.

In addition, we learned that this graduate level work must be designed so that teachers can develop and take ownership of their own integrated curriculum. Teachers, like the rest of us, are far more likely to embrace fundamental change in their work habits when they can be part of the change process themselves and make it fit with what they are already doing. And, as we found in subsequent schools where we have worked, as soon as teachers become excited about an innovation, they will naturally reach out to parents and others to include the wider community in the learning process. Creating that level of enthusiasm for deep-seated change schoolwide among teachers, administrators, and school board members is the great challenge of our work.

The centerpiece of the course at Barnet was the development of a schoolwide journey of seasonal thematic units based on the unique story of the Barnet community. The notion of developing curriculum around the story of a local place was crucial for creating a consistent and meaningful context for practical, ecological learning through the grades. From past experience, we saw how easily curriculum can splinter into disconnected subjects without the unity of a central focus or overriding theme. We have been particularly influenced by the work of Myles Horton, the founder of the Highlander Center in Tennessee, and his thoughts on building curriculum based on a holistic approach.

> The universe is one; nature and mind and spirit and the heavens and time and the future all are part of the big bell of life. Instead of thinking that you put pieces together which all add up to a whole. . . you have to start with the premise they're already together and you try to keep from destroying life by segmenting it, over-organizing it, and dehumanizing it. (1978, 14)

At the same time, we noticed how few opportunities schools provide for students to experience and learn about the communities in which they live. Indeed, our educational process seems designed to do quite the opposite by rewarding abstract patterns of thinking and learning that serve ultimately to remove children from their familiar immediate environment.

At the Barnet School, we merged these twin needs—providing a central theme to integrate the curriculum and basing the school's learning activities around tangible, familiar places and things—by recreating the story of the Barnet community through the grades. This proved to be a key link in making this very different style of teaching and learning work for Barnet teachers and, equally important, for Barnet students.

We have found that recreating the story of the very community in which the students themselves live provides an ideal context for meaningful learning. Now for the first time, the teacher can say to the curious child just entering school that we are going somewhere. Each season we are going to live the lives of the people who first lived here, we are going to walk their footsteps and learn from their lessons—how they survived and sustained themselves over time. We are going to discover the foods they grew and the ways that they grew them. We will explore how they related to and used nature in balance or out of balance, constructively or destructively. We are going to explore their culture using arts, dance, theater, music.

We shall walk in these woods and meadows, and learn what grows here and what animals live here. We will learn about the houses and neighborhoods and families that have sprung up in this town over the generations. We will meet the people who live here, talk to the men and women who themselves went to school in this place, to hear their words and stories and worries and questions. In addition to understanding their perspectives on the past and their concerns about the present, we will discuss their hopes and dreams for the future. This, children discover, is what we call learning. This is the starting point of formal education. All of this we see as the three legs for cultivating a literacy of place—food literacy, ecological literacy, and cultural literacy. As an old farmer told us later at a harvest meal at one of our Common Roots schools, "If you don't know where you came from, how are you going to know where you're going?"

Developing the Context for the Common Roots Story

In the Common Roots graduate course, we recreate the local community's story by exploring with teachers five basic questions:

- Where are we?

  We began our coursework in recreating the story of the Barnet community by asking this simple question: Where are we? geographically? ecologically? historically? demographically? culturally? Typically at this early stage we will invite in an area historian from the historical society along with various elders to share their stories about the local history and changes in the land over time.

- Who are we?

  Here we take a detailed look at the needs, strengths, and challenges of the school, students, families, and the local environment. We conduct a rigorous community/school profile, which includes a thorough needs assessment. This stage culminates in a wide-ranging discussion of the implications of this profile for teaching and learning. For example, if we have a forty percent rate of children on free or reduced lunches—What should we be teaching these children? How do we respond to their immediate and longer-term needs?

- What are we doing?
  This phase focuses almost exclusively on the existing school curriculum, identifying all relevant programs and curricular units that address the needs outlined in the needs assessment. These include food, environment, and community-service learning activities that are already underway, as well as professional development coursework, areas of parent and community involvement, examples of multidimensional assessments and other pertinent information about the current climate and culture of the school. An additional task in this stage is to identify the natural and cultural resources that exist locally.

- Where can we go?
  What is our vision for transforming the school into a center for community learning that meets the relevant needs of all students? How do we educate our children without diminishing or harming the habitability of this watershed for future generations? How do we grow our own food, learn the traditional knowledge passed down from our elders, and be of service to others? How do we find our own unique niche in our local ecosystem? At this stage, the group develops a vision statement describing the specific plans of the indoor and outdoor educational landscape. This includes the expectations of students and families as participants and co-learners in this lifelong learning process.

- How do we get there?
  What skills, knowledge, activities, and methods do we need to prepare us to teach in a more ecologically sustainable way? What is our action plan and timeline for implementing the Common Roots framework? Once this local context has been developed, we have a fuller account of local history, geography, ecology, and demographics, and have conducted a thorough needs assessment. With this understanding of place and needs, teachers are ready to identify the Thematic Areas for building a grade-by-grade continuum of practical, hands-on learning opportunities that form the skeleton for each grade's seasonal journey.

Designing the Schoolwide Framework

Based on the information gathered from these questions, the major Thematic Areas of the grade-by-grade developmental framework are identified, forming the outline of the schoolwide journey through the seasons. Examples of Thematic Areas teachers have incorporated into their framework include: Historic Theme Gardens, Schoolyard Habitats, Community Service Learning, Entrepreneurial Opportunities, Stories from our Elders, Celebrations and Festivals, and Appropriate Technologies.

Teams of teachers then begin to articulate the journey through the seasons. As they write this narrative, they use their grade level curriculum content designated by district and state guidelines. Additionally, teachers identify state and district standards that they must teach to as part of their standard teaching requirements. This ensures that all prescribed content in traditional subject areas as mandated by the district and state are covered through each of the Thematic Areas.

Our curricular strategy for building a pedagogy of place has been to create a grade-by-grade story following the near-to-far developmental social studies framework in place throughout the United States and most of Europe. The Barnet story starts, then, in kindergarten with the study of the self. In grade one, the focus is on homes of Barnet and in grade two, Barnet neighborhoods. Grade three students study the wider Barnet community, and grade four concentrates on the history of the Barnet region and state of Vermont. In grade five, U.S. history (from a Barnet perspective) is studied, consistent with most other Vermont public schools, and grade six studies world history focusing on its implications for Barnet and rural life in Vermont. This framework provides a consistent grade-by-grade foundation for telling a story unique to each community.

For example, kindergartners enter the world exploring the garden, the "child's garden," and nature as it relates to the self. Grades one and two look at the indigenous peoples of their community as part of the first homes and neighborhoods. Grades three and four create a community heritage garden to bring to life regional and state history. Grades five and six explore the sustainable garden ecosystem as it relates to U.S. and world history, grappling with more complex global issues such as: How do we feed six billion people by the year 2000?

Three Sample Thematic Areas of the Journey

In keeping with the natural ecological sensibility characteristic of so many indigenous societies that have sustained themselves over time, the Thematic Areas provide a focus for building a continuum of ecological awareness, knowledge, and action.

Historic Theme Gardens. As we moved from a single-grade garden at a middle school to a schoolwide approach to food gardening, we needed a way to make each year new and exciting for the student. We were also concerned with telling the story of each community's agricultural legacy, a heritage that has been under siege for decades. The near-to-far social studies approach has provided the ideal vehicle both for telling the local story through the grades and making that story relevant to students, teachers, and community. By developing different historic gardens for each grade, this approach allows teachers to link their existing social studies themes—on Native Americans, European explorers, the local community, and regions of the United States—by creating a logical historical progression to these units that parallels the agricultural history of the community.

Food Works offers a three-credit graduate course in garden curriculum certification designed to integrate historic theme gardens across the curriculum. Because the historic theme gardens serve as a visible demonstration of the history of the community, parents and community members are eager to become involved in the building, planting, summer care, and harvesting of the gardens. Margaret McLean, a principal at a Common Roots school in Peacham, Vermont, has said, "The greatest advantage to this kind of learning process is that it brings the community into the school. Today we have a great number of community people actively involved in our school who never would have entered the building without Common Roots."

We have found these gardens to be powerful vehicles for hands-on learning because children are naturally drawn to and deeply curious about the wonders of all living things, especially when they are cultivating that life themselves. For many children it is their first chance to have contact and responsibility for something alive. With carefully planned seasonal activities, a Historic Theme Garden nourishes the curiosity of children throughout the year.

Using food in daily lesson plans also serves to reinforce and add meaning to the overall story of a community. Students can feel that they have gone back in time, for example, by using recipes of days gone by for cooking and baking activities. Nutrition, too, takes on new meaning when students have their own garden to grow foods that many may have never tasted before. During the cold months, an indoor winter garden provides students with daily contact with plants. Growing lettuce, sprouts, beans, peas, and radishes indoors gives children year-round access to fresh, healthy, and nutritious foods. Also, classroom earthworm farms are excellent garden teaching tools for learning soil science, the life cycles of worms, and the decomposition process.

Schoolyard Habitats. Schools are surrounded by a wide variety of habitats that are home to a diversity of fascinating life. Many schools in Vermont now are beginning to use their schoolyard habitats in order to explore the delicate interrelationships between all living creatures and the unique ecosystems that support them. Food Works is working in schools and communities across the state to develop a series of schoolyard habitat learning centers, nature trails, and indoor habitat stations that are introducing students to their natural heritage, which they had never before dreamed was possible to explore in school.

We have found that the outdoor classroom is a powerful tool for teaching across the curriculum as teachers discover first-hand how traditional subject areas such as math, social studies, science, language, and creative arts can be naturally integrated through investigations in Schoolyard Habitats. Forests, meadow-thickets, marshes, and streams are just a few habitat learning centers near schools that are providing excellent opportunities for real-life investigations and experiments across the curriculum.

To spearhead this initiative for broadening the classroom to include the school's natural surroundings, Food Works offers a three-credit hour graduate course specifically on schoolyard habitats to develop the schoolwide framework, seasonal projects, and hands-on activities based on the school's natural environment. From these courses, teachers are learning how to use dynamic outdoor habitats as vehicles for integrated learning.

Through the Common Roots process we introduce teachers to the concept of adopting a schoolyard habitat at each grade level so students can move from one habitat to the next with each successive year. Included in each grade's year-long journey are seasonal explorations of the relationship of human settlements to the land through history. Students gain practical first-hand experiences in observation, data collection, habitat monitoring, and strategies for preserving the diversity of their own natural ecosystems. Students carry this excitement back to the classroom with a blend of learning activities documenting their findings, analyzing data, drawing field maps, and researching flora and fauna. Additionally, we have developed a telecommunications system, RootsNet, linking up classrooms doing habitat research with other schools and communities. Our goal is to engage students as local field ecologists, documenting sensitive, threatened, and endangered species, and strategizing ways to protect their immediate natural environment.

Cultural Literacy. Very early on in our work in public schools, we recognized that children were learning little, if anything, about the customs, traditions, and lifeways of the cultural and ethnic groups within their community. With each passing generation, local wisdom, traditional knowledge, stories, and oral histories are disappearing.

> As places of local learning, schools must somehow respond to this daunting challenge: How do we, as educators, begin to develop the languages of dance, painting, music and narrative that primal peoples used as a means of encoding the moral templates for living in ecologically sustainable relationships, and providing members of the community the experience of transforming the ordinary into an extraordinary, transformative sense of reality? (Pinar and Bowers 1992, 21)

One aim of the Common Roots process is for schools themselves to become the repository for collecting the rich cultural legacy of the peoples who once lived here and who live here now.

Over the course of the year at the Peacham School in Caledonia County, for example, two multi-age classrooms focused on the roots of the Peacham community. Students took field trips to the historical society to research Peacham history, and contacted local elders to speak to them and share stories. Thelma White, an eighty-year-young school board member and former schoolteacher, was the catalyst for the project, and she contacted many of her friends to ask them to come in and have lunch with the students and share a story or two. As a bridge between generations, Thelma has taught us all about how to stay young in life from her keen interest in birds, insects, gardens, and the wonders of nature.

Another interesting project Thelma has been spearheading is creating learning materials both to prepare children to be with an older person and to prepare elders to be with children. Thelma led morning circles with students discussing what it is like to grow old and how to ask socially appropriate questions. On the other end, Thelma also made sure that her older friends took time to prepare for their visits with children by thinking about short stories and unusual experiences that students would be interested in.

Working with any school on cultural literacy projects, our goal is to catalogue elders' stories, local lore, crafts, and traditional skills so that the school can preserve and pass on this way of life to future generations. The Peacham School, for example, has hosted a series of seasonal events bringing elders and children together for a broad range of activities including bread baking, birding, composting, applesauce canning, making balsam pillows, planting potatoes, and drying apples. All of this has been videotaped, and Food Works is producing a short guidebook to assist other schools in reconnecting to their cultural roots.

So many elders have experiences to share that can easily fit across any curriculum. Unfortunately, however, they often perceive schools as a place for professionals and for children who are so busy preparing for the future that they are no longer interested in the past. But with Common Roots we have made the exciting discovery that once a teacher sees the intergenerational connections in their curriculum, and once an elder is given a meaningful opportunity to participate in the life of the community, a wonderful thing happens. Young and old become connected once more.

THE COMMON ROOTS STORY THROUGH THE GRADES: TEACHERS' VOICES

Here are the comments of a few Common Roots teachers describing their K–8 journeys.[1] The journey begins with the indigenous peoples (K–2), continues with the early colonial settlers (3–4), moves on to the multicultural fabric of contemporary communities influenced by U.S. and world historical patterns (5–6), and progresses to current and future relationships of communities to their natural and cultural heritage (7–8).

Indigenous People's Homes and Neighborhoods

Alecia Hingston, an early childhood educator at the Barnet School, was among the first Common Roots teachers to pilot the notion of a year-long journey to create meaningful, hands-on learning opportunities for young children. She uses her Three Sisters Garden curriculum to teach through the seasons of the year. Each community story begins with the peoples who first lived and walked this land. She explains:

> The Three Sisters Garden takes the students through a Native American journey. I weave this theme throughout the school year, with literature, social studies, the garden harvest, nutrition, science, drama, the indoor garden, etc.
>
> Through a garden we can show the whole of life, the full cycle instead of only pieces. I find I can also teach nutrition in the context of the story of the first inhabitants of Barnet where the food was gathered and hunted locally and people knew about the food they ate. With our garden, students develop an awareness of health and nutrition, a lifelong skill in making good food choices.
>
> The study of the indigenous peoples of Barnet is about a way of life that we are rapidly losing contact with. It provides a foundation for future learning. Today children sit down at a computer and have no idea that we once commu-

nicated with a smoke signal or a drum beat. As we look into the future I think we need to be aware of the continuum of the past.

There is a lot of gloom and doom relating to how we have treated the earth, and I want to give them a way to be pro-active in showing their care and concern for the earth. If they are able to experience this early love for the earth, they will care and become good stewards. The health of the earth will be relevant to their lives.

The most important thing is the stewardship in teaching the children about the earliest days of Barnet. The harmony that needs to exist between all people and the earth can be demonstrated by exploring Native Peoples' relationships to food, environment, and towards each other. My reasoning behind teaching this is that the students will bond with the earth and hopefully take care of it as a result.

The Three Sisters Garden enables students to use all of their modalities as whole beings. The multiple intelligences come to life and they gain a rite of passage moving from one Historic Theme Garden to the next. With the gardens right outside our classroom it is so visual to them—they watch it each day, changing through the seasons, and they document this.

The Community Heritage Garden

As a teacher in a multi-age grade 3–4 classroom, Alex Houston has brought to life the heritage and ecology of the Duxbury community by integrating the historical class garden, food cooking and recipes from elders, and studies of their Winooski River watershed into the story of Duxbury's history. The Duxbury Roots Program was started in 1992.

Duxbury Roots has been a perfect focus for hands-on learning experiences for children to make a connection between then and now. In teaching local history, when you say to children, "Imagine what it was like with no TV, no cars, etc."—they just can't do it. But when they plant a garden just like the gardens that the early settlers here had, and when they use the seeds they saved over from last year to grow their own food, that they can imagine because they're doing it in their own garden.

When the children research the foods the settlers grew, and then go out and grow it in their own garden, it puts a whole new perspective on history. It makes the learning real for them.

Just using their hands changes their learning. The things they find in the earth spark so many other inquiries—about insects, rocks, artifacts. They've found pottery and old nails on our garden site. We now have our own box of artifacts that we found in the garden. It really makes kids stop and wonder, "Wow, who was here before us?"

Then they use those foods to cook and make a meal. Picking potatoes is like finding treasure for them. When they go out in the cold to harvest, they experience the hard work of farming—digging, pulling, washing, storing; then seed saving and experimenting with local potato recipes. After we harvest we prepare the garden for winter by turning the soil and broadcasting winter rye as a cover crop, which we turn into a green manure in the spring.

By January we start to plan what we are going to plant in our outdoor garden. The students read historical novels and research what people ate and planted then.

In the fall we have a schoolwide harvest festival called "Dining out in Duxbury," where the students harvest, cook, and serve meals to over 300 parents and community members. Each class turns its classroom into a cafe, and they work together taking orders, serving the meal, cleaning up, demonstrating what they have learned. It really brings out the spirit of the community.

The Sustainable Garden Ecosystem

The Newport Town Roots Program has incorporated a number of interesting innovations into its Common Roots curriculum, including an outdoor bread oven typical of traditional community bread ovens of New England and Quebec. In order to teach U.S. history, Cynthia Lafoe, the fifth-grade teacher at Newport, worked with her students to design, build and plant the fifth-grade garden in the shape of the United States. Cynthia was honored as Vermont Teacher of the Year for the 1995-96 school year.

This year I used our Historic Theme Garden as a challenge for my class to research and design an outdoor replica of the United States. We used a 21' X 33' lawn area next to the entry of the school for our design process. It became a math portfolio problem that we had to solve. We wrestled with the question, "How do we get the whole United States out on the lawn?" We quickly decided that the most effective way was to use graph paper and trace squares onto the lawn.

This process was part of my "emergent curriculum" where I facilitate the inquiry of students towards finding the answers to their questions. On this project the students kept finding more math, geography, and ecological problems as they had to research the regions of the U.S. and reproduce them on our replica. Students learned about the direct application of math concepts such as perimeters, grids, scale, mapping. The biggest thing was that they were able to practice what they were learning, applied learning.

We felt it was important to put in the major rivers, mountains, and land forms. They recreated the Rockies, the Sierras, the Appalachians, the Mississippi, the Columbia, and other major mountains and rivers in a way I've never gotten across before. By the end of this, 100 percent of them knew the geography like never before.

After studying the geography of each region, they researched the climate, the people, and the major food crops. By using food as the focus of the curriculum, I found students gain a whole new respect for food. They develop a vested interest in being able to participate in every step of the food-growing cycle. It gives a sense of fulfillment that you don't get from going to a food store. The subjects that this theme brought together—math, geography, history, social studies, science, climate, writing, research, arts—it has been a beautiful, glorious project.

Culturing an Ecological Ethos

Ed Good is an avid birder and a grade 7–8 teacher at Washington Village Elementary School where we have conducted our course on schoolyard habitats. Ed feels that cultivating an environmental ethos depends entirely on whether or not children are allowed to develop a real intimacy with the natural world.

Here's my take on how ethics works. The thing that builds an ethical human being, an ethical child, is not reasons, but *feelings*. The energetic base of morality is compassion which requires being in touch with things, feeling empathy. That's not just environmental ethics, it's any ethics. And you cannot feel empathetic toward something until you're intimate with it somehow. Intimacy is the key word here.

And these students that are going out into the woods year after year are establishing a certain intimacy with that habitat by developing a personal connection to a place. Every year they become more aware about what's going on; they really know the relationships not just intellectually, but they can sense them. That's where environmental ethics comes from.

SUMMARY

There is no simple formula for transforming public schools into community learning centers based on sound ecological principles. Indeed, our own "transitional tool kit" of curriculum development strategies is itself being continually transformed as parents and educators from communities around the country adapt their own unique earth-centered approaches to teaching and learning. Through all of our best strategies, practices, and methodologies we return to our common work at hand:

To sense ourselves to be one with the world, surely, awakening that realization must be a central task for an education which would heal the fractures wrought by our disassociation from other life forms with whom we share this small planet. (Kesson 1995, 3)

It is this imperative to reintegrate ourselves into the greater whole which guides our day-to-day activities out in the world.

Each week we receive phone calls from teachers, principals, school board members, and students across the United States and Canada, intent on initiating a holistic process for school change, requesting the practical, community-based teaching that we have to offer: graduate courses for teachers on comprehensive curriculum development; hands-on workshops on historic theme gardens, schoolyard habitats, or watershed studies; introductory presentations about how to get started with the Common Roots process; or our Common Roots curriculum guidebooks offering seasonal stories, activities, and projects for curious young minds.

At the very least, we feel that this growing demand demonstrates that we have found several powerful methods and approaches that can assist schools and communities to nurture more creative, passionate, and self-motivated children for the tremendous challenges of the near future. A brief summary of the fundamental elements to this process follows:

First, educators, together with the community at large, must collectively recognize the massive ecological changes their own region and the entire planet have undergone in the past century. Further, we must acknowledge the role of our educational system in that process. This central issue must continually be the focus of school change and community development, an issue that must be returned to again and again through the process of conscious, guided inquiry. By linking education and ecology at the very heart of the school development process, we are both providing schools with a real-world context for learning to take place and building the foundation for holistic education that honors the natural interconnectedness of all things.

Equal to this, we have found that it is crucial for schools to focus curriculum locally, even while using resources, teaching materials, and lesson plans that come from far away. We have discovered that by learning "the basics" in the context of their own community, students are more eager to take ownership of their learning process. At the same time, they learn to value and treasure the place where they live, which contemporary educational practices tend to undermine. If teachers are giving children the unconscious signal to disregard their own history and homes and neighborhoods and woods and rivers in school, then they will tend to disregard those of the rest of the world as well.

In creating a context for local curriculum, we have seen the power of unifying the curriculum through the unique story of each community. Not only does a story help place each teacher's disparate units in a logical continuum, but a local story speaks clearly to parents and community members about honoring their roots through a journey of discovery. The teaching power of stories is a time-honored tradition which our culture ignores at its own peril. Theologian Thomas Berry speaks to the power of story in giving meaning to our lives on a more universal level:

> For peoples generally, their story of the universe and the human role in the universe is their primary source of intelligibility and value . . . . It communicates the most sacred of mysteries . . . . The deepest crises experienced by any society are those moments of change when the story becomes inadequate for meeting the survival demands of the present situation. Such, it seems to me, is the situation we must deal with in this late twentieth century. (Berry 1988, xi)

As the central catalysts of the school change process, teachers should be given far greater opportunity and assistance to collaboratively plan, design, and implement their curriculum within a local context of ecological sustainability. The failure of schools to develop consistent unifying themes that are meaningful to students is not the fault of teachers. It is a design problem inherent in the structure of the larger educational system, which itself is reflective of modern socioeconomic processes that created that system. To address this enormously complex issue at the micro level, teachers must be allowed to break down the institutional walls that separate and isolate them in school in order to work together cooperatively *as part of the normal school day*. Besides being a useful strategy for creating consistent curriculum through the grades, our on-the-job research has shown that from sharing their experiences of success, struggle, frustration, and inspiration, teachers are able to nurture among themselves the kinds of communication and cooperation they are trying to cultivate in children.

Finally, as we open ourselves to more earth-centered ways of knowing and being in the world, it is only natural to feel a certain fear, resistance, and anxiety. Questioning the dominant story or mythos upon which our civilization's belief system is founded can be a painful process that challenges our personal sense of security. But we feel, along with millions of others, that this questioning process is healthy and good as we collectively awaken to our intuitive connection to nature and to one another. This unfolding of consciousness demands courage, strength, and desire in order to let go of conventional patterns of learning and knowing that society supports and schools teach. We are finding this process of letting go of old patterns—personally, professionally, socially—more and more compelling as we experience how these routines and habits are exhausting us physically and emotionally while failing to nurture our inner life.

Increasingly, educators are recognizing the power of nature as our teacher in both content and method. No longer isolated into compartmentalized units, we can be free to discover the vital life force that exists in each of us, in the land itself, and in every family, neighborhood, community, and bioregion. Our challenge is to allow this natural impulse to take form in our everyday lives and make this learning our lifelong curriculum.

Notes

1. An evaluation report sponsored by the Vermont Department of Education includes numerous students' comments about the Common Roots Program. See Kathleen Kesson, *The Barnet School: A Case Study in School Restructuring* (Vermont: Vermont Department of Education, 1995).

References

Berry, Thomas. (1988). *The dream of the earth*. San Francisco: Sierra Books.

Bowers, C.A. (1993). *Education, cultural myths and the ecological crisis*. Albany: State University of New York Press.

Gore, Albert. (1992). *Earth in the balance*. New York: Penguin Books.

Horton, Myles. (1987). *Highlander Center promotional calendar*. Tennessee: New Market.

Kesson, Kathleen. (1995). Holistic education and the ecologically responsive mind. Paper presented at the Education for a Green World Conference, Rutland, Vermont. October.

Orr, David. (1994). *Earth in mind*. Washington, D.C.: Island Press.

Pinar, William F., and C.A. Bowers. (1992). Politics of curriculum: Origins, controversies and significance. In Gerald Grant (Ed.), *Review of Research in Education 8*, pp. 163–190. Washington, D.C.: American Educational Research Association.

2 Deepening Children's Participation through Local Ecological Investigations

Paul Krapfel

My associates and I develop biology investigations that draw 4–8th grade classes into field studies of plants and animals common on playgrounds of northern California. We decided to use local species for three reasons. First, we wanted the kids outside. Second, declining school budgets made bus trip–dependent field classes rare. Third, we believed that the deepest lessons are the ones we practice on our own; we wanted to focus kids' attention on things they would continue to encounter on weekends and vacations.

An awareness of "deeper lessons" developed when I was a naturalist with the National Park Service giving campfire programs and nature walks. My goal was to inspire in my audiences the same enthusiastic love and awe for the natural world that nature inspired in me. Because I presented the same programs week after week, I could experiment with different presentations and styles. Different responses from my audiences taught me that some formats create deeper learning than others. I came to have respect for the Zen saying about how the finger pointing at the moon is not the moon. I wanted my audiences to focus on "the moon" (the natural world), not my "finger" (my words) pointing to it.

One reason I especially wanted to do this was that so many of the programs I listened to made the National Park sound completely known. We rangers were so busy presenting concepts about nature we didn't realize that silently we were saying that this world was now uncovered and understood. The scientists I met working in the National Parks never had this attitude. They, more than anyone else I met, exuded with every breath an awareness of how much they didn't know. This paradox fascinated me. Those people our culture viewed as knowing the most viewed themselves as knowing only a little. I wanted to instill that combination of wonder and humility in my audiences.

When I became an educator for a natural science museum in northern California, I participated in many teacher-training sessions. I quickly became dissatisfied with most of the environmental education curricula (such as *Project Wild* or *Project Learning Tree*) because they were "generic." Since they were intended to be used by teachers anywhere in the United States, they could not focus on the specifics of the living things right around us. Although the activities were about nature, they could be done in such a way that students remained completely isolated from the natural world.

In working with teachers, I also learned that most lacked knowledge of the world around their school. This was partly because many were teaching in a different place than where they had grown up and partly because most of them had never learned to view the natural world with intellectual wonder. These two reasons interact in a way that can bleed our culture of engagement with the natural world. If families and teachers are moving around too much to learn about the region they are living in, then the next generation lacks adults to lead them into fascinated learning about this world. I wanted to help reverse this process, so we began a museum project developing science investigations that used phenomena specific to our region.

The response of teachers to these investigations has been positive enough to maintain this project for seven years. During that time we have developed ten curriculum units.[1] The most popular have been ones dealing with birds of northern California, volcanoes, ants, energy flow through spring ponds, filaree (a common name for *Erodium,* a spring wildflower), and autumn oaks. We have field-tested these curricula both in our museum programs and in classrooms throughout our region. We have given a variety of inservice presentations to more than one thousand teachers.

Our work has several characteristics. One is a focus on science. This focus stems partially from the fact that we are a natural science museum. But another reason is that most of the people I've met who are emotionally bonded and committed to the preservation of the natural world have been scientists. The scientific approach can lead an investigator into an emotionally deep relationship with the world. We wanted to try creating that experience for students doing our investigations.

Another characteristic is an emphasis on the immediate schoolground. While working to promote Adopt-a-Stream, we had found that teachers who did not have a stream within walking distance of the classroom were limited by school budgets and structures in what they could do. Our curricula therefore focused mostly on phenomena that were right on the school grounds. This allowed us to incorporate investigations, for example, in which students did daily monitoring over a week or two. One advantage of this is that it permitted students to continue observations and experiments during recess and on their own time. It also allowed the activities to spread like wildfire throughout the student body, something we always delighted in each time we went to field test a curriculum. At lunch and recess, we could watch many of the students continuing the momentum of their investigations with kids from other classes. This momentum had a wonderful feedback loop because the ability to teach one's peers helped make the investigations even more fun.

In the course of doing this work, the interactions between students and nature have sensitized us to a dimension of learning that is important to environmental education. Education that moves in one direction along this dimension leads student into deeper participation with the world. Movement in the other direction leads them toward intellectual and emotional detachment.

We are still learning to navigate our teaching in terms of this dimension which has several attributes. I will use various anecdotes to demonstrate these, incorporating the graphic motif above to visually unite the different parts of this chapter.

TRANSCENDING THE OBVIOUS

Let me begin by describing a well-received technique we have used again and again: marking something that is slowly changing—such as a flower. An advantage of using locally common species is that investigations are dirt cheap, which makes our investigations attractive to teachers who have limited budgets for science investigations. Every student can mark his or her own flower. A student ties a piece of yarn lightly around the base of a specific flower and then writes her or his name on a piece of masking tape which is attached to the yarn.

Several things happen during such an investigation. The first is focused attention. Most of us, when we see a field of flowers, see only the flowers that are in colorful bloom. Day after day we notice the blooming flowers and so, somehow, we assume each particular blossom stays there day after day. Only when we mark a specific flower so that we can observe it on a daily basis do we discover that the flowers of many species have dropped their petals by the next day. The flowers we see the following day are new ones that were not open the day before. A blossoming flower is ephemeral, often lasting only a few hours.

Once students are aware of the ongoing changes happening to specific individuals, then they can begin measuring and graphing the changes. For example, students can be asked to measure the rate at which a flower's pistil lengthens as its seeds develop. Or whether leaves decay on the scale of days, weeks, months, or years. They might also examine the rate at which daylength and shadowlength change through the year. Rate is a very important concept which, unfortunately, is not taught well in our schools. Until high school, "rate" remains mostly a set of arithmetic calculations of "miles per hour" or "financial interest."

This is unfortunate because virtually all of our environmental problems are rate problems. The problem is often not the kind of change but the rate of change. Changing the rate at which solar energy flows out through our atmosphere underlies the "greenhouse effect." Changes in the birth and death rates can lead to exponential population growth. Many of the processes that underlie environmental problems are as natural as life and death. Pollution is quite natural; life has been dumping toxic wastes into the environment for billion of years. Animals defecate all over the place and exhale carbon dioxide. Our current problem with pollution lies in the rate at which we are dumping toxic wastes and the slow rate at which many of our manufactured toxins break down.

Marking things also helps students become aware of slow changes. Too often we think of nature as "always there," or we think of changes as too slow to see. We don't practice looking for the changes. Therefore, change remains an intellectual abstraction rather than a visual reality. As the graphic below suggests, awareness is limited to the obvious. But all the world is just a transitory stage within larger but "invisible" processes of growth, decay, succession, and evolution. By marking specific objects, we focus students' awareness on this deeper level. Science truly is consciousness-expanding. Kids' awareness is usually limited to changes that happen at a rate that can be observed within a few seconds. Many kids are impatient even with these changes and will try to accelerate them. They poke the slowly moving snake; they create a flood on a stream table. Common changes happening over many days are little-known to them unless, by marking, attention is focused on specific examples.

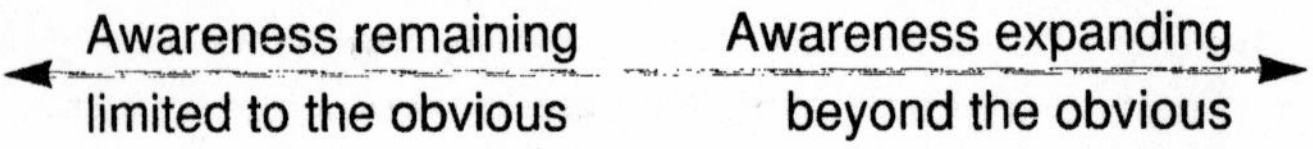

EMBRACING THE COMPLEX

When I began this work, I tried to design classic "recipe" experiments. I tried to control variables so that all students would obtain the same unambiguous results and therefore reach the same conclusion that the experiment was designed to teach. But despite my efforts, students could not get uniform results. There is simply too much interconnected variation, both in the natural world and in the way different students proceed with their investigations. Unfortunately, my desire for certain results, when it encountered variation, led me into bad teaching. I found myself saying phrases like "What you should have gotten was . . ." or, "We can discount that result because . . ." or, "If we had done this right, what we would have found was . . ." And I would see blank faces and feel ebbing interest. I could imagine an internal dialogue within the students. "Why are we supposed to pay attention to some variables and not to other variables? I don't understand. I think I don't like science."

In wanting to focus on one variable that would teach a chosen concept, I was discounting the effects of all the other variables. I was discounting the opportunity for students to directly experience how complexly interconnected the world really is. This happened enough times for me to begin loosening up. Rather than jumping in to discount "extraneous" variation, I found myself holding back and nourishing group discussions about what the results meant. This change began leading to class discussions concerning all the variables that might be shaping the results and the different possible interpretations that could explain them. These discussions often led to a class-designed second experiment to move our understanding beyond the ambiguity. As I loosened up, I found it easier to revel in the messiness of experimental results, to see them as "first drafts" that would lead to "second drafts." But usually the teacher in each new classroom I field-tested investigations in had not loosened up. What was it I had learned that they hadn't had a chance to yet discover?

What I had learned is that kids instinctively give the teacher more slack out in the field. The classroom is a teacher-controlled environment. Which subjects are taught when, which activities are done, and what is marked correct or incorrect are controlled by the teacher. But kids realize that the teacher cannot control what is happening in the field. A teacher is expected to know the answer to every question asked in a textbook, but students do not expect a teacher to know everything in the field. The entire focus shifts from question-answer dialogue to sharing and wondering. A more collegial relationship is possible in the field. Rather than the teacher examining the student, they both stand together examining the world in wonder. This especially happens when the teacher shifts away from a one-time-only recipe experiment (either you get the right result or you did something wrong) to an ongoing series of experiments, each growing out of the discussion of results from the previous experiment. The following quotation from a junior high student in a class I taught reveals how a face-to-face direct investigation of the natural world influences his awareness. Notice how the teacher is completely missing—especially in terms of providing motivation or determining when the investigation is completed.

> Well, I think that the first thing that I learned from science is that the only way to prove something is to try, try, and try again until you come up with some kind of results. The only way to learn something is by studying something, and in science you have to have your full concentration on what you are doing because a moment's lapse of attention could mess up your whole experiment. Also, when you start a new experiment there isn't a lot that you can assume. For example, in our experiment when Jon said that when he breathed hot air on the fruit that it unwound, we could have assumed that hot air was the cause but that would have been wrong. In an experiment you must explore all the possibilities, otherwise nothing has been proven.

A quotation from another student demonstrates how science is extending and deepening his concentration in an enjoyable way.

> I have learned that science takes a long time to get one answer and science is a very slow process. I think that I am beginning to like science. You have to be very observant while doing science or else you might miss something that happens.

Student-generated experiments led us into developing a certain trick that I call "turning demonstrations into investigations" or "investigating at a deeper level than you plan to teach." I first became aware of this when I wanted students to experience plant transpiration as one of the many "flows" that connect oak trees with their environment. Together we bound plastic baggies around clumps of leaves and found moisture within the bag a few hours later. Some bags had a lot of moisture; others had only a few drops. What could cause the variation? This led to student-generated follow-up experiments. Half the students would put bags on the south side of blue oaks, and the other half on the north side. Or half the students would put bags on valley oaks, and the other half on interior live oaks. By teaching in this way, we drop to a level below the concept of "plants transpire." Grappling with whether north side leaves transpire as much as south side leaves, students learn about transpiration at a deeper level than if we had simply explored plant transpiration with one bag on some leaves. We find ourselves increasingly using experiments to investigate such fundamental natural relationships.

The important point is that kids respond better to the real thing with all of its complexity than to a simplification. When I began this work, I was trying to make the world more understandable by simplifying it for students. I now believe this was a mistake. I have great faith in children's ability to grapple with the complex as long as they are given opportunities to talk about it and do follow-up investigations. In fact, I have come to believe that complexity attracts and invigorates their minds. Participating in these discussions makes me believe deeply that the human mind evolved and is right at home within nature's incredible complexity. What we call "science" is the exercised, collective mental practice that is a natural trait of our species. When people decry science as "reductionist," they refer more to recipe science than this real stuff. I am reminded of a wonderful passage from Michael Waldrop's book, *Complexity,* describing an interview with John Holland, a computer scientist researching adaptation:

> What captivated [Holland] wasn't that science allowed you to reduce everything in the universe to a few simple laws. It was just the opposite; that science showed you how a few simple laws could produce the enormously rich behavior of the world. "It really delights me," [Holland] says. "Science and math are the ultimate in reduction in one sense. But if you turn them on their heads, and look at the synthetic aspects, the possibilities for surprise are just unending. It's a way of making the universe comprehensible at one end and forever incomprehensible at the other end." (1992, 153)

In my personal growth during this work, I have come to revel in the true complexity of the natural world. Here is one way to picture this dimension of learning.

THINKING SYSTEMICALLY

Another way to describe the dimension of complexity is in terms of systems thinking. Peter Senge (1990) mused that there were two essential steps in making the transition to this way of thinking. The first is shifting from seeing the world as "snapshots" to seeing it as processes. Marking flowers is an example of how our investigations help students make this first transition. The second is shifting from seeing cause and effect relationships as linear to seeing them as spirally built to create feedback loops. Studying how variation in our results arises from the interaction of multiple relationships usually leads to this. So our field biology investigations have the effect of moving students toward systems thinking.

It took us several years to recognize this effect. The delay was partly due to the way my thinking had been circumscribed by the classic debate among educators between teaching "content" and teaching "process." I started this project believing that these investigations were rightly skewed towards "process." For example, several investigations focused on the way an *Erodium* carpel plants its seed by twisting and untwisting in response to moisture. Kids are fascinated by this behavior, and in the course of the investigations, they engaged in many of the processes of science: measuring, graphing, averaging, and analyzing data. In terms of content, however, no science framework or standard calls for knowledge of carpel behavior. Science standards are made of terms such as magnetism, astronomy, plate tectonics—not *Erodium* carpels. But I felt I could justify a class spending time with these investigations because they gave students direct experience with the process of science.

A deepening awareness of systems thinking, however, has led me to change my sense of what the content really is. The content is not how filaree carpels behave; the content is how this behavior leads us to deeper understanding of the influence of weather patterns, soil conditions, and other species on this wild flower. The content shifts from objects to the relationships between them and the processes that connect the world. Understanding how this particular phenomenon is shaped simultaneously by many variables is the content. In so many "content versus process" debates, content is presented in terms of unchanging, independent, discrete concepts. But the world is richly interconnected; by understanding this interconnectedness, the concepts come alive. As systems thinking develops, we learn that much of the world's dynamics lie in the connections. So yet another way I could characterize the dimension of learning that leads to participation rather than detachment is that systems thinking points toward one of its poles; at the other are static, disconnected "things."

World as Disconnected and Static ◄——————► World as Interconnected and Dynamic

A comment from another junior high student illustrates the kind of understanding that emerges when processes become the content.

I've especially learned that science is very odd but it works so perfectly. Everything fits together in so many ways to make something work. I have learned that in the deepest crevices there is always something that makes things do what they do. From flowers to cells, everything has a way of working out.

FUSING EMOTION AND INTELLECT

A fourth thing that happens during these investigations is that many students emotionally bond with their flower or leaf. They name their flower; some students build little fences around their plant. The next day virtually all students ask whether they can go out and check on their flower. This personal interest is part of the power of students having their own flower or leaf to study.

The emotional power of these investigations was brought home to me as a class was engaged in an activity we often do after students have marked individual flowers and watched them change over time. This activity is done with very common, introduced "weed" species. I pick two samples, one at an early stage, the other at a later stage, and ask the class which one comes first. They can easily point to the earlier stage. Then I pick a third stage and ask them where it fits in. Then a fourth stage. Where that one fits in usually generates a bit of discussion before agreement is reached. Then I give them the assignment of picking at least eight different stages of the flowering process and arranging them in sequence from earliest to latest. After I have checked their sequence, the students can tape them onto paper so that by running their eyes over a sequence that occupies a few inches of space, they can observe a sequence that occupies a few weeks of time.

A fifth-grade boy came up to me frustrated. He had three earlier stages and three later stages, but he was very aware that there somehow was a gap between them. He could easily see how the earlier stages changed from one to the other and the same with the later stages, but the two different sequences might as well have been two different species. There was no "missing link" to connect them. So we looked together. I found a perfect, intermediary stage. He studied it for several seconds before he saw the transition. Suddenly an emotional "That is so cool" burst spontaneously out of him.

That spontaneous, strong emotion helped me understand a profound observation of Henri Bortoft, teacher of physics and philosophy: "In a moment of intuitive perception, the particular instance [that particular flower and its place within the sequence] is seen as a living manifestation of the universal [the fascinating process by which flowers develop into seeds]. . . . As an authentic discovery, this moment can only be experienced directly; it cannot be 'translated' adequately into the verbal language of secondhand description" (in Seaman and Mugerauer 1989, 299). I had tried to describe what the "missing link" would look like and how it would bridge the gap between the other two groups of flowers, but my words could not communicate the aesthetic impact of the actual sequence. Bortoft goes on to contrast this approach with the more common educational approach. This moment of perception ". . . is not to be thought of as a generalization from observations, produced by abstracting from different instances something that is common to them. If this result were the case, one would arrive at an abstracted unity with the dead quality of a lowest common factor . . ." (in Seaman and Mugerauer 1989, 299). An example of "an abstracted unity with the dead quality of a lowest common factor" would be textbook drawings of a generalized flower showing seed development. Such a drawing has educational purpose after students have directly experienced several examples of the process, but the drawings are no substitute for this experience. Instead, such drawings tend to lead to an emphasis on terminology with little understanding of what the terminology refers to.

This contrast between generalized abstractions and "particular instances" echoes Holland's "ultimate in reduction" and "possibilities for surprise" depending on how one looks at things (Waldrop 1992). Again we are encountering the same dimension possessing the same possibility for moving in two directions. However, this time a new characteristic is emphasized: the perfect fusion of intellectual understanding with aesthetic emotion. It is this fusion which creates the love of learning that drives scientists ever onward. A junior high student expressed this nicely.

I have found science very complicated and wonder how do they find out all of these small things within something that people usually pay no attention to. Science finds things very interesting no matter what it is. Like a little flower. We see a flower, but they see what its purpose is, what it does, how it works, and other things that make each individual plant seem like a whole new world. Science studies the things within things and makes everything seem interesting.

This fusion was also nicely expressed more simply by a fourth-grade student in one of our field tests. This boy, who occupied the classroom niche of class clown and distractor, wrote, "I like science now because I've learned that it can astonish your mind."

Separation of Intellect and Emotion ←	→ Fusion of Intellect and Emotion

Awareness of this dimension is important because curriculum frameworks for environmental education often have an affective component (an emotional response to the natural world) and a separate intellectual content component (an intellectual response to the world). If we think of these as separate, we will tend to teach them separately. We will miss the opportunity to practice both experiencing and teaching the two components as one fused unity.

We lose something when our minds and hearts become separated. I encountered this separation with an eighth-grade boy. On the first day of field testing, he had been a bit rebellious in a good-natured way. But he had come around and was now quite intrigued by both the flowers and the process by which the class was learning new things about them. By the fourth day, he stayed inside during recess, simply to talk with me alone about the investigations we had been doing.

After several minutes of good conversation, I asked, "Well, what have you learned from these investigations?" He thought about it for several seconds and replied in a somewhat tentative voice that had lost the sparkle it had carried up to that point, "That the coily seed thing is called a fruit." At first I was disappointed by this response (and the falling out of emotion in his answer). His noncommittal statement did not match the depth of our previous conversation. Then a new interpretation came to me. He was trying to translate his week's experience into something that would fit the slot he assumed I meant by "What have you learned?" What, out of this whole complex experience, would a teacher consider "learning?" Judging by his answer, he must have decided that I meant terminology, something that could be captured by a multiple-choice or fill-in-the-blank or match-the-word-with-its-definition type assessment.

There is a truism in education: "What you test for is what you get." This boy's response made me realize it goes deeper than that. Through our decisions of what to test for, we communicate to our students what, out of all the world, we believe is important and should be especially attended to. What we adults pay attention to is a profound form of communication to children. Students don't come to school knowing what it is they need to know. On the contrary, trying to understand what adults want is one of the most powerful communications children encounter as they organize the mélange of their experience into what they hope will be a socially responsible, productive life. Perhaps part of the disaffection many students fall into by junior high is related to their sense that the only thing the adult world esteems (based on the students' experiences in school) is sitting inside and learning a series of definitions and recitations of the packaged known, disconnected from emotionally powerful experiences.

The boy's response made me worry whether all the other students in the class were sticking only terminology in their mental file labelled "learning" and were putting all of the other things that were happening in these investigations into some other file that was *not* labelled "things I learned at school that will be useful to know sometime in the future."

So after recess, I shared our conversation with the class. I told them that what I was trying to teach them was not something that would fit into a typical test, so they should pay attention to what lay beyond vocabulary and other testable content. I then tried, for the first time, to state explicitly what I was hoping to teach with these investigations. I pointed out that we had learned, as a class, answers to questions students had asked. I asked the students to pay attention to and think about the process by which we were finding answers to our questions. At the end of the field testing, I gave that class my standard assessment instrument. "Describe what you have learned about science during this week? Not what have you learned about flowers (or oaks or ponds or ants) but about science." The replies from that class were the most powerful I ever received from any class. The students I quote throughout this article (except for the fourth grader) are from that class. Here are responses of three other students that describe their perception of the learning process:

Through these past few days I've learned a lot more about what the point of science really is. I always thought it was boiling liquids and blowing up of chemicals. When we first started this unit I was sure it would be boring and melodramatic. Yet it's not, although a few parts were confusing. I learned science is the search for truth. It is a study of the world which will never end. I think there are a few parts of science I could truly enjoy.

Also, you always have many reasons to why you are getting what you are getting. You may not know the reason so you must discover what it is. In science you must expect to sometimes be proven wrong or have to show your theory and prove its existence.

You have to do many tests if you are a scientist to find out things. Once you find out something then the question is why. You can't find a certain answer by people telling you things. You have to look to the world and find out things for yourself. If you are a scientist and you have a question, then do tests and figure out the answer.

That class taught me the importance of being explicit about the meta-lessons I am trying to teach. So often I have heard older students ask their teacher, "Why do we have to learn this?" It's a legitimate question to which I have heard several poor answers such as, "because it will be on the test" or "because you need to know this in high school." Their question is one we should think about deeply. What is it we want students to learn through environmental education and why?

EMERGENT DIVERSITY

This question leads us into a tricky area: the relationship between what we want students to learn and the structure of our schools, between what is taught and how it is taught. Our current school structures tend to produce learning that is centered on what Bortoft describes as "an abstracted unity with the dead quality of a lowest common factor"(in Seaman and Mugerauer 1989, 299). The curriculum frameworks and content standards are formulated as abstract generalizations; this leads to textbooks, lesson plans, teacher mindsets, and unit tests that emphasize known verbal formulas rather than student-centered perceptual breakthroughs. Our top-down hierarchies and mandates tend to create classrooms that are uniform in curriculum in which there is little space or time for students to pursue emotionally powerful discoveries.

The concept of "teaching about place" nicely illustrates this relationship between school structure and learning outcomes. The phrase *teaching about place* is an abstraction that, if turned into a standardized curriculum by mandate, would be a disaster. Imagine what a nationally distributed textbook designed to "teach about place" would look like. What questions could be asked in the end-of-the-unit tests that students from Alaska to Florida could answer based solely on the material in the text? A textbook could present a variety of bioregions (probably targeted on major urban areas) and describe how the physical characteristics and histories of different places interacted with the living things of that place. But such a cultural geography program is very different from what most advocates mean by "teaching about place." This mistranslation is caused by an educational infrastructure designed for a different purpose. On the other hand, if we leave this infrastructure and reorient our thinking away from what concepts will be taught and emphasize instead what students will learn through experience, then "teaching about place" means teaching what is here and now: what is touch-able, see-able, smell-able, hear-able, taste-able.

If "teaching about place" means learning about what is right around students, then this concept creates reverberations throughout the educational infrastructure. For example, local knowledge, by definition, could never be incorporated into nationally distributed standardized examinations. Therefore, assessment of students and evaluation of a school's program could not rely simply on tests of standardized content. Evaluation would have to look more closely at the local and nonstandardized. "Teaching about place" puts a foot in the door so that classes find it easier to go outside and look around for themselves and learn directly from the world. Classes would spend more time outside, which would leave less time for rote-learning drill sheets. Students would grapple with more complexity than most currently do. Teacher training would include methods for investigating the local environment.

There is a relationship between what is taught and the structure by which it is taught. Since most environmental educators believe that our society needs to make a mid-course correction, it's to be expected that there will be a mismatch between current school structures and the content environmental educators want taught. The simplest example is that the current school structure conditions children to associate being outdoors with unstructured play time. In order to focus academic attention, most classes need to begin within classroom walls. Therefore, there is a very strong tendency among teachers to remain indoors if the content area is considered academic. This can lead to either of two undesirable consequences. Content dear to environmental educators that is translated to inside paperwork might end up producing learning that is not considered important by the students, or curriculum taught outdoors might be viewed by the teacher as nonacademic activities peripheral to the essential core curriculum.

This mismatch between educational goals and educational structure is important. For example, in a mood of urgent crisis, one wants so much to have the power to change every classroom so that every child will become ecologically literate within a few years. This great desire can seductively draw a person to the upper echelons of educational administration, where resides the power to mandate changes throughout entire systems. However, if one steps back and watches carefully, one notices three intertwined characteristics of this power. The first is that mandates constrain teachers. Centralized power structures, regardless of their aims, work to create an educational monoculture in which each classroom replicates the same curriculum. The second thing one notices is the ineffectiveness of this power. Teachers resist the mandates out of their need to teach from their hearts. Mandates grow attenuated the closer they move to the classrooms and fade soon after their funding ends. The third is that such mandates lead to nonlocal, generic, paperwork-heavy curriculum because that is the only cost-effective kind of curriculum one can give to all teachers, many of whom will be teaching this mandate against their will.

It is hard to turn one's back on this power because the siren song of improving the education of all children and making society a better place through the implementation of a mandated curriculum is so tempting. I, however, have come to believe that the true path of environmental education lies not in changing the mandates, frameworks, curriculum standards, and generic textbooks but in changing the educational structure that currently expends its energy in creating mandates, frameworks, curriculum standards, and generic textbooks. Rather than requiring all teachers to teach environmental education, I would rather give teachers the freedom to teach from their hearts and give parents the freedom to choose the teaching approach they want for their children. I then want to help develop and demonstrate that an education that studies the world right around us is superior to a standardized, generic education. If we can demonstrate this convincingly, then there will be a growing demand from parents for teachers who teach this way.

By inserting the above diagram, I imply that the dimension we have discussed concerning a student's learning experience somehow has a cultural analog. Could it be that the educational structures that currently constrain environmental education are the product of the same cultural outlook that has created our environmental problems? Could it be that the work of changing school structures to better accommodate environmental education is one of the many tasks that will help our culture grow beyond our environmental problems? This possibility (along with the pitfalls mentioned earlier) deepens my meditation on the question: What is it I want students to learn through environmental education and why?

My answer is strongly shaped by my background in the tradition of science. My answer has co-evolved with my relationships with students. My current answer to "Why do we have to learn this?" is: So you can learn to read the story directly for yourselves. The world is a vast accumulation of fascinating stories. Through careful observation and sharing with others, we can learn to read these stories for ourselves. We don't have to depend on some established authority to tell us the story. That was the revolution science created! If you don't learn how to read the world, then you will be dependent on others to tell you the stories, and you will live your life according to their stories. But learning to read the stories for yourself will allow you to choose your own course.

This is my current answer. It leads me to avoid environmental curricula that preach or that present generalized concepts without examples that students can experience directly. My answer leads me outside with teachers and children to mark flowers, to see how and where and when they grow, to try figuring out why flowers here grow bigger and more numerous than flowers over there, all the time enjoying good air, sunlight, the smell of earth, and blossoms. Beyond the classroom, we are able to revel in both the order and messiness of the world around us.

WORK IN PROGRESS

The student responses included in this chapter came after ten hours of such experiences. How would students respond if they had this level of natural science investigations throughout their school career? Fascination with this question led my wife and me to create "Chrysalis"—a charter school focused on natural science investigations. We are using the freedom of our charter to explore to what extent nature study can form the backbone of a school's entire curriculum. As I write this chapter, the school has been in existence for half a year, so it is too early to draw conclusions, but working with the school makes us acutely aware of other educational issues that are peripheral to this article. Can computers be used to deepen students' understanding and appreciation of nature? What "outdoor" rules and structures need to be in place if a class is to work productively outside for extended periods of time? How much of the time should the teacher be following the interest of the students and how much of the time should the students be following the instructions of the teacher? (This is not an either-or question; there is room for much overlap.) What is the most productive blend of "place-based learning" and "nonplaced-based learning" (such as learning about ancient Greece)?

I will conclude with some tentative extensions based on our work at Chrysalis. Children are fascinated by the concept that they are surrounded by stories they can learn to read. A powerful phrase that sharpens students' perception is "tracks of the past." We are always finding tracks of the past that tell a story, whether it is a rotting log, strata in rocks, or the foundations of a pioneer's cabin. Almost all of the younger students that come to us have never practiced seeing the world in this way, and within a half a year most of them are developing the expectation that there are stories to read.

Systems thinking, on the other hand, is not a quick take. It is not developed within a few months. Systems thinking involves becoming aware of general principles that arise from complex specific examples. Like fine shale, this kind of understanding is laid down one layer at a time. Students need to encounter example after example of how systems thinking provides insight into dynamics that would otherwise remain invisible. Judging from students who have been with us in museum programs that preceded Chrysalis, we think it probably takes two to three years until students are spontaneously and accurately applying systems thinking to novel situations. However, given that systems thinking is not easy or common among adults, we believe the results we are seeing in pre-adolescent children are significant.

We are learning that repeated short experiences outdoors are best. It is better to go outside for one hour every day rather than on an all-day outdoor field trip once a quarter. There are two main reasons for this. One is that students' attention to their surroundings stays high throughout an hour trip whereas attention fades after a few hours. Second, repeated trips allow students a chance to get to know certain places well enough that they become sensitive to changes happening there. Repeated visits open up numerous opportunities for marking slow, subtle changes such as the changing diameter of a young tree or the eroding outside edge of a stream bend.

We have found that reflective writing or drawing while outdoors is a powerful way to bring the place, experiences, and lessons firmly into the mind. Short speculative discussions outdoors can help sharpen students' focus but lengthy, summarizing discussions are best saved for the classroom. Students find it hard to focus on a discussion when there are so many fascinating things lying and crawling on the ground.

Though outdoor investigations won't work with every student every time, our confidence is growing that if we take the kids outside, a lesson will present itself. Often we have a specific investigation in mind, but if we don't, that should not stop us from leaving the classroom. Nature is such a complex system, something interesting always occurs. And with each trip, students accumulate more stories and experience the participation from which both wonder and scientific analysis emerge.

Notes

1. In all of our curricula, we want students to look more closely at the world. Therefore, the *Ornithology* curriculum focuses on a common bird each week with a coloring page, species account, and observational challenges. The *Energy Flow through Spring Ponds* curriculum contains directions for transforming a $10 wading pool into a lively study pond that attracts an amazing amount of life. *Autumn Oaks* has students observing many of the ecological processes involving the most common group of trees in Northern California. Curricula are available at Carter House Natural Science Museum, 800 Arboretum Drive, CA 96001.

References

Seamon, David, and Robert Mugerauer (Eds.). (1989). *Dwelling, place and environment.* New York: Columbia University Press.

Senge, Peter. (1990). *The fifth discipline: The art and practice of the learning organization.* New York: Doubleday.

Waldrop, M. Michael. (1992). *Complexity: The emerging science at the edge of order and chaos.* New York: Touchstone.

3 From Human Waste to Gift of Soil

Madhu Suri Prakash
and Hedy Richardson

With the introduction of Mr. Crapper's "flushed with pride" device for "crap," the lives of modern people all over the world have been radically transformed.[1] This transformation has been at least as radical as those engineered by the automobile, train, or plane. Modern technologies of the latter kind habituate people to transporting their bodies over large distances in a very short span of time. Mr. Crapper's technology, on the other hand, "educates" or habituates people to another type of transportation: that which creates an instantaneous and complete distance between themselves and the products of their intestines and kidneys—their so-called "human waste." At a very tender and impressionable age, the moment they learn to balance their bodies on the water closet seat, modern people are educated to acquire the attitudes and dispositions of those who not only cherish but are in fact totally dependent upon the state-of-the-art descendants of Mr. Crapper's device which, with one deft, easy movement of the flush toilet's handle, transports the "unpleasantness" evacuated from their intestines so far away in a matter of some seconds that they do not have to waste another thought on their "waste." In the large cities of the "civilized" world, millions of gallons of "purified" water are "consumed" every single day in transporting human faeces and urine.

Today's human waste, however, is not alone in using modern means of transportation for rapidly travelling far and wide. *Qua* food, in its earlier incarnation prior to ingestion or excretion, it is already a well-heeled traveller of the "civilized" world. The "typical mouthful of American food travels 2,000 kilometers from farm field to dinner plate" (Durning 1991, 159). Furthermore, in the obsolescent age of "Long Distance, Short Life" (Fairlie 1992), razor blades, cameras, newspapers, and all the other disposable "goods" that define modern life are also intrepid globe trotters—moving many thousand miles from source to sink in frivolous, brief life spans, amounting to no more than the mere twinkling of an eye. A convoy of ten-ton garbage trucks used to transport only a part of the waste annually produced in the United States alone, if placed in single file, would reach halfway to the moon.[2]

This is called "progress" or "development" (Sachs 1992). It is also said that "ignorance is bliss." The bliss of such progress is expressed in the oft-repeated adage: "out of sight, out of mind"; that is, once out of their bodies, modern individuals never have to see or give any serious thought to their own excrements ever again—unless they fall sick or the plumbing fails. In the case of the former, physicians generally ask them to start paying attention to what they evacuate. In the case of the latter breakdown, a professional sanitation "engineer" or flush toilet "doctor" (yet another modern expert), working in conjunction with an elaborate centralized sewage bureaucracy of the State or the Market has an appropriately expensive treatment for a decidedly modern, economic commodity or good: waste. Like other modern commodities, it is transported, packaged, treated, bought, and sold, making major contributions to the expansion of the economy, national, international, and global.

Mr. Crapper's nineteenth-century water closet (or W.C.) took hold of the industrial world after World War II, totally reformulating the urban environment. Today, the W.C. and its sewage system are the very expression of modern life, urban as well as rural. Modern identity is defined by it. We have been informed about numbers of draftees honorably discharged because they suffer from the inability to perform an essential human function in the absence of the water closet. They are habituated not only physically, but emotionally as well—convinced that it is a "basic human need," and therefore, a legitimate moral claim or "right." In the worldview of international development experts, whether in the fields of education, economics, health, manpower, or city planning, "civilized" human beings "need" Mr. Crapper's device as much as they need classrooms, health centers, airports, highways, factories, refrigeration, and all the other pieces of the package called progress or development. Peoples and places still lacking this package of "goods," "needs," and "rights" are classified as primitive, underdeveloped, or failures of development.[3]

The private water closet, tying the self to the vast and intricate system of the state's sewage pipes, is an apt metaphor for the logic of contemporary sociopolitics. Like industrial eating, modern sewage ties people's intestines to several centralized bureaucracies. In doing so, it breaks them off from their communal commons. The individual self, shaped, defined and dis-membered from community by the water closet (and other industrial inventions) is forced into increased dependencies on the market or the state; constituted by institutions and technologies so complex and large that they disregard the limits that define the human scale. Opacities that hide ecological or cultural damage and destruction are the "natural" result.

Being as opaque as all other modern technologies, modern sewage systems fail to reveal to their users that by promoting convenience today, they are inconveniencing those yet to be born; that by absorbing vast proportions of the water piped into private homes and public institutions, involving an inordinately high consumption of energy, they are creating scarcities of drinking or irrigation water for those that constitute the Two-Thirds World ("social majorities"). Equally opaque for their users is the fact that the technology designed for the privacy of individual selves (demythologized as far back as de Toqueville), transforms them "down the tubes" (so to speak) into millions of alienated atoms, constituting "the masses" of the modern State. Urban planners reduce W.C. users into a numerical or statistical unit of volume: the amount of faeces generated per head count. Instead of a communal responsibility that belongs to peoples' commons, human waste is now transformed into a state matter, controlling all citizens required to follow official regulations. Opacity, privacy, and atomization prevent individual selves from seeing that every time they pull the chain for what they believe is another modern "liberation," hidden strings pull them into conformity with State norms.

In the "age of cultural evaporation," describing the violence involved in manufacturing "One World" through the project of global development, Wolfgang Sachs (1992) writes: "At present, roughly 5100 languages are spoken around the globe. Just under 99 per cent of them are native to Asia and Africa. . . . Yet many indicators suggest that, within a generation or two, not many more than 100 of these languages will survive" (102). Neocolonialism, through five decades of development "aid," spreads abroad the cultural damage and destruction already wrought at home. "It is, after all, scarcely an accident that Europe, the home of literacy as well as the nation-state, has only 1 percent of all languages left. Whichever way one looks at it, the homogenization of the world is in full swing. A global monoculture spreads like an oil slick over the entire planet" (Sachs, 102).

All state institutions, and especially the educational system, destroy not only linguistic diversity, but also the diversity of cultural practices regarding defecation or urination. Part of the furniture of the global monoculture carried abroad by electronic mail, the World Wide Web, and the jumbo jet is the W. C. As a basic human need, the W.C. is offered or imposed upon the social majorities, justified as progress; a mode of privacy and convenience that they seemingly lack; and that they are expected to aspire to and achieve as a human right.

Most of those who constitute the Two-Thirds World have never used the W. C. and probably never will. What do these billions of people do to maintain, enrich, and regenerate their cultural practices of defecation or urination? How have their richly diverse traditional practices evolved in this matter over the centuries? For the "educated," these are usually not pertinent questions. They do not constitute modern studies of multiculturalism or cultural diversity. The relevance of such questions is usually buried under the burden of evangelisms for saving the underdeveloped; or doing something for the poor.

WASTE NOT, WANT NOT: BEYOND THE UNIVERSE OF MODERN WASTE AND ILLITERACY

The indigenous, traditional, or nonmodern peoples of every continent have evolved their own cultural practices and traditions for cleansing their bodies without creating waste (matter, human or other, that is out of place or inappropriately placed). Bodily ejections are returned to the soil of commons and communities, composted in ways as diverse as those that differentiate their cultural and physical soils. Making soils with tools that are convivial, communal, simple, and transparent, they dispense with the elaborate, opaque, and expensive hardware of subterranean sewage pipes. Neither do they waste nonrenewable resources like water.

In places as far apart as Vietnam and Guatemala,[4] communities have evolved "dry latrines": ecologically responsible and benign ways of composting faeces and urine without the wasteful and toxic creation of modern "black waters," requiring the proliferation of disastrous chemical treatment plants. Their latrines avoid waste and toxicity by preventing the combination of three naturally beneficent elements—faeces, urine, and water—into the odorous, toxic, polluting mixture that is transported as modern sewage. These dry latrines, cheaply and ingeniously constructed, separate faeces from urine. Rich in fertilizers, urine is used in the household garden to water and fertilize fruits, flowers, and vegetables. Faeces dropped into a dry chamber in the toilet, protected from humidity, odor, or flies through a dusting of layers of soil, ash, and lime, sprayed after each motion, composts over a period of two or more years into a rich manure. These indigenous technologies enable people the safety of keeping their evacuation at home, protecting themselves and others from pollution and toxins. Separated from each other, neither urine nor faeces need to be shipped off or transported anywhere. They stay within the precincts of home economics and communal commons. Kept within the horizon of their users, dry latrines encourage every household to take full responsibility for their human waste without relying on "experts," with their expensive, centralized, and opaque bureaucracies.

Grassroots Postmodernism: Pedagogies of the Oppressed

For the masses, the common people, the marginals who constitute the Two-Thirds World, the water closet emerges as a need only when urban friends or relatives come for a visit to the village and cannot accommodate themselves to "primitive" local conditions. Some members of the social majorities have undoubtedly been taught that the water closet is a basic human need, and, therefore, a legitimate political claim. While a few have succeeded in getting their claims met, most others are not even waiting for a solution to an artificially created modern predicament. By now, many have learned the hard way the consequences of this scientific improvement. Living in the places where the social minorities transport their black waters, the social majorities are learning how these pollute their soils and rivers, creating problems for which they have no solutions in their own traditions. Furthermore, the social majorities are fast learning that, despite the promises of state functionaries seeking election (or re-election), sewage systems remain an impossibility. The masses know that state budgets for water or energy are not designed to provide them the privileges taken for granted by the social minorities. No doubt some marginals resent this fact; most others seek alternative solutions that help them retain their common sense—particularly their sense of community. Those experimenting with dry toilets and other alternatives to the W. C.'s sewage system are rediscovering nature's ways for transforming their "waste" into valuable community soil, participating with full autonomy in the organic chain of life. Instead of using expensive water and energy to transport and treat their faeces, they are not producing waste (black waters) but life (compost). Inexpensive, decentralized, transparent, and "environmentally friendly," these allow the social majorities to enjoy a renewed sense of local responsibility.

San Luis Beltrán offers one of many such grassroots postmodern initiatives.[5] It became a *barrio* of the city of Oaxaca in southern Mexico during the last two decades when the city's growth extended itself into neighboring hills and valleys. Like other suburbs of Oaxaca, it lacked a modern sewage system. In 1987, the people of this *barrio* learned of the experiences of other communities that had opted for dry latrines as a result of confronting shortages of water. With the help of outsiders from these pioneering communities, they built their first twenty-five dry latrines. To construct the remaining 200, they needed no outside help; they had each other. Once dry latrines began to be publicly discussed in Oaxaca, villagers visiting the city, eager to learn the best available techniques for building and using this specific tool, began to arrive in San Luis Beltrán, now quite famous in the region for its dry latrines. In 1992, city authorities announced that San Luis Beltrán was being included in the government's plans for extending the sewage system of Oaxaca. The people of San Luis Beltrán opposed that plan, knowing that Oaxaca lacks a treatment plant; that its black waters are contaminating everything, including the Atoyac river—which, for many centuries, used to be the source of water and pleasure for all the inhabitants of the city. Their community explored the consequences of transporting their sewage onto the lands of neighboring communities. Their response to the city authorities was: "No, thanks." Following that specific decision, they confessed that their original acceptance of dry latrines had initially been provisional: until the time they succeeded in acquiring modern facilities. After their experiences with dry latrines, however, they came to appreciate the meaning this technology has for communal autonomy. They chose not to fall victim to the W. C.

While the social majorities of the Two-Thirds World are regenerating traditional knowledge to pioneer paths beyond modern unsustainability and waste,[6] postmodern educators are also designing educational projects to shorten "supply lines for food, energy, water, and materials—while recycling waste locally—impl[ying] a high degree of competence not necessary in a society dependent on central vendors and experts" (Orr 1992, 92). David Orr's *Ecological Literacy—Education and the Transition to a Postmodern World*, for example, offers a theory and practice of education that attempts to reverse the evolutionary wrong turns taken to create the unsustainable modern era (Prakash 1995). By composting and remaking communal soil, these take us beyond the waste caused by modern ecologically unsound practices.

Ecological Literacy and Dry Latrines

For several months during Spring 1994, we studied *Secundario "Instituto Patria,"* a small junior high school located in the town of Xico, Chalco Valley, a few miles southeast of Mexico City (Prakash 1994). Only a few decades ago, before its transmogrification by economic development, the valley of Chalco was prodigiously fertile, rich in diverse agricultural traditions that had evolved over centuries. The destruction of its natural and cultural wealth started during the colonial period. It was violently accelerated because of the development projects of the post–World War II era. In the last two decades, the population has more than doubled. A fever of construction projects overtook the region perpetrated through massive investments by public and private developers. These have created enormous ecological and social damage. This damage and violence to ecology, culture, community, and commons is nakedly exhibited to residents of and visitors to the Chalco Valley—as it is in Love Canal, Bhopal, and other disasters of modern civilization. Located minutes away from the "black waters" of Mexico City, this bleak, treeless, odorous, and grimly grey settlement, a human overflow from other overpopulated urban centers, has become home to 400,000 people, desperate for a place on earth they can call their own. Less than an hour away from Mexico City, Xico-Chalco has successfully acquired many of the so-called modern goods and services.

While modern transportation, along with other technologies and institutions, is a part of life in Xico-Chalco, Mr. Crapper's device has failed to make its inroads into this suburb of Mexico City. In the majority of Xico-Chalco homes, the modern waste of their kidneys and intestines goes nowhere. Evacuated into a hole dug in a corner of their house lots, it stays where it is dropped. Because of its ever-present odor, students and their families are forced to pay close attention to it through the seasons, daily applying industrially manufactured deodorants; more so during the rainy season when the water table of Xico-Chalco rises dangerously—often forcing above ground the faeces that were sent under during previous days and weeks. Every few years, the families are compelled to dig a new hole in the ground in another part of their property after the old one fills up.

After two decades of failed electoral promises, most people in Xico-Chalco are still awaiting the arrival of modern facilities, including flush toilets—even though these would be more disastrous for the ecology of this place than they have proved to be in other parts of the world. The Chalco valley lies on top of an aquifer and at the bottom of what was formerly one of Mexico's loveliest lakes. Since the aquifer is being drained at an alarming rate to supply the unending water demands of the residents of Mexico City, it is sinking as much as a quarter meter every year. Given that Chalco is located in a basin lower than its surroundings, its problem of sewage is reaching untreatable proportions. Promises for development and progress in Chalco include some of the biggest pumps on earth, requiring multimillion dollars of investment and very complex engineering works—despite the knowledge that the peat soil under Chalco, when drained, could sink, making sewage systems buckle. The domestic water presently used in Chalco or accumulated during the rainy season has by now reached the foundation level of its houses, many of which are at the point of collapse. All this portends catastrophic floods to the whole urban area—threatening to mix potable and black waters. "Educated" to embrace all modern/Western expectations, they await the sewage system—an election-year promise continually reneged. The situation in Xico-Chalco provided an ideal opportunity to develop among students an awareness of the ecological consequences of generally unquestioned modern assumptions and technologies.

Sanitario Ecologico

At the school, *Secundario "Instituto Patria,"* in Xico-Chalco, different groups of teachers and students have started several projects for sustainability and ecological literacy: daily composting all organic matter; recycling nonorganic school waste; growing and cooking organically grown macrobiotic foods, etc. Complementing these projects, we initiated an interdisciplinary curriculum and pedagogy for ecological literacy: to study and research the production, distribution, and improvement of *sanitario ecologicos/latrinas secas* (dry latrines). This project develops the knowledge, skills, attitudes, dispositions, and habits required for regenerating communal soil—physical and cultural. Pioneering teachers at the school have embarked on a radical postmodern path: instead of waiting for a modern sewage system, they are learning how to resist and liberate themselves from this modern technology; opting for ecologically friendly ways of making cultural and physical soil from the same substances that modern peoples call "waste."

The dry latrine project simultaneously develops theoretical and practical skills. History, English, Spanish, social studies, natural sciences, journalism, community development, recycling, waste "management," and other disciplines are taught in the integrated manner essential for engaging in moral education and ecological literacy. Through their extended participation in Chalco's *Sanitario Ecologico* Educational Project, teachers, staff, and students are challenged to teach as well as to learn from each other in and through particular activities that demand cooperation. The mutuality of learning and teaching among teacher-students and student-teachers challenges all participants to acquire more than abstract, theoretical knowledge. They gain the concrete, practical skills needed to transform their homes and community. The theory and practice of dry latrine installation needed to solve the sociopolitical, economic, and ecological problems of the local community do not require the teachers, staff, and administrators to be experts. All the adults involved learn in cooperation and conjunction with the students. While learning the standard academic or theoretical skills, teachers, students, staff, administrators, and parents are breaking new ground. By bringing an alternative, postmodern technology into their community, they are overcoming the modern ignorance and indoctrination engendered through advertising and other forces pushing economic development.

The dry latrine project involves "learning by doing." The school day is divided into two parts. During the afternoon, teams constituted of students, supervising teachers, parents, and neighbors install at least one dry latrine a week for the entire academic year in the homes of community members. This is key to communal learning. The mornings focus on theoretical explorations of this postmodern technology. The theory and practice of producing, promoting, constructing, and installing dry latrines involves several elements: (a) curing themselves of the ignorance and apprehensions regarding dry latrines—including fears of odor, disease, plagues, dysfunctionality, underdevelopment, or backwardness; (b) liberating themselves from their blind faith that the flush toilet of the developed world is superior or more desirable; (c) emancipating themselves through the discovery that even if the flush toilet were made available to the population of Xico-Chalco, it would not be desirable; that, in fact, it would prove to be a catastrophe for a whole set of ecological, economic, political, health, moral, and educational reasons; and (d) developing leaders in the community for the production, promotion, installation, and construction of alternative postmodern ecologically friendly technologies.

Theoretical, in-class investigations during the morning offer a wide spectrum of issues and disciplinary perspectives:

- The history, sociology, and anthropology of mainstream technologies, including the flush toilet
- The social and natural sciences as well as language arts needed to understand the social significance of experiments (like those of Mr. Crapper) for promoting modern science and technology, while destroying and co-opting "people's science" and indigenous technologies
- The critical sociopolitical investigation of the kinds of colonialist practices that brought the Crapper device to the whole world in

the context of developing it; or, worse yet, the latrines created for the poor by the rich—as modes of "false charity"[7]

- The latent/hidden ecological problems of water use and treatment associated with the installation of modern sewage treatment plants and the flush toilet
- The careful study of why these problems have been kept well hidden by the scientific establishment, the national governments, as well as the corporate structures that produce and market the products worldwide
- Alternative cultural practices and traditions for human waste disposal that have flourished and continue to survive all over the world
- The history, anthropology, and sociology of dry latrine installation in different parts of Mexico as well as other countries in an attempt to bring in postmodern technologies
- The theoretical and practical exploration of ways to communicate or spread the word through pamphlets, cassettes, *talleres*, and other projects in order to educate the community about alternatives to their present expectations of the provision of sewage systems by the government
- The systems study of the soil and general geography of Chalco in order to understand and explain to the public why the installation of sewage systems by the state and the market, even if it were to take place as promised, would actually be dangerous, further destroying the already devastated ecology of the region

This project of constructing and installing dry latrines develops knowledge of the different subject areas in an integrated manner. The social and natural sciences are used for understanding the politics and economics of disseminating modern sewage systems. The knowledge of these sciences can also be used to understand reasons for replacing modern waste systems with postmodern systems that draw upon traditional wisdom. Mathematical and other numerical skills are developed in comparing different sanitation systems as well as alternatives to sanitation or in studying epidemiological impacts and economic costs. English skills are developed through the translation of the literature that is now available on the problems of the flush toilet and the modern sewage system, and the alternatives that are being conceived and experimented with all over the world, including Chalco. Spanish skills are developed not only to understand the literature, but to conceive and implement creative ways of spreading the word within different subsections of the local community, as well as in neighboring regions. By producing cassettes and magazines that cover local stories of change, improvement, and experimentation, students learn documentation techniques while keeping a careful register of the whole spectrum of educative experiences that constitute this project.

An important element of the project is its economic design. It strengthens the bioregional economy of husbandry and care, generating local sources of income and self-sufficiency through the production and installation of the dry latrine pots. Students earn while learning. "Promoters" get a "profit" (a margin included in the price of the dry latrine pot) to pay for their work in launching the idea within the local community, educating neighbors and the public, and supervising the construction and use of the dry latrines. The dry latrines are constructed through a revolving fund. This fund was set up during a meeting at the school in 1994. It provides soft credits of three to six months.

Innumerable educational, economic, ecological, and sociopolitical benefits stem from this project for students, teachers, parents, and other members of the community. They improve their community by addressing one of its most pressing needs. They enjoy greater communal autonomy, freedom, or decentralization. They increase their knowledge of their place: its soils, its waters, its waste, and its neighborhoods. They deepen their understanding of the different subjects required to make sense of their concrete problems, whether ecological or sociopolitical, as well as how to address them with practical common sense. The sensibility that emerges is communal.

FROM SOUTH TO NORTH: THE REVERSE TRANSFER OF POSTMODERN TECHNOLOGIES AND PRACTICES?

The dry latrine project in Xico-Chalco has taught us much about "grassroots postmodernism." From the perspective of those interested in making transitions to a postmodern world, we discovered why and how the so-called "disadvantages" of "underdevelopment" or "poverty" should actually be viewed as advantages and opportunities. In the absence of huge existing investments made in the elaborate infrastructure of modern sewage systems, for example, Xico-Chalco is ideally located for launching revolutionary alternatives to modern "waste" technologies. Neither habituated to nor trapped by modern sewage systems, the people of "underdeveloped" places like Xico-Chalco can more easily consider and experiment with simple, small scale, decentralized, low-tech technologies for going beyond destructive, modern waste.

It might be asked, however, what relevance, if any, the dry latrines of Xico-Chalco have for life and learning in our modern, developed suburbs of the North. Is it desirable to import the dry latrines of Guatemala or Vietnam into the neighborhoods where we live or the schools and universities where we teach in the North? Is it even possible to do so?

Tangled within the vast opaque and rigid chains of metallic subterranean sewage pipes and administrative bureaucracies (municipal and other), the simple act of installing a dry latrine even in our own suburban homes or apartments seems daunting, if not impossible. How would we go about gaining the permission to do so in our countries where violation tickets are issued for dandelions that grow six inches above the norm ordained for lawn grass height? Counties where it is still illegal to compost uneaten broccoli flowerets, carrot ends, or empty egg shells? Furthermore, from where would we obtain the dry latrine pots, so abundant in Xico-Chalco but never glimpsed in the Wal-Marts of the North?

While some of us remain daunted when confronted by these questions, others are already moving ahead as courageous pioneers. They have started taking small but sure steps beyond Mr. Crapper's device. In our region, for example, our community farmers, creators and sustainers of Community Supported Agriculture (CSA), have, for years, saved their urine in old gallon milk containers. Instead of flushing it away to be chemically transformed in sewage treatment plants, they have been gifting their urine to the fruit and vegetable plants they grow for us every year. Living a few miles outside the dictates of city codes, on their farmlands they are enjoying the freedom of improvising alternatives to the dry latrine by composting their faeces with grass and leaves.

Over the years, we have sent a steady stream of undergraduate, graduate, and grade school students to study these experiments that transmogrify human waste into gifts of soil. Learners who experience these alternatives first hand suddenly find their imaginations liberated from the chains of Mr. Crapper's contraption. They begin to gaze beyond the cemented sidewalks and sewage pipes of modern suburbs to landscapes of soil and streams where humans are naturally rejoining nature's cycles; where no industrial infrastructure is needed to ecologically return dust to dust.

Notes

1. Thomas Crapper was most likely the manufacturer and popularizer of the flush toilet rather than its inventor, contrary to Reyburn's (1971) story. In

Old English the word "crap" referred to the husk of grain or the dregs of beer or ale (*Oxford English Dictionary*).

2. To understand the big business of modern waste, creating jobs and other goods and services, see also Wendell Berry (1990); Simon Fairlie (1992); Dan Grossman and Seth Shulman (April, 1990); John Young (1991).

3. For the most incisive deconstruction of these and other related words see Sachs (1992).

4. While working with refugees in the jungles of Guatemala, we studied how even when displaced from their places, their village soils, these indigenous peoples find ways to properly place their "gift" (*atujual* in Quiche) protecting it from degeneration into modern "waste." Communities of refugees dig separate trenches in the forest for men and women. Menstruating women have their own separate trenches. Their gift to the land is covered not only with ash and soil, but also the bark of a particular tree indigenous to the region. Long fronds are used to cover the ditches at night and are removed in the morning. After two years, the gift, now fully composted, is used to create mounds on which corn is planted. These refugees have created these ways to grow their own corn even in the midst of the jungle's inhospitable soils, far from their homes and villages.

5. For other examples, see Esteva and Prakash (1997).

6. Jean Robert has conducted an extensive theoretical and practical research on other grassroots communities experimenting with dry latrines and other related alternative technologies. He is part of an informal network of people working at the grassroots to prevent faeces from being transformed into human "waste." With Cesar Anorve, he has created a technological variant to the Vietnamese latrine. He has written several essays on the history of the water closet as well as on the theoretical issues involved and the alternative technologies available.

These experiences stimulated lively public debates in Mexico. In association with groups from Guatemala, Colombia, and other countries, two world seminars were held in the late eighties: the first in Medellin, Colombia, and the second in Mexico City. The organizers were at first surprised by the kinds of response they got to an informal, open invitation. The presentations of "experts" from a dozen countries revealed advanced "scientific" alternatives for addressing the modern production of human waste. They have created the Latin American Network for Alternative Technology (RETA, for its acronym in Spanish: *Red Latinoamericana de Tecnologia Alternativa*). Several books and extensive materials, documenting experiences all over the world and describing the most recent advances, have been published. The documentation is available from Jean Robert, Opcion, S.C. Cordobanes 24, San Jose Insurgentes, Mexico, D.F. C.P. 3900.

7. For example, in the times of *Punta del Este* when the big and powerful were concerned with the impact of the Cuban Revolution, the World Bank formula for development of the "underdeveloped" included massive latrinization. On that occasion, Che Guevara denounced the "solution" as the modernization of poverty; giving poor solutions to poor people, instead of struggling

against poverty itself. The latrines promoted by the World Bank and many other governmental and nongovernmental organizations since then are not only ugly and uncomfortable—full of flies, odors, and disease—they are also polluting the aquifers. Postmodern alternatives reject those latrines as they do the W.C.

References

Berry, Wendell. (1990). Waste. In *What are people for?*, pp. 126–128. San Francisco: North Point.

Durning, Alan. (1991). Asking how much is enough. In Lester Brown (ed.), *State of the world: 1991,* pp. 153–169. New York and London: Norton.

Esteva, Gustavo, and Madhu Suri Prakash. (1996). Grassroots postmodernism. *Interculture* 23(2): 3–52.

Esteva, Gustavo, and Madhu Suri Prakash. (1997). *Grassroots postmodernism: Beyond human rights, the individual self, and the global economy*. New York: Peter Lang.

Fairlie, Simon. (1992). Long distance, short life. *Ecologist* 22(6): 276–283.

Grossman, Dan, and Seth Shulman. (1990, April). Down in the dumps. *Discover*: 36–41.

Orr, David W. (1992). *Ecological literacy: Education and the transition to a postmodern world*. Albany: State University of New York Press.

Prakash, Madhu Suri. (1994). Chalco's *Sanitario Ecologico* educational project. A paper presented to *El Centro de Desarrollo Communitaria Secundario "Instituto Patria,"* Xico-Chalco, Mexico, July 1994.

Prakash, Madhu Suri. (1995). Ecological literacy for moral virtue: Orr on (moral) education for postmodern sustainability. *Journal of Moral Education* 24(1): 3–18.

Reyburn, Wallace. (1971). *Flushed with pride: The story of Thomas Crapper*. New Jersey: Prentice-Hall.

Sachs, Wolfgang. (1992). *The development dictionary*. London: Zed.

Young, John. (1991). Reducing waste, saving materials. In Lester Brown (ed.), *State of the world: 1991*, pp. 39–55. New York and London: Norton.

4 From Margin to Center

Initiation and Development of an Environmental School from the Ground Up

Dilafruz R. Williams and Sarah Taylor

In the spring of 1995, the Portland School Board approved a proposal that allowed a group of parents, students, teachers, and other community members to start a new Environmental Middle School in the Portland Public School District, in Oregon.[1] Facing a financial crisis due to changes in tax structures passed by Oregonian voters in 1990, the school district had begun the process of "downsizing" with impending staff and teacher layoffs and program cuts.[2] As public confidence in supporting schools was becoming questionable, many feared that parents would withdraw their children from public schools. To regain public confidence, from 1995 on, the school district began to offer, with the support of the superintendent, new *alternatives* in education to provide choice to parents within the public school system.

Despite fiscal uncertainties and the fact that were there were no schools in the district that had their curriculum and pedagogy centered on the environment, the Environmental Middle School (EMS) opened in September 1995, with the mission of weaving ecology into education to make schooling meaningful for young adolescents. Here we present a formative story: (1) the sowing and rooting of EMS; (2) the joys of nourishment and growth of EMS as a fertile community that links with the local community and place; and (3) the challenges for EMS of confronting on one hand, the tough soil of modernism with its urban realities, and on the other hand, state/school district policies which regulate the school's tenor, bearing, rhythm, and pulse.

EMS began as coauthor Sarah Taylor's dream that brought interested teachers, parents, students, and community members together to embark on a creative journey with a shared vision. This fluid and loosely knit collection of dreamers and planners, whose core group included eight members (including the coauthors), met to discuss and imagine the possibilities of alternatives in education that would specifically address care of the earth and also meet the needs of young adolescents in a *public* school setting. There was common interest in creating a "small" middle school unlike the district's "large" ones, which had five hundred to more than a thousand students. As planning began, an unexpected turn took place. A Native American elder joined the group, providing insight into Indian understandings of human-environment relationships. His participation also made the group realize the needs of Native American students, their high dropout rates, and the curricular match that the Native American children and parents would potentially find in a school such as EMS. Discussions about structure and curriculum were approached with Native American and other culturally diverse students in mind.

A number of beliefs surfaced in the group that helped define key characteristics of the school. First, environment would be at the core of the educational program. Second, since all children, including adolescents, have a natural and compelling affinity for the outdoors, the program would ensure direct experiences with nature. Third, civic pride would be nurtured by connecting youth to the bioregion. Adolescents are at a time in their lives when they struggle with developing a sense of self. Tied in with this struggle is, on one hand, high-risk behavior; on the other hand, there is idealism and commitment to friends, family, and community. If the program was dedicated to fostering an environmental ethic and interest through community service it would likely prevent high-risk behavior, even as it motivated adolescents to take responsibility for Portland, its greenspaces, and its communities, including the elders. The school would break barriers of isolation by extending into the community and by being permeable to the community. Finally, cultural representation would be ensured by reaching out to various neighborhoods and a special curricular strand would be offered to attract Native American students. Excited about the prospects of shifting environmental education from the margin to the center of the educational experience, and of building a middle school from the ground up, the following questions became central to developing EMS's mission:

- How could our urban middle school be designed to respond to the pressing ecological problems that we encounter today?
- How could a safe and nurturing educational community be created where adolescents could learn from their relationship with the natural environment and the community?
- In what ways could we ensure that this middle school would have an integrated and holistic approach to environmental education rather than a piecemeal and add-on one?

- Since the financial scenario of Portland's public schools was not promising, in what ways could local greenspaces, parks, and community resources be used to supplement what textbooks, computers, or special classes have to offer?

Since the proposed Environmental Middle School was not an independent charter or private school, the dreamers often had to come down to earth and confront certain realities. Being a public alternative school, some of the structures within which the sowing of the dream was to occur were already in place in the school district. The district's developmentally appropriate curriculum framework, and the state education department's new benchmarks for eighth graders were taken into consideration so that on graduating from EMS students would be ready for regular high school. Furthermore, the district's staff hiring and layoff policies were also strictly adhered to. As the proposal was passed by the school board, and as the seeds of EMS were sprinkled and began to germinate and establish roots, the above factors along with the realities of the urban social and political climate also had to be faced.

LOCATING A SITE

On sowing, dreams need fertile soils in order to germinate and flourish. Sometimes we can find soils that are already fertile; sometimes we have to "work" the soil to enrich it. The condition under which the proposal for the new school had been approved by the district was that it would be housed in an already existing school building. As the search for a site began, we considered the following to be important factors: (1) the school had to be in a central location so that students from all neighborhoods could participate; (2) there had to be land around the school for naturescaping and building gardens; and (3) the school had to be on an accessible local public bus line so that students and teachers could use public transportation to reach the various greenspaces and the community. Not only would public transportation dispense with the need for extra funding for private buses, but students would learn to value public transportation and learn the norms of public behavior. After several efforts, we found an elementary school that had many empty classrooms due to dwindling enrollment and whose location and grounds met the above criteria. On approval by the school district, EMS took up residence as a separate middle school sharing the site with the existing elementary school. The process of dwelling began even as we, the strangers, sprouted roots often to be entangled in a mesh of hostility and discomfort that outsiders are accustomed to experiencing. The soils of coexistence were often deeply fissured around a variety of matters: territorial—such as sharing classrooms, resources, staffing, gardens, and so on; developmental differences—adolescents' needs clashing with those of elementary school children; or educational philosophies—differing orientations to curriculum and pedagogy. Working the soil has been a critical venture; sometimes territorial fissures are sealed but new ones develop from time to time.

STUDENT AND STAFF SELECTION

As the site for EMS was sought, brochures and application forms were developed and sent to all fifth graders in the school district. Special efforts were made to reach inner-city neighborhoods and local Native American organizations. In their applications students are required to present an essay describing their experiences with nature. They have to explain why they want to be in a school such as EMS with its special focus. We had decided to take only 120 sixth- and seventh-graders during the first year and to increase the enrollment to 150 for grades 6–8, in the second year. However, the first time the school was presented to the public, the event drew more than 300 parents and children. Due to this overwhelming public interest in the new school, which took us by surprise, we included some eighth graders the first year. In the third year, we raised the enrollment to 180 students because of the school district's configuration for staffing; the student-teacher ratio had to be increased in order to be able to save the positions of a teacher/coordinator and a secretary.

Staffing has been an edgy issue for the school. In the first year, selections had to be made from applicants, some of whom were new to the school district, with first preference given to those teachers who were tenured and had requested transfer to another school within the district. EMS needed specific qualities in its staff, both in skills for interdisciplinary middle school teaching and also qualifications for environmental science-related fields. Fortunately, during the first year, three new teachers who were appropriate matches for the school were hired. However, at the end of the first year, these new EMS teachers were among 300 the school district had targeted for dismissal.

This uncertain fiscal scenario and related staffing issues have been among the biggest challenges for EMS. Following the district's policies for hiring, it has been difficult to maintain continuity and staff morale.

How can teachers be enthusiastic about teaming when they do not know whether they will have jobs at EMS? If preference for hiring is to be given to transfers within the district, whether or not they have the special skills needed to teach in a school such as EMS, can the integrity of the program be maintained? When there is lack of staff continuity, to what degree can the curriculum for mixed-age classes be developed and implemented? Furthermore, how can a new school such as EMS operate without a funded position for a coordinator when this position is crucial for supervision of added curricular and pedagogical responsibilities for outreach in the community? These shortcomings have left the soils of EMS eroded on many an occasion. However, the regular assessment of implementation, along with its hurdles and successes, brings the EMS community together even as its members get frustrated or invigorated to work with a renewed sense of mission.

OVERALL FRAMEWORK, CURRICULUM, AND PEDAGOGY

On the national and international scene, environmental education, if included at all in the curriculum, has long been marginalized (OECD 1991; OECD 1995; Andrew and Robottom 1995). Considered one more subject to be added to the already dense curriculum, environmental education is usually reduced to the transmission of a body of knowledge or facts related to nature study (Elliott 1995, 33). Largely predefined by syllabi and textbooks approved by school districts, environmental education has been subjected to the same dominant culture that requires mastery of textbook facts or mastery over information processing. To counteract this, in recent years, some K–12 environmental education programs have included field studies and interdisciplinary curricula along with practical guidance on addressing environmental problems in their communities in order to provide a more holistic understanding of the relationship between self and environment (OECD 1991; OECD 1995; Traina and Darley-Hill 1995). The Environmental Middle School is in keeping with this more compelling philosophy. Developing a sense of awe and wonder about nature—that is, appreciating the *poetry* of nature—is just as important as comprehending its *science*. Equally needed is an understanding of the social, political, and economic conditions of modern life so that environmental issues are contextualized. In order to provide opportunities for students to create meaning about what they are learning, EMS has taken an active hands-on approach with the curriculum and pedagogy centered on context and locale. As a study of environmental programs in a number of countries states:

> Young people need to feel that they can do something in society that is respected, that they can influence the reality in which they live—in short, that they matter. They need a framework to gain experience in investigating, reflecting, and acting on their environment. This is most important . . . because meaningful activities motivate learning. (OECD 1991, 11)

It has long been established that students learn best when they can make connections between what they are learning and why (Dewey 1916). What matters to them? Why are their environment and communities important? How are the connections between self and environment to be made? What happens in day-to-day ordinary activities that empowers adolescents to make personal and emotional commitments to their education? At EMS, environmental education forms the core through which other subjects are addressed. On one hand, students feel a sense of beauty and wonder about their natural surroundings. On the other hand, by addressing real-life environmental problems related to their own community, they become sensitized to and gain practical experience for dealing with local situations. Recognition of environmental problems and exploration of ways in which these can be addressed and solved requires that thinking not be restricted to any one particular discipline. Nor can learning stop with mere cognitive understanding of the problem; emotional commitment to the process of learning is also needed.

An important feature of EMS is that it is a loosely planned learning community. While the general structure and curriculum framework are in keeping with the school's philosophy, there is enough flexibility to permit connections with the community as opportunities for engagement arise; and, rather than have discipline policies that must strictly and consistently be adhered to "by the book," the approach taken by the coordinator is that each child is unique and each child's discipline-related issue needs to be dealt with on its own merit. This loose structure, both in terms of the curriculum and in dealings with students, has had its advantages and disadvantages. Let us consider the curricular advantage first. For example, one cannot plan ahead for floods in the community; however, when there is a loose structure, a school can respond to floods and community needs by addressing questions of why floods occur in the first place and how erosion can be controlled in practice. Flooding and community service can thus become curriculum matters linked to the interdisciplinary theme of "rivers." As we present examples, it will be clear that the kinds of experiences students have had in the community would be impossible were it not for a variety of nonlinear ways of connecting EMS with community events and needs as they arise. Similarly, if one adhered strictly to discipline policies, some of the students who have traditionally been left out of the mainstream of schooling would drop out. By addressing each student as a unique person, the EMS community finds ways to deal with behavior problems that only a handful of students seem to consistently exhibit. Yet, a few teachers and parents, especially those who have never operated without strict guidelines and year-long plans, find it difficult to cope with the uncertainties and the flux in which they find themselves due to EMS's flexibility. A large proportion of students come from diverse urban neighborhoods and backgrounds and have innumerable needs; this diversity, lack of supervision and absence of a caring adult at home, and the modern lure of gangs and peer pressure attract some adolescents who adopt inappropriate behaviors. Some of the staff feel that the lack of a structured curriculum aggravates behavior problems; and since no special staff are available to attend to these students' needs, teachers find the loose discipline policies to be a challenge.

At present at EMS there are 180 adolescents, seven teachers (including coauthor Sarah Taylor who serves as a teacher/coordinator), and many parents and volunteers. Six mixed-age classes of grades 6, 7, and 8, undertake the study of environmental core themes such as rivers, mountains, or forests that are used to integrate the curriculum. Math, environmental science, health, language arts, history, music, dance, and literature are connected with an intention to make learning meaningful. Spanish is taught as a second language. Community service plays a significant role as do direct experiences with nature. With block scheduling, students go outdoors twice a week to participate in a variety of environmental and community service projects. Students assemble daily in the auditorium for morning meeting which begins with everybody singing songs especially of peace, love, and care for the earth. This ritual of singing is critical to the formation of the collective, and to the attachment of students of all grades to the school as a whole. For adolescents, singing with others their own age and with adults can help them loosen up and dissolve barriers of communication due to peer pressure. Many songs also incorporate wit and humor that are appropriate for this age; they serve a purpose for celebrations, too. Morning meetings have served another important function: a variety of people from the community come to the school to present topics related to environmental, health, and other issues; elders, seventy to eighty years old, who come to these assemblies tell the history of place through their stories.

Once a month, a class takes on the responsibility to make a community meal for the whole school. Students, teachers, and parents plan these special meals, often shopping at a nearby Nature's store that sells organic foods. The very act of cooking can bring people closer; we have seen a sense of efficacy in adolescents' faces when the class in charge of community meal plans, cooks, sets up the classroom to serve food, and welcomes parents and community members including elders, providing ample opportunities for intergenerational conversations while eating together.

These in-school and out-of-school activities have been possible because more than fifty percent of parents and a large number of elders from the community are actively involved with EMS. When possible, these elders accompany the classes all day on field study twice a week. Student teachers and practicum students from Portland State University and Lewis and Clark College are often found learning jointly with EMS students and teachers both in the classroom and in the community. There is also a community-based partnership program for stewardship administered by Portland State University and the city's Bureau of Environmental Services that has made possible the adoption of the Tideman Johnson Park, which is in the school's watershed, for streambank restoration work. In addition, a number of environmental projects which include monitoring, mapping, removal of invasive ivy, or on-site gardening, recycling, and composting, are possible because of the support of organizations such as the Audubon Society, National Wildlife Federation, City Community Gardens, Green City Data, and Friends of Trees. In the next section, we present examples of curriculum and pedagogy and the voices of students, parents, and teachers, which demonstrate the intermeshing of community service and environmental studies in order to develop a sense of place.

PERMEABLE GROUNDEDNESS: COMMUNITY BUILDING AND CONNECTEDNESS

Much of the literature on urban public schools captures youth's disconnectedness from their communities and from their educational experiences. To counteract this trend, many proposals have been put forth to create schools themselves as communities of support in order to promote students' bonding with and attachment to school (Wehlage et al. 1989). Drawing upon the Deweyan notion of community, Raywid (1988, 3) argues that interdependence, communication, sharing, and mutuality are essential qualities of community. Communities come into being when individual members come together to pursue common interests. EMS, with its special focus on the environment, is at an advantage in that parents and students choose to come to this school. Furthermore, its small size, mixed-age classes, loose and somewhat flexible curriculum, requirement of teaming from teachers, and field activities provide a strong framework for what we refer to as "permeable groundedness." While EMS is grounded in its local community and place, it is also permeable to its community which helps to shape its direction and bearing; simultaneously, the community counts on EMS's members to provide vitality and service when needed. A school can reach its community best if its own texture symbolizes the experience of what it means to be a community.

The Willamette River, the Columbia River, and many of the creeks in Portland are accessible from school by public bus within five to sixty minutes. Many parks can be found in the heart of the city and within a twenty-minute bus ride. The accessibility of green spaces and the commitment to use public transportation (not special buses) have been crucial to the symbiotic relationship between the community at large and the school community. We should add here that although EMS emphasizes the local, it does not mean that students do not learn anything beyond their local region. For example, during one academic term, the entire curriculum was integrated around the theme of "rivers." Besides studying their local watersheds, students picked a river in the United States and conducted historical research on the impact of that river on humans and also ways in which humans had changed the course and nature of the river. They read novels in which rivers play a significant role, did art projects and painted murals, sang songs about rivers, conducted experiments and studied water properties, learned about water conservation techniques in their own homes, and monitored streams as they participated in streamwalks. Students wrote poems, which were compiled in a book, *A River of Words*. The culminating activity of this unit was a "River Festival" at the school, where students displayed their art and writing and the EMS community came together to celebrate the promising developments of the new school.

Building Historical and Cultural Gardens on School Grounds

To learn about rivers and watersheds is to learn about one's location and place, including the school site and the grounds. A local foundation provided funding for one of the first EMS projects. Joseph Kiefer, who describes the Common Roots Program in this volume, was invited for staff development in construction of gardens on site. One weekend, students, parents, teachers, EnviroCorps staff, and community volunteers gathered together to convert a portion of the school grounds into gardens. The initial efforts were some of the strongest ways in which members of the new school came together to become a community: digging out decades of sturdy grass; carting away the newly lifted turf; building raised beds; filling the beds with cartloads of compost and organic soil to enrich the garden; using recycled bricks and concrete blocks to create paths; setting recycled rubber tires into the soil to create circular beds; and building a shed to store the garden tools. The first steps toward becoming caretakers of the earth had begun. One parent commented: "It is important to give time and energy as a volunteer. I think it is great that EMS seeks opportunities [such as starting gardens] for kids and parents to have a positive impact, and for others in the community to see kids do good things." Such intergenerational interactions are contrary to the age-segregated schooling typically experienced in modern times. Tuesdays and Thursdays, which are field-study days, are spent weeding, sowing seeds, making interpretive signs, creating wetlands by channeling water from downspouts, and planning, designing, or simply maintaining the variety of gardens on the school grounds, including the cultural gardens, the medicinal and herb gardens, and the native plant garden. For the cultural gardens, Native American elders have played a significant role in providing guidance and wisdom.

Native Plants Outreach to Community

Local grants have been used to buy grow-labs for each classroom for propagating native plants in particular, since there is a high demand for these plants in Portland. A group of EMS students did research on the native plants in the region and prepared brochures showing why native plants were good for wildlife and for restoration and preservation activities and which plants were native to the region. One student wrote in the brochure: "Native plants are good because they add natural beauty, and animals like to come to your garden too. Your young children will like to see native animals in their natural habitat. Native plants keep out weeds, too." Another student wrote: "Being in a natural garden is more peaceful, relaxing, and fun than being in a nonnatural garden, where you can't even move without feeling that you just ruined a day's worth of gardening work just by running through the flowers." A sample sheet from the brochure is presented in Figure 4.1 to show how students explain why native plants should be used in a garden.

With the help of a teacher, students also designed a quilt with imprints of native leaves from the native garden at the school. A few months later, a booth was set up at a local nursery on several Saturdays

Why Use Native Plants?

Native plants are good to use in a garden because they are beneficial to the gardener and the environment. Nonnative plants often require much work to maintain, and they destroy the native habitat. English Ivy is an example of a nonnative plant that is taking over some of the natural habitat of our region. The ivy spreads quickly and strangles trees if it is not removed. This is one reason why we should plant native plants instead of exotics. But this is not the only reason.

- Gardening with native plants is inexpensive
- Native plants do not need fertilizers
- Native plants do not need to adapt to a new environment therefore they grow easily
- Plants native to Oregon will naturally thrive
- Native plants keep out weeds
- Buying native plants is the same price or cheaper than nonnatives
- Some native plants can be edible and be used for food or cooking
- Native plants will not kill other plants
- Native plants attract native wildlife to a garden
- Using native plants brings a garden back to its natural heritage
- Native plant landscapes conserve energy and water

Fig. 4.1. Landscaping with native plants. Sample page from brochure developed by students.

where EMS student volunteers, with parental support, distributed brochures they had designed, and explained to the general public the importance of using native plants. A woman, who had stopped by the booth out of curiosity and was now leaving with a cart full of native plants, exclaimed: "I came in merely to buy two tomato plants and look at how many natives I am leaving with! Thanks, kids, for all this information—I never knew that native plants required less effort and that they would bring wildlife to my backyard!" Students have also presented the project to the general community at a local conference on watersheds. Presentations such as these have given EMS students the opportunity to develop public speaking skills and to learn that their work is appreciated by the community and that they are not alone in becoming stewards of the watershed.

Urban Bounty Farming and "Salad Day"

A "Salad Day" project has also been started with local farmers[3] at Zenger Farm in a poor neighborhood close to a wetland along Johnson Creek. Students are learning about sustainable agricultural practices as they help plant lettuce. This project serves as a prime example of conservation and revitalization of farming in urban areas. The land at Zenger Farm is surrounded by fast-food drive-ins, wrecking yards, machine shops, an abandoned drive-in movie theater, and a suburban housing development. There have been intense community efforts to revive this land which had once been the source of food for much of Portland. For EMS students involved in getting their hands dirty at the farm, "It's hard work, but it's fun." The bounties of their labor provide motivation.

The farmers have taught EMS students how to prepare raised vegetable beds and how to start seeds in trays and cultivate them under grow lights in their own classrooms. Last year, one class harvested the vegetables they grew at the farm and also on school grounds for their community meal, calling it the "salad day." The intent is that the EMS community will appreciate organic farming and harvesting and using food grown locally instead of that shipped thousands of miles before it gets to our tables.

The project has been expanded to include three classrooms, with a variety of activities at Zenger Farm, including painting murals on an old dilapidated tractor shed: (1) Salad Day is continuing with students starting seeds, transplanting lettuces/exotic greens, and harvesting; (2) Pumpkin Patch: Students will be learning not only how to grow and care for pumpkins but will also be involved with market research and sales. Before seeds are ordered, the students will investigate which pumpkins sell in the local farmers' market with a view to raise funds for EMS; and (3) Stinking Rose Garlic: EMS students are assisting the farmers in getting their next crop of garlic planted and mulched and will help maintain the crop during the season.

Care of Consumption and Waste on Site: Composting, Worm Bins, Recycling, Energy Audit

Committees of students have been formed to deal with composting, recycling, and worm bins. Garbage produced at the school is weighed and charted, helping students to apply the mathematics they have learned. Presentations of the information during morning meeting and through newsletters have led to curtailing garbage that is not recyclable. All students are encouraged to bring cloth napkins, mugs, and thermos bags rather than "throw-away" lunch items. They are also encouraged to ask for lunch items that they are likely to eat. Worm bins and several compost piles have been set up in the schoolyard. A workshop was held to teach parents how to use worm bins at home. An energy audit was done by the school district, and EMS has won a prize for conservation. This year, the school has been selected through a grant to become a center for recycling education. To show how such activities are included as part of the curriculum, a recent assignment in math is presented in Figure 4.2.

We have found some indicators of transfer of knowledge into action, and also of the holistic ways in which students are connecting the different aspects of the curriculum. For instance, one parent stated in an end-of-the-year survey: "During the floods, [my son] was helping out with sand bags. He looked at the garbage floating in the flooded areas and said: Boy, now I am glad there is an Environmental Middle School, obviously recognizing respect for the environment and where trash ends up." For an assignment that dealt with keeping an account of water usage in the family, a sixth-grade girl made connections between consumption and waste:

> I learned about water waste. Where the water in my house goes. We measured the amount of water consumed in my family—like showers, dishwashing, toilets, doing clothes, etc. This was a class assignment. Measuring water consumption for ten days I was able to see the wastage of water in our family. I had never really linked this consumption with [the] Willamette River, how what we do at home impacts wildlife and our rivers.

Responses such as these highlight what it means to "know" one's place and to become a "dweller" as Berry (1981), Orr (1992), and Snyder (1993) have argued. At EMS, efforts are made to link curriculum in ways that can help the students and their families understand the local place that they inhabit. Environment, in this sense then, is not simply about "enjoying" nature; rather, it is also about recognizing how we are implicated in the use of resources.

Math in the Environment: An Assignment

One of our classes conducted a garbage audit at EMS so that we could see exactly what we are throwing away and what we are recycling. For homework, please save all of your family's "throw-aways" for two whole days. Make a graph that shows what your family wastes are composed of. It may be a bar graph, a pie graph, or any kind of graph. It must be attractive and neat. When you are finished, please help with your family's recycling!

TYPE	WEIGHT	PERCENT OF TOTAL WASTE (ESTIMATE)
Plastic with thread neck recyclable at curbside		
Other plastic you recycle		
Glass		
Tin		
Pop cans		
Newspaper		
Recyclable paper		
Cardboard		
Compost		
Garbage (not recyclable)		

Fig. 4.2.

Ecological Restoration in the Watershed

The school has adopted Tideman Johnson Park by Johnson Creek in the watershed where EMS is situated. Students and teachers collect data and map, monitor, and identify plants and other wildlife in that area. With the assistance of the city's Bureau of Environmental Services, they have learned about Combined Sewage Overflow (CSO), and a group of students has helped disconnect downspouts and make signs by drains to prevent eventual dumping into the river. For one of the sites, the school's Green City Data team was involved in feeding the collected data into the city's comprehensive data bank about the watershed. Students have also presented their findings and their activities at local and regional conferences. Elders from the community have come to the school to share their personal stories about the history of the park, dating back fifty to sixty years.

Beyond the technical and scientific know-how, there are other kinds of equally important activities that occur. Undaunted by rain and extremely cold temperatures in Winter 1997, one of the teachers and his class responded to a community request for salvaging native plants, as part of their environmental science and community service, from an area where new construction was to begin shortly. As they extricated and dislodged frozen root balls, the students were filled with mixed emotions of sorrow and pride. One seventh-grade girl, who was cradling in her arms the mule's ear plant she had salvaged with her classmates, sighed: "I just wish it could be here forever!" From one point of view, the class was energized at the thought of "saving" the native plants that they would then replant in the gardens they had constructed on the school campus; but they were also sad that the native plants simply could not live in their present habitat—a plot of land meant for native vegetation, which had occupied that area for some time. Because the developers' bulldozers were coming soon and they would dig, flatten, and shape the earth for new construction, the students and their teacher recognized that if those native plants were not salvaged, they would end up in a trash dump somewhere. Concentrating on the task at hand, the middle schoolers pushed on their shovels as they tried to dislodge the roots. Wearing thick gloves, they also worked on removing their treasure of native plants from entangled blackberries. This sense of purpose filled their faces with pride as they carried their bounty to replant in their native garden and the newly constructed wetland on school grounds.[4]

After three months, many of these native plants found a "home" in Tideman Johnson Park, where the entire school has been involved with the city in stream-bank restoration. Johnson Creek is notorious for flooding portions of southeast Portland. To hold the banks of the stream from erosion, students have been working in a specific area in the park targeted by the city for restoration. They have cut back invasive Himalayan blackberries and extricated their roots. They have seeded the clearing with native grasses, and covered the area with jute netting. Next, they have planted natives—bare root and potted ones—in anticipation that these will grow, hold the banks, prevent erosion, and bring wildlife to the park.

These experiences are being carried over by students to their homes and life outside the school setting. One parent said, "My child is so into pulling ivy that he started pulling it from areas where it was growing around our house. He has been very enthusiastic about what he learns and sees on trips." Another parent shared this about her sixth-grade daughter: "Her view of the ecology of the world has grown, how intertwined it all is." Yet another parent was amazed at her son's "incredible interest in ballot measures that affected the environment. He read them and instructed me on how to vote. He also insists we recycle. [He] doesn't want me to rip out the old bushes around the house." The intergenerational communication and transfer of learning is evident in comments such as these. One parent was delighted that her daughter was "much more aware of consequences and thoughtful about how her everyday life affects the environment. She loves working in the garden, especially the wetlands, and feels more connected to the environment in that way, definitely." Further, reflecting on his involvement in the watershed, a student explained: "We have cleaned up garbage at Johnson Creek and did creek restoration by planting trees. We also built bird houses for native birds. Most of my studies last year were in the watershed. We learned about CSO and removed downspouts and spray-painted storm drains that said: *Dump no waste—drains to river*."

Besides the service component of environmental science, students are encouraged to experience nature in a variety of ways such as sitting quietly and reflecting. They carry their writing pads and art materials to complete certain assignments, an example of which is provided in Figure 4.3.

In response to assignments like this one, students have done paintings and/or have written poems and essays. Below we present three poems, *Questions*, *The Grass between My Fingers,* and *Finally I Am Free* written by sixth graders. These capture their feelings as well as their understanding of environmental conditions that they face.

Assignment: Field Trip Activity at a Creek

Compare four areas: The slope under the bridge; a grassy meadow; the banks of the creek; and a wooded hillside. Next, do close up observations: Choose a spot along the creek. You should be alone but within sight of the adult in your group. Sit quietly and use all your senses to absorb what is going on around you. Write down five sounds that you hear. Close your eyes and identify two smells. Describe them. What animals can you see in the water? On land? What plants do you see? Are they different as you get closer to the water? How has the creek changed the land? Using colored pencils or crayons, draw a picture of your place. You can draw closeups of small things. Try lying on your back and draw a tree from that perspective. Write down how you feel sitting here. Write a poem, if you feel inspired.

Fig. 4.3.

Questions

Have you ever sat in the dark cool forest
Or on the bank of a trickling stream or raging river
And asked yourself, Who am I?
What am I doing here? Where do I fit into all this?
Does it really matter what I do? Does anybody even care?

Well, I can't speak for the humans
but I will speak for the world.
For the beavers, and the foxes, and the birds,
and the salmon,
For the river and the creek, the trees and the salmonberry,
For all those who cannot speak for themselves.
Everything you do matters, whether you turn
Off the lights or clean up the neighborhood.
If you've asked yourself these questions,
You know there's something wrong.
And it's your job to make all those

Who never wondered, wonder,
Those who never asked, ask,
And those who never cared, care.

The Grass between My Fingers

I stand before the great Columbia
as I smell the pine trees with their great old smell
as I touch the cold cool grass
and the wind howls at my ears
I hear the birds beneath my feet
I see a deer feeding her young
I never know what I'm going to see
at the great old Columbia
. . . try some more.

Finally I Am Free

Tall golden grass quivers
in the crisp wind
as I plow through.
Beautiful mustangs spin around and bolt
as I approach.
The sweet smelling air
blows through my hair
as I hop atop a warm boulder.
Flinging off my shoes and socks
I roll up my pants and wade into the cool, deep, placid water.
I stoop down and splash my face with the icy water
enjoying every second.
My beak grows and my feathers sprout
I blink a golden eye
I spread my wings and cry
I soar above all others
Finally I am free.

Other Environmental Core and Community Service Activities

Student responses, whether in the form of poems, essays, or stories, clearly indicate their connection to nature and to their own bioregion. This is primarily because environmental core/community service activities have been undertaken during Tuesday and Thursday blocks. Besides the projects mentioned above, there have been others such as planting trees at the local arboretum; distributing brochures in the neighborhood to save elms from Dutch Elm disease; building raised garden beds for the elderly; creating handicapped accessible community gardens; feeding the hungry at a local homeless shelter; building bird and bat houses and distributing these to the elderly; being guides at the local zoo; and naturescaping other school grounds. Student responses to these experiences have been positive. Comments such as the following are common: "We get to work with our friends and we have more responsibility. We can decide how we want to do stuff to be more productive. We get more hands-on, too"; or, "[We like] being outdoors, helping the environment, and working to help others. Working yet having fun." One of the students' favorite community service projects has involved a Native American elder who takes groups of students to a homeless shelter to feed hungry and homeless people. After visiting the shelter a student wrote in an essay:

> In just two Tuesdays, we [EMS students] served 775 homeless people at Blanchet House. The Blanchet House runs on donation from organizations like Fred Meyer and Safeway which donate salads and pastry. Sage donates 100 gallons of chile [sic] a week. Blanchet holds dinner days like Christmas and Thanksgiving; they served 58 turkeys at the Convention Center on Thanksgiving. . . . [This shelter] helps people get jobs, ID, education, and even a mailing address. . . .
>
> I think poverty is terrible but it is a reality. Seeing it makes me realize how selfish I am to have all this luxury and stuff. I'm glad I got to experience it and to realize that my expectations can be just silly and piggy. I hope I will be able to realize this feeling forever so I can feel lucky for my security and understand that not everyone has what I have taken for granted. Being cold and hungry makes it harder to care about anything but warmth and food. But it seems that through all of it they [the homeless] still find hearts to be caring. For that I think that we should all respect them.

Teachers have commented that the "block" approach to environmental core/service activities provides opportunities for continuity and flexibility in establishing relationships with the community. One teacher explained that his students were simultaneously getting "training in observation and analytical skills, and [in] small group skills." Another teacher mentioned that he and his class loved "being outside in a beautiful place, walking, drawing, writing, and . . . stopping to observe something special." Parents, too, have noted that there is greater awareness and sensitivity in their children; they appear to be more interested in Portland as a place, and in local environmental issues.

Teachers and parents have said that in classes and in the school as a whole, there is a sense of community based on this connection to place and concern for the environment. One teacher reflected at the end of the third quarter, "I see students become inquisitive about environmental issues and then writing about them in classwork. We bring in speakers, films, and experiences at the school to enhance the students' academic content. We collaborate to create deep lessons for the kids which offer inquiry and open-ended projects to meet various needs. Our whole approach is challenging, open-ended, and diverse." Moreover, another teacher acknowledged that EMS is "a place where people feel safe, nurtured, motivated, and understood." Concurring with the teacher, a parent commented in an end-of-the year survey that she viewed EMS as a "healthy community" since it was based on "trust and communication. [EMS] includes and values everyone's opinion equally and fosters a shared vision of success." To many involved with EMS, there is consensus that the school is a comfortable enough place to be called a "home." Here parents, teachers, and students take joy and pride in their work and relationships in an atmosphere of respect for others, including nonhuman beings. By establishing strong roots they are developing a sense of place and community.

STRENGTHENING THE CENTER, ENRICHING THE SOIL: INTERPLAY OF COGNITION, AFFECT, AND SKILL

David Orr (1992) argues that much of education has traditionally focused on teaching the skills to read and use road maps—drawn by "expert" others. The living landscape and its contours are seldom captured on this road map curriculum. Nor does the culture of learning and teaching promote an understanding of, attachment to, and concern for our complex web of life sources. While soil, water, and air are taken for granted, community and place are largely invisible in education. Symptomatic of this neglect, modern humans are used to being "residents" instead of becoming "dwellers."

To address the ecological illiteracy emanating from such neglect, in recent years various approaches have been adopted within the framework of "environmental education"—which is largely at the margins of education. These include the acquisition of knowledge as facts from texts; inquiry-based knowledge where students discover the environmental problems they confront; and construction of knowledge based on an understanding of context and locale through active engagement. However, mere knowledge about the environment does not necessarily change behavior or provide practical skills to deal with problems in one's own community and locale (Hungerford and Volk 1990). Acknowledging this, the curriculum and pedagogy at EMS pay attention to the interplay of cognition, affect, and skills instead of focusing on only one domain; this is in keeping with the conclusion, from a study of fifteen years of research on environmental education, that relying on any one of these domains is not sufficient (Zimmerman 1996, 43). By being embedded in the local, EMS provides relevance and context to adolescents who are at a time in their lives when they question their notions of self and relationship with the other (Gilligan 1982). Being small, and providing innumerable opportunities for students to learn in group settings and in community, is what makes students describe the school in the following way to new students exploring EMS as an option: "EMS is better than a rough school with a thousand kids. Every day we have morning meeting to start the school. Every kid goes to it and we sing songs and stuff. . . . I have been here two years and plan on going next year, too." "This is a good school if you like hands-on activities. We work in our school garden. We go on field trips. . . . We clean parks. We are making a class museum. We work together. Everyday we clean the room. This isn't the school for you if you don't like to get dirty." "On field studies we go to places to clean up garbage and storm damage or study water and animals. I really think this school is cool." Teachers and students alike are involved in solving local problems as they integrate various disciplines around environmental themes. In the process, not only do they learn about environmental science, but they also obtain practical skills as they try to grasp the complexities of human-environment relationships.

By moving environmental science from the margin to the center of education, and by grounding students' experiences in their own place, students at EMS are provided with a framework that enables them to create context-based knowledge and to "feel" their place. As the OECD report on a study of environmental education in European countries stated, environmental awareness develops not only by passively contemplating a problem but by taking action to resolve it (OECD 1991, 27). Comments by parents and students indicate that this awareness is being translated into action. At EMS, practical wisdom is obtained through hands-on community service and interaction with elders. Instead of becoming "information processors" about the environment and about environmental degradation, the approach taken by EMS enables the school community to form and to develop civic sense, efficacy, and responsibility.

Can the center hold? Given the fiscal scenario for the school district, there are uncertainties about continuation of staff from one year to the next. This is likely to affect curriculum planning and the carry over of experiences for students. While revisiting the implementation of school goals is important, new staff bring new vision for the school without having a historical sense of its mission. Building relationships with parents, students, and the community takes time. Will there be long-term commitment for staffing on the part of the school district/state or even on the part of the staff? Will teachers be willing to learn anew, give up their comfort for control, and explore the curriculum of place with renewed energy every year? Will there be compromises of inclusion because of the challenges posed by student diversity, in terms of background knowledge, commitment to environmental education, cultural understandings, class differences, and emotional needs? Further, a school of this kind requires many community members to give freely of their time and energy. So far, parent volunteers, other elders, and community organizations have provided strength and support. As years go by, and the newness of EMS fades, will enthusiasm wane? How will EMS reconcile the normal requirements of district and state tests with the environmental curriculum? How will graduates from EMS fit into the regular high school? While these challenges would appear to weaken the center, paradoxically, as resources—communal and fiscal—diminish, they are also likely to engage the public in questioning commonly held assumptions about schooling, staffing, financing, and curriculum. Most of these concerns are primarily about dwindling resources and loss of community in our urban areas. They are not separate from environmental concerns; hence, the soils will need to be worked and enriched even as environmental education grounds itself at the center of education. Only then can the intricate web of context and meaning, bonding and attachment, recognition and action, be woven to bear promises and hopes for the future generation.

Notes

1. We acknowledge the assistance of many community members, parents, volunteers, students, and EnviroCorps staff who have dedicated their energies to this vision. Special thanks go to Jan Zuckerman, whose support was critical for Sarah Taylor to explore implementation of her dream for EMS, and to John Richter for his invaluable insights in developing this chapter. Zuckerman and Richter are also teachers at the school. EnviroCorps staff were funded through a federal grant (similar to AmeriCorps); in its first year, Portland State

University provided partnership services to EMS through the support of twelve EnviroCorps staff.

2. In 1990, Ballot Measure 5 passed in Oregon, reducing the rate of increase of property taxes, thereby reducing funding for many public schools. This has had a devastating effect on public schools in Portland in terms of massive cuts in support programs, reduction in resources such as textbooks, and increase in class sizes due to teacher layoffs. For a detailed account of the impact of this measure see Gregory A. Smith (1995).

3. Urban Bounty farmers Beth Roasgorshek and Marc Boucher-Colbert have volunteered their time to create this partnership, and have provided project information.

4. See also Inara Verzemnieks, "Native Plants Get New Home," *The Oregonian* (January 17, 1997), which reported on this community service project.

References

Andrew, Jennifer, and Ian Robottom. (1995). *Environmental education across Australia*. Geelong, Victoria: Australian Association for Environmental Education and Deakin University.

Berry, Wendell. (1981). *The gift of good land*. San Francisco: North Point Press.

Dewey, John. (1916). *Democracy and education*. New York: Free Press.

Elliott, John. (1995). Environmental education, action research, and the role of the school. In Organization for Economic Cooperation and Development. *Environmental learning for the 21st century,* pp. 65–78. Paris, France: OECD.

Gilligan, Carol. (1982). *In a different voice*. Cambridge, Mass.: Harvard University Press.

Hale, Monica, (Ed.). (1993). *Ecology in education*. Cambridge: Cambridge University Press.

Hungerford, Harold R. and Trudi L Volk. (1990). Changing learner behavior through environmental education. *The Journal of Environmental Education,* 21(3): 8–21.

Organization for Economic Cooperation and Development. (1991). *Environment, schools and active learning*. Paris, France: Author.

Organization for Economic Cooperation and Development. (1995). *Environmental learning for the 21st century.* Paris, France: Author.

Orr, David. (1992). *Ecological literacy: Education and transition to a postmodern world.* Albany: State University of New York Press.

Raywid, Mary Anne. (1988). Community and schools: A prolegomenon. In Jim Giarelli (ed.), *Philosophy of Education 1988*, pp. 2–17. Normal, Ill.: Philosophy of Education Society.

Smith, Gregory A. (1995). Living with Oregon's Measure 5: The costs of property tax relief in two suburban elementary schools. *Phi Delta Kappan* 76(6): 452–461.

Snyder, Gary. (1993). Coming in to the watershed. In Scott Walker (Ed.), *Changing community,* pp. 261–276. Saint Paul: Gray Wolf Press.

Traina, Frank, and Susan Darley-Hill, (Eds.). (1995). *Perspectives in bioregional education*. Troy, Ohio: North American Association for Environmental Education.

Zimmerman, Laura. (1996). Knowledge, affect, and the environment: 15 years of research (1979–1993). *The Journal of Environmental Education,* 27(3): 41–44.

5 Exploring Children's Picture Books through Ecofeminist Literacy

Elaine G. Schwartz

Whatever befalls the earth,
befalls the sons and daughters of the earth.
—Ted Perry

The above quotation, inspired by the well-known speech attributed to Chief Seattle, serves as a prescient reminder of the critical times we now live in. We and our students face an unprecedented ecological crisis and the development of a global monoculture. As educators, we must strive to address these issues in a mindful and caring manner by artfully interweaving theory and practice. Our pedagogy should lead students to become well informed and active in the struggle to preserve the ecosystem and humanity's diverse cultures. As part of my theoretical and pedagogical response to these critical issues I will discuss: ecofeminist literacy (Schwartz 1997); critical inquiry; and the manner in which children's picture books may support the enculturation of the values inherent in ecofeminist literacy. I will focus specifically on children's picture books although the same pedagogical approaches are appropriate across the full range of children's literature.

ECOFEMINIST LITERACY

Concerned primarily with the domination of women and nature, ecofeminist literacy represents the interweaving of ecological literacy, multiculturalism, and critical ecofeminism. The concept of ecological literacy has been developed by David Orr (1994), Professor of Environmental Studies at Oberlin College. Ecological literacy begins in childhood when we delight in a sense of kinship with the living world. The goal is not just a comprehension of how the world works, but, in the light of that knowledge, how we come to live our lives. This knowledge applies to our place-based realities, as well as to our understanding of the interdependence of all living and nonliving entities on planet earth. Orr (1992) explains that ecological literacy implies "a broad understanding of how people and societies relate to each other and to natural systems, and how they might do so sustainably" (92). He is critical of conventional education that emphasizes the human and neglects to account for nature—in the design of buildings within which education takes place, in the content of education, in the delivery of education, and in the lack of civic competence for dealing with environmental concerns. By virtue of what is included or excluded in education, individuals are taught a certain way of being in relationship with the environment. Thus, "all education is environmental education" for Orr (90). On becoming ecologically literate, individuals can gain a broad and deep understanding of the root causes of the global crisis. Such understanding will empower students to both envision solutions and act upon rectifying local manifestations of the crisis. Interwoven throughout ecological literacy are issues that address the intersection of culture, language, knowledge, power, and ecology. A number of these issues may also be found under the rubric of multiculturalism which includes a deep understanding of the ways in which the complexities of power interact to define and marginalize diverse peoples within and across cultures (Sleeter and McLaren 1992). While multiculturalism provides a comprehensive analysis of the complexities of power relations in societies, it does not specifically address the ecological crisis, nor the twin oppressions of the domination of women and nature.

All of these issues are addressed through ecofeminist literacy. In order to fully comprehend its theoretical basis, it is necessary to take a cognitive leap and conjoin the conceptual underpinnings of ecological literacy, multicultural literacy, and what I term critical ecofeminism (Schwartz 1997). Ecofeminists, tied by their common understanding of the related oppression of women and nature, approach the issue from diverse perspectives (Birke 1994; Birkeland 1993; Merchant 1980, 1992, 1995; Starhawk 1987). There are a number of strands of ecofeminism such as liberal, Marxist, cultural, and social (Merchant 1996). Each strand has "been concerned with improving the human/nature relationship and each has contributed to an ecofeminist perspective in different ways . . ." (Merchant 1996, 5).

Political scientist Irene Diamond (1994) gives a succinct and readily useful definition of ecofeminism:

> The primary insight of ecofeminism is that all issues of oppression are interconnected, that to understand how to heal and liberate our world, we must look at the relationships between the various systems by which power is constructed. In an ecofeminist vision, there is no such thing as a struggle for women's rights separate from a struggle to repair the living systems of the earth that sustain life, or a struggle for gender equality that can be divided from a

struggle for equality along lines of race, culture, economics, ancestry, religion, sexual orientation, or physical ability. (ix)

I have chosen to call this strand critical ecofeminism. Critical ecofeminism focuses on "reproduction, rather than production" (Merchant 1996, 15) as central to an ecologically sustainable future by placing women and nature at the forefront. It provides a standpoint from which to analyze and act upon social and ecological transformations that lead toward a socially just, culturally diverse, and ecologically sustainable future.

Critical ecofeminists wish to address the root causes of the universal domination of women and nature across all cultures—from First to Third World, from northern to southern hemisphere. By adopting a global perspective, critical ecofeminism offers us inexhaustible opportunities to approach issues of injustice from our own vantage points. Ecofeminist Vandana Shiva seeks to address the inequitable distribution of power by placing "women and children first" (Shiva 1994, 16). This may be understood literally and metaphorically as one way of expressing the life-enhancing, feminine values that constitute the core of critical ecofeminism. By placing the welfare of women and children in the foreground, we focus on the inalienable human right to food, shelter, and a safe and healthy environment. In essence, the critical ecofeminist position proposes to emphasize the basic needs of women and children in order to ensure that all life on earth receives equitable and just treatment. This perspective has led to what I term ecofeminist literacy.

Ecofeminist literacy involves cultivation of the ability to discern diverse forms of domination as they affect the lives of women, members of Western and nonWestern societies, and the planet. Although ecofeminist literacy draws upon ecological literacy, multiculturalism, and critical ecofeminism, these theories are not necessarily interwoven equally in all instances. The focus we may take is contingent on specific social, historical, and political contexts. We might investigate the local impact of environmental racism (Bullard 1990). Perhaps students would be interested in the focal role of women in the development of the United Farm Workers movement. We might also look at the historical significance of ecofeminism rooted in feminism (Merchant 1996, 185; Plumwood 1992, 12–13).

To fully understand the significance of ecofeminist literacy means that we acknowledge and actualize its values in our personal lives and through our practice as educators. What is most important is that within the context of a pedagogy based on ecofeminist literacy students will come to recognize and critically analyze systemic injustices, both to humans and the nonhuman world, within and across cultural boundaries. Ultimately, the goal of ecofeminist literacy is to empower students and educators to become visionaries who question, analyze, reflect, critique, and engage in forms of nonviolent social action that will lead toward a socially just, culturally diverse, and ecologically sustainable future for all life on earth. However, within the context of schooling, it is the educator's role to provide a pedagogical framework that will open the pathway toward ecofeminist literacy. Such a framework is informed by a process of critical inquiry (Schwartz 1992).

My interest in critical inquiry grew out of my concern with the ahistorical and acultural pedagogical frameworks that educators often receive in the context of their professional education. This is based on my understanding of the interrelationship of culture, nature, knowledge, language, and power in the construction of social reality. Educators, as cultural beings, consciously or unconsciously demonstrate their belief systems through their practice. Those who understand this are forthright about their beliefs and ask themselves: Where do our questions come from? How is reality socially constructed? If educators understand the social construction of knowledge and the ideological control of popular culture, then they may begin to comprehend the social construction of their own questions. This critical questioning stance is fostered through a pedagogical process that is dialogic and dialectical. Critical inquiry is dialogic in the sense that dialogue, both internal (Bohm 1992) and in the context of small and whole class settings, forms the basis for the interrogation of concepts and the building of a classroom community. It is dialectical in the sense that continuous dialogue and reflection contribute to the building of new knowledge as well as to the rediscovery of knowledge from past traditions.

It is this deliberate aspect of the process of critical inquiry that led me to develop a number of generic questions: In whose interest is any given custom, tradition, or law? Are the interests of women and children placed in the foreground? Is this life-affirming? Who benefits and/or who is harmed? Is democratic decision making valued? Whose voices are heard or marginalized? Is this issue understood in terms of its historical, global, or local context? Does this promote the common good? How do we define the common good? If problems are posed, are they presented in terms of individual or systemic solutions? What form of social action might we undertake in light of any of the above questions?

This process of critical inquiry, when combined with the conceptual base of ecofeminist literacy, has the potential of fostering an understanding of the following principles:

1. All forms of life on earth are part of a living organic system.
2. Natural geographic regions define the social, political, and economic realities of our society.
3. Mind/body and nature/culture are not separate but interdependent.
4. Knowledge is multidimensional, influenced by diverse epistemologies and cultural traditions.
5. Human beings have the capacity to create and recreate the world by recognizing their own subjectivity and agency.
6. Creating a world in which neither humanity nor the earth is in jeopardy requires an ethic of Gandhian nonviolence because the means are as significant as the ends.

These principles can serve as a vehicle for the development of curriculum and selection of books and teaching approaches capable of contributing to the creation of a socially just and ecologically sustainable world.

ECOFEMINIST LITERACY AND CHILDREN'S PICTURE BOOKS

Imagine a fourth-grade classroom in a moderate-size city in the great Sonoran desert of the southwestern United States—a classroom in which literature is integrated across the curriculum. Our reading of children's stories centers around literature circles (Harste, Short, and Burke 1988, 299–304).[1] Literature circles include four to five students who collectively read a shared book set (all read the same book) or a text set (a diverse, yet thematically related group of books). Students write literature response journals and meet periodically to discuss their readings and possible future inquiries that arise from these readings. The following discussions of children's picture books are embedded in this curricular framework that is appropriate for all age levels.

Maps and the significance of sense of place are the central foci of *My Place* (1988), an exemplary children's picture book by Nadia Wheatley and Donna Rawlins. It addresses, explicitly and implicitly, many of the principles inherent in ecofeminist literacy such as: bioregionalism, bioregional narrative, the multidimensional nature of knowledge, and valuing the cultural traditions of the past. This picture book, constituting the first shared book set of the school year, sets the ideological framework for future readings and student inquiries.

My Place provides a child's-eye view of the ecological, multicultural, social, and political history of one urban Australian neighborhood over the span of 200 years. The authors begin with the year 1988 and move backwards in time to 1788, that is, from modern industrial civilization to aboriginal times. Included in each time period is a hand-drawn map of the neighborhood. This map undergoes profound changes as we travel backward in time. In 1988, nature, which is tamed or polluted, is almost invisible amongst the buildings and roads, whereas the 1788 map representing aboriginal times shows nature as the dominant feature and humans living in complete interdependence with nature. The years between 1788 and 1988 show the progression of this change. Not only is the physical landscape included in this picture book, the multiplicity of cultures that constitute modern-day Australia are also represented.

The stories, told through children's voices, evoke the essence of "my place" at each historical decade. These girls and boys refer to their daily connections with the natural world, discuss their observations of the degradation of their neighborhood through the process of industrialization, share their responsibilities for a diverse variety of animals, and discuss the social issues of the times. Victoria speaks of her desire to "be something when I grow up" (22), a subtle reference to her understanding of the difference between ladies and the single women she knows who must work for a living. In the midst of the Depression in 1938, Cal describes the eviction of a local family and their relocation to the unemployed camp. In 1968 Sofia refers to the draft and the Vietnam war. All of these issues are relevant to classrooms in the United States as well as Australia.

Each decade holds many teachable moments when educators can grasp the critical opportunities found throughout this book. For example, the technique of mapping and the format of the picture book serve as a template that may be reproduced across all grade levels. Students of all ages can map their worlds. For some, this may mean beginning with the school grounds while others may wish to map their neighborhoods or towns. An oral history project would be another appropriate response to this picture book. Students could very well conduct oral histories of their schools, their neighborhoods, or their towns. Some students in upper elementary, middle, and high school may wish to expand upon this by creating historical maps representing ecological changes that have occurred in their towns or bioregions.

The power of mapping one's place and thus delving into the social, political, and ecological aspects of the world is strong. The most significant understandings to come from reading this picture book will arise through students' response journals and discussions of the picture book in their literature circles. Through these experiences students will have the opportunity to connect their own knowledge of place to the diverse bioregional narratives found throughout *My Place.*

The second literature circle experience consists of a text set, i.e., a group of diverse yet thematically connected pieces of literature. The picture books chosen for this text set are: *The People Who Hugged the Trees* (1990) by Deborah Lee Rose, *Forgotten Forest* (1992) by Laurence Anholt, *City Green* (1994) by Diane DiSalvo-Ryan, *La Calle Es Libre* (1981) by Kurusa, and *The Table Where Rich People Sit* (1994) by Byrd Baylor. Principles of ecofeminist literacy are interwoven to different degrees throughout these five picture books.

The People Who Hugged the Trees (1990) by Deborah Lee Rose is more evocative than didactic in nature. Rose's adaptation of this 300-year-old classic Indian folk tale depicts the ancient roots of an ecologically sustainable world. Amrita, the girl who came to love the trees, is the central character. Through the magic of story, we come to learn of the intense interdependence between her people and the forest. The forest guards the village from desert sandstorms; its very presence indicates water, the source of life itself. In this first Chipko or tree hugging movement, Amrita and her fellow villagers risk their lives to save the forest from the Maharajah's woodsmen. However, it is Amrita and the other women who take the lead in protecting the very lifeblood of their existence: the forest.

This story demonstrates the necessity of a land-based ecological ethic and presents a deep understanding of humankind's interdependence with other forms of life. It values nature in terms of her nurturing qualities and exemplifies humankind's ability in the past to live in harmony with the environment. *The People Who Hug Trees* emphasizes the need for personal and collective nonviolent social action in the struggle to provide a sustainable future for all life on earth. Women's ancient ecological knowledge, moral and political insights, and willingness to engage in social action form the basis of the struggles depicted in this picture book.

This reading and subsequent discussions constitute the beginning of further inquiry into the connections between this book and the social realities of students. Students might begin by looking closely at the role of nature in their school. Questions that may arise are: How might we create a balance between our presence in the school and nature? Are we native to this place (Jackson 1994), or does our presence represent intrusion? An understanding of the interdependence of all life forms is an integral part of these questions. What is the role of nature on our playground? Are there any wild places (Nabhan and Trimble 1994; Pyle 1993)? What might we do to "green" our playground? That is, how might we transform it into a "naturalized area" (Mutton and Smit 1993, 33–36). These questions represent the valuing of wilderness or the wild side of nature. Who can aid us in this inquiry? What diverse funds of knowledge (Moll and Diaz 1987) are available in our neighborhood? Might the neighborhood women, who maintain traditional gardens in this arid southwestern bioregion, help us? In what ways has their knowledge been transferred across generations? These questions demonstrate an awareness of the valuing of traditional and personal place-based knowledge and narratives. They also acknowledge the positive value of women's knowledge of and connection to the earth.

Students may decide to expand on this by researching and writing ethnographic narratives based on the traditional roles of women and nature among their own Latino and Native American families. In the process students may begin to make connections between the protection of Amrita's forest and the need to protect the fragile bioregion of the Sonoran desert. Students may inquire into the urbanization of this desert environment. They may wish to know who benefits from the destruction of this fragile Sonoran bioregion. This could lead into more extensive inquiries into the fate of the flora and fauna of this region vis-à-vis the global ecological crisis. This would take students full circle as they look at the global ecological crisis in terms of its local context (Pyle 1993). Based on what they have learned, students could then investigate possible courses of local action. Their inquiries will have led them into the area of action research (Fals-Borda and Rahman 1991).

The Forgotten Forest (1992), a picture book by Laurence Anholt, is a delightful cautionary tale. A city is born, and with it comes the loss of the wild open spaces that preceded it. However, in the midst of this large noisy city is a forgotten forest, a forest that had somehow missed the onslaught of progress. Not everyone has forgotten the forest, certainly not the children. The forest, hidden behind high walls, serves as an enchanting wilderness playground for the children throughout the four seasons of the year. Anholt's joyful and bright water colors emphasize this ambience. One day the children arrive to find that the forgotten forest has not really been forgotten. Adults and earth moving machines are there in abundance. However, they are not about to destroy the forest. They are there to tear down the fence and plant new trees around the perimeter. The forest is no longer hidden, but is to be shared by children and adults alike.

This book speaks to the students in our classrooms as well as to child in all of us. It exemplifies, through the lives of the children, the intimate relation that exists between mind and body, and nature and culture. It begs us to follow that urge to climb a tree and swing from a limb, to regain that form of freedom that the modern Western adult mind has deemed untameable and childlike. The children's delight in and need for the forgotten forest come from deep within their souls. For them, it serves as a refuge from the concrete covered urban environment surrounding it.

Anholt's picture book provides an opportunity to search for our own forgotten forests, or "ecotones, those places in the natural world where differences come together in the richest of habitats" (Krall 1994, 4). In our desert environment this may mean that students will discover volunteer cacti growing beneath the officially planted school shrubbery. Or it might lead to a new understanding that the empty weed-strewn lot across from our school is, in reality, a haven for wildflowers, cacti, and burrowing desert animals. This book will encourage students to further inquiry as they begin to view their world through the eyes of budding young naturalists.

Diane DiSalvo-Ryan's fictional picture book, *City Green* (1994), aids us in understanding the realities of life in urban America. An old building is torn down, leaving behind memories of lives long gone and a multicultural neighborhood facing urban blight. This serves as a rallying point for the community. People old, young, able, disabled, and of diverse ethnic backgrounds organize, lease the lot from the city, and create a community garden which beautifies the neighborhood and further solidifies the sense of community.

This book exemplifies the power of human agency in the creation of this community garden. The diverse people involved in this garden come together to create a microcosmic urban bioregional narrative. This community brings together a multiplicity of gardening traditions as they come to work together to reclaim this piece of land. It recounts the power of people to come together across differences to create that which will be of benefit to all.

The struggle of this community may inspire a similar effort by students. Perhaps students will propose a school garden or even a community garden. Students may also connect this book to the local reclamation of a historically significant African-American school in a nearby neighborhood that will soon become a culture center with a community garden. Fictional and real-life examples provide further inspiration and appreciation of people's ability to work together toward positive social change.

La Calle Es Libre[2] (*The Street is Free*) by Kurusa (1981) is a monolingual Spanish picture book based on the realities of barrio life on the outskirts of Caracas, Venezuela. This is a child's-eye view of progress in a Third World or southern hemisphere country. The metropolis of Caracas is surrounded by what in Venezuela are called barrios, i.e., makeshift slum housing. (In the United States the term "barrio" means neighborhood.) The children who live here can no longer roam the hills, climb trees, fly kites, or fish from clear streams as their ancestors did. All that is left are the streets. Everywhere they go they are told, "*la calle es libre*." A group of children decide to band together and petition the municipal government for a park. The initial response to their requests is that the streets are free. As they stand in front of the city council headquarters a squadron of police descends on them. The children sit down in an act of nonviolent resistance. Fortunately, there is a local reporter at hand. Under the watchful eyes of this reporter, the city council calls the police back and also has a change of heart regarding the park. A few days later a ribbon-cutting ceremony announces the construction of a children's park in a nearby vacant lot. Yet nothing else happens. It was an election year, and the ceremony was simply for the benefit of the press.

Inspired by the children, the barrio community organizes, liberates the vacant lot, and creates its own community park. Throughout this tale boys and girls are given equal status. As the community organizes, the power of women's informal networks takes hold as a powerful community organizing tool. The story ends as the children place a large banner on the fence: *El Parque Es Libre, Pasen Todos Muy Felices* (*The Park is Free, Enter All in Happiness*). The children and the barrio community have learned the significance of self-reliance and self-determination through this experience.

The most prominent of the ecofeminist principles that run throughout this book is that of valuing human subjectivity and agency. The community as a whole participates in the struggle to create a park. Women take a strong leadership role in this struggle, and their informal networks are integral to their community organizing. They epitomize the power of human agency and nonviolence, even under the most trying conditions. When faced with unjust and corrupt governments, no matter how minuscule the issue, one's integrity is at stake. Gandhian nonviolence, while not articulated as such, is exemplified as the children come face to face with the police. Social change and nonviolence are inextricably interwoven throughout this book.

The final book in this text set is Byrd Baylor's (1994) *The Table where Rich People Sit*. Peter Parnall's ink and water color illustrations effectively evoke the feelings of the shapes and colors of the Sonoran desert setting. This story is told by Mountain Girl, the girl child in this family of four. Mountain Girl's parents have chosen a lifestyle outside of mainstream American culture. They prefer to live simply, yet enjoy the bounties of the great outdoors. Their family motto is, "We have to see the sky" (9). Mountain Girl was named for the mountain on which she was born and whose vista she observed when only eight minutes old. Her brother, Ocean Boy's first view was a great expanse of vast blue ocean.

Mountain Girl, feeling somewhat impoverished in comparison to her schoolmates, becomes dissatisfied with the lack of money in her family. She calls a family meeting around their homemade wooden table. During the course of this meeting her parents skillfully guide her to understand that one cannot place monetary value upon the most meaningful aspects of their life style: sunsets; working outdoors; coyotes howling; the long vistas, shadows, and colors of the desert; cactus blossoms; the sounds of the day and night birds; the wild animals in their natural surroundings; the pleasure of wandering through open country; and the nights they can safely fall asleep under the open star-studded sky. At the end of this book Mountain Girl realizes that such riches cannot be measured in monetary terms; their homemade wooden table is truly the table where rich people sit. For Mountain Girl's family lives a rich, yet simple life. They tread lightly upon the land and relish nature's bounties.

This book provides opportunities to explore the place of human beings in nature and the virtue of humility. Mountain Girl's family gained its riches from living in harmony with nature, rather than through its exploitation. Mountain Girl's ability to wander freely throughout the desert might very well bring up the issue of personal safety to students whose environments do not offer such a refuge. One can only speculate upon the interesting responses to the notion that riches lie in nature's bounties rather than in the accumulation of money. And the corollary to this, as this picture book so aptly demonstrates, is that there is no shame in wearing patched clothes or in not being able to keep up with the latest designer styles. Rather, real wealth lies in our relationship with the natural world. We must hone our diverse intelligences to appreciate the possibilities inherent in such wealth.

The six books discussed in this chapter are representative of a rapidly growing body of children's literature that addresses the global ecological crisis and/or the development of a global monoculture. While my discussion centered around their use in a fourth-grade classroom, children's picture books, as well as the diverse genre of children's literature, may be used with students of varied levels. This body of literature includes picture books, wordless picture books, children's fiction, and a variety of nonfiction formats. Their use is contingent upon the educator's purpose and the needs and ages of the students.

My purpose has been to share the potential inherent in the mindful and theoretically based use of children's literature in the classroom. The principles of ecofeminist literacy aid in furthering the power and the promise of children's picture books by fostering a critical understanding of the current ecological crisis and the development of a global monoculture. However, critical understanding is not enough. As these books demonstrate, we must go beyond this to social action as we collectively work toward the creation of a socially just, culturally diverse, and ecologically sustainable future for all the inhabitants of the earth.

Notes

1. For further information on literature circles and their place in literature-based classrooms see the following: Kathy G. Short, Jerome C. Harste, and Carolyn Burke, *Creating classrooms for authors and inquirers.* (2nd ed.) (Portsmouth, N.H.: Heinemann, 1996).

2. *La Calle Es Libre* (1981) is available through Kane/Miller Book Publishers. This publishing company specializes in foreign children's books. Catalogues may be obtained by writing to: Kane/Miller Book Publishers, Box 310529, Brooklyn, New York 11231.

References

Anholt, Laurence. (1992). *Forgotten forest.* San Francisco: Sierra Club.

Baylor, Byrd. (1994). *The table where rich people sit.* Ill. Peter Parnall. New York: Atheneum.

Biehl, Janet. (1988). What is social ecofeminism? *Green Perspectives* 11: 1–8.

Birke, Lynda. (1994). *Feminism, animals and science: The naming of the shrew.* Philadelphia: Open University.

Birkeland, Janis. (1993). Ecofeminism: Linking theory and practice. In Greta

Gaard (ed.), *Ecofeminism: Women, animals, nature*, pp. 13–59. Philadelphia: Temple University Press.

Bohm, David. (1992). *On dialogue*. Ojai, Cal.: Author.

Bullard, Robert D. (1990). *Dumping in Dixie: Race, class, and environmental quality*. Boulder: Westview.

Diamond, Irene. (1994). *Fertile ground: Women, earth and the limits of control*. Boston: Beacon.

DiSalvo-Ryan, Diane. (1994). *City green*. New York: Morrow.

Fals-Borda, Orlando, and Mohamad Anisur Rahman. (1991). *Action and knowledge: Breaking the monopoly with participatory action-research*. New York: Apex Press.

Harste, Jerome, Kathy Short, and Carolyn Burke. (1988). *Creating classrooms for authors: The reading-writing connection*. Portsmouth, N.H.: Heinemann.

Jackson, Wes. (1994). *Becoming native to this place*. Lexington: The University of Kentucky Press.

Krall, Florence. (1994). *Ecotone: Wayfaring on the margins*. Albany: State University of New York Press.

Kurusa. (1981). *La calle es libre*. [*The street is free*]. Ill. Monika Doppert. Caracas: Ediciones Ekare-Banco del Libro.

Merchant, Carolyn. (1980). *The death of nature: Women, ecology and the scientific revolution*. San Francisco: Harper Collins.

Merchant, Carolyn. (1992). Ecofeminism. In Rosiska Darcy de Oliveira and Thais Corral (eds.), *Terra femina*, pp. 2–22. Rio de Janeiro, Brazil: Companhia Brasileira de Artes.

Merchant, Carolyn. (1996). *Earthcare: Women and the environment*. New York: Routledge.

Moll, Luis C. and Stephen Diaz. (1987). Change as the goal of educational research. *Anthropology and Education Quarterly* 18:300–311.

Mutton, Miriam, and Debbie Smith. (1993). Establishing a naturalizing area. *Green Teacher: Education for Planet Earth* 34:33–36.

Nabhan, Gary P., and Stephen Trimble. (1994). *The geography of childhood: Why children need wild places*. Boston: Beacon.

Orr, David. (1994). *Earth in mind: On education, environment and the human prospect*. Washington, D.C.: Island Press.

Perry, Ted. (1992). *How can one sell the air*? In Eli Gifford and R. Michael Cook (Eds.), *How can one sell the air?—Chief Seattle's vision*. Summertown, Tenn.: The Book Publishing Company.

Plumwood, Val. (1992). Beyond the dualistic assumptions of women, men and nature. *The Ecologist* 22 (1):8–13.

Pyle, Robert M. (1993). *The thunder tree: Lessons from an urban wildland*. Boston: Houghton Mifflin.

Rose, Deborah Lee. (1990). *The people who hugged the trees*. Niwot, Col.: Roberts Rinehard.

Sale, Kirkpatrick. (1988). *Dwellers in the land: The bioregional vision*. San Francisco: Sierra Club Books.

Schwartz, Elaine. (1992). *In the spirit of inquiry: Milton Meltzer, whole language and critical theory*. Unpublished Master's Thesis. The Department of Language, Reading and Culture, University of Arizona, Tucson.

Schwartz, Elaine. (1997). *Weaving a postmodern tapestry: Ecological literacy, ecofeminism and curriculum theory*. Unpublished Doctoral Dissertation. The Department of Language, Reading, and Culture. University of Arizona, Tucson.

Shiva, Vandana. (1994). *Close to home: Women reconnect ecology, health and development worldwide*. Philadelphia: New Society.

Short, Kathy G., Jerome C. Harste, and Carolyn Burke. (1996). *Creating classrooms for authors and inquirers.* (2nd ed.). Portsmouth, N.H.: Heinemann.

Sleeter, Christine, and Peter McLaren. (Eds). (1995). *Multicultural education, critical pedagogy, and the politics of difference*. Albany: State University of New York Press.

Wheatley, Nadia, and Donna Rawlins. (1994). *My place*. New York: Kane Miller.

6 Education Indigenous to Place

Western Science Meets Native Reality

Angayuqaq Oscar Kawagley
and Ray Barnhardt

Students in indigenous societies around the world have, for the most part, demonstrated a distinct lack of enthusiasm for the experience of schooling in its conventional form—an aversion that is most often attributable to an alien school culture, rather than any lack of innate intelligence, ingenuity, or problem-solving skills on the part of the students. The curricula, teaching methodologies, and often the teacher training associated with schooling are based on a world view that does not always recognize or appreciate indigenous notions of an interdependent universe and the importance of place in their societies.

Alaska Native people have their own ways of looking at and relating to the world, the universe, and each other. Their traditional educational approaches were carefully constructed around observing natural processes, adapting modes of survival, obtaining sustenance from the plant and animal world, and using natural materials to make their tools and implements. All of this was made understandable through thoughtful stories and demonstration. Indigenous views of the world and approaches to education have been brought into jeopardy with the spread of Western social structures and institutionalized forms of cultural transmission.

Recently, however, many Native as well as non-Native people are recognizing the limitations of the Western educational system, and new approaches are being devised. In this chapter we contribute our understanding of the relationship between Native ways of knowing and those associated with Western science and formal education, so we can devise a system of education for all people that respects the philosophical and pedagogical foundations provided by both indigenous and Western cultural traditions. While the examples used here will be drawn from the Alaska Native context, they illustrate the issues that emerge in any context where efforts are underway to reconnect education to a sense of place (Orr 1994).

INDIGENOUS KNOWLEDGE SYSTEMS

While Western science and education tend to emphasize compartmentalized knowledge which is often decontextualized and taught in the detached setting of a classroom or laboratory, Native people have traditionally acquired their knowledge through direct experience in the natural environment. For them, the particulars come to be understood in relation to the whole, and the "laws" are continually tested in the context of everyday survival. Western thought also differs from Native thought in its notion of competency. In Western terms, competency is based on predetermined ideas of what a person should know, which is then measured indirectly through various forms of "objective" tests. Such an approach does not address whether that person is really capable of putting knowledge into practice. In the traditional Native sense, competency has an unequivocal relationship to survival or extinction. You either have it or you don't, and survival is the ultimate measure.

Native people do a form of "science" when they are involved in subsistence activities. They have studied and know a great deal about flora and fauna, and have their own classification systems and versions of meteorology, physics, chemistry, earth science, astronomy, psychology (knowing one's inner world), and the sacred. For a Native student imbued with an indigenous, experientially grounded, holistic perspective, typical approaches to teaching can present an impediment to learning, to the extent that they focus on compartmentalized knowledge with little regard for how academic disciplines relate to one another or to the surrounding universe.

To bring significance to learning in indigenous contexts, the explanations of natural phenomena should be cast first in Native terms to which students can relate, and then explained in Western terms. For example, when describing an eddy along the river for placing a fishing net, it should be explained initially in the indigenous way of understanding, pointing out the currents, the movement of debris and sediment in the water, the likely path of the fish, the condition of the river bank, upstream conditions affecting water levels, the impact of passing boats, etc. Once the students understand the significance of the knowledge being presented, it can then be explained in Western terms, such as flow, velocity, resistance, turgidity, sonar readings, and tide tables to illustrate how the modern explanation adds to the traditional understanding (and vice versa). All learning should start with what the student and community know and are using in everyday life. The Native student will become more motivated to learn when the subject matter is based on something useful and suitable to the livelihood of the community and is presented in a way that reflects the interconnectedness of all things.

Since Western scientific perspectives influence decisions that impact every aspect of Native peoples' lives, from education to fish and wildlife management, Native people themselves have begun to take an active role in reasserting their own traditions of science in various policy-making arenas. As a result, there is a growing awareness of the depth and breadth of knowledge that is extant in many Native societies, and of its potential value in addressing issues of contemporary concern. The following observation by Bielawski (1990) illustrates this point:

> Indigenous knowledge is not static, an unchanging artifact of a former lifeway. It has been adapting to the contemporary world since contact with "others" began, and it will continue to change. Western science in the North is also beginning to change in response to contact with indigenous knowledge. Change was first seen in the acceptance that Inuit (and other Native northerners) have knowledge, that is "know something." Then change moved to involving Inuit in the research process as it is defined by Western science. Then community-based research began, wherein communities and native organizations identified problems and sought the means to solve them. I believe the next stage will be one in which Inuit and other indigenous peoples grapple with the nature of what scientists call research. (18)

Such an awareness of the contemporary significance of indigenous knowledge systems is beginning to impact policy development in the North, as is evident in the following statement in the Arctic Environmental Protection Strategy (1993):

> Resolving the various concerns that indigenous peoples have about the development of scientific based information must be addressed through both policy and programs. This begins with reformulating the principles and guidelines within which research will be carried out and involves the process of consultation and the development of appropriate techniques for identifying problems that indigenous peoples wish to see resolved. But the most important step that must be taken is to assure that indigenous environmental and ecological knowledge becomes an information system that carries its own validity and recognition. A large effort is now underway in certain areas within the circumpolar region, as well as in other parts of the world, to establish these information systems and to set standards for their use. (27)

The incongruities between Western institutional structures and practices and indigenous cultural forms will not be easy to reconcile. The complexities that come into play when two fundamentally different worldviews converge present a formidable challenge. In an analysis of the beliefs and practices of indigenous people from around the world, Knudtson and Suzuki (1992) identified the following characteristics as distinguishing their worldviews from the predominant beliefs and practices in Western society. We invite readers to explore the differences in the indigenous and Western worldviews in the following observations adapted from Knudtson and Suzuki (1992, 13–15):

- Spirituality is embedded in all elements of the cosmos;
  Spirituality is centered in a single Supreme Being;
- Humans have responsibility for maintaining a harmonious relationship with the natural world;
  Humans exercise dominion over nature to use it for personal and economic gain;
- Need for reciprocity between human and natural worlds—resources are viewed as gifts;
  Natural resources are available for unilateral human exploitation
- Nature is honored routinely through daily spiritual practice;
  Spiritual practices are intermittent and set apart from daily life
- Wisdom and ethics are derived from direct experience with the natural world;
  Human reason transcends the natural world and can produce insights independently;
- Universe is made up of dynamic, ever-changing natural forces;
  Universe is made up of an array of static physical objects;
- Universe is viewed as a holistic, integrative system with a unifying life force;
  Universe is compartmentalized in dualistic forms and reduced to progressively smaller conceptual parts;
- Time is circular with natural cycles that sustain all life;
  Time is a linear chronology of "human progress";
- Nature will always possess unfathomable mysteries;
  Nature is completely decipherable to the rational human mind
- Human thought, feelings, and words are inextricably bound to all other aspects of the universe;
  Human thought, feeling, and words are formed apart from the surrounding world;
- Human role is to participate in the orderly designs of nature;

Human role is to dissect, analyze, and manipulate nature for own ends;

- Respect for elders is based on their compassion and reconciliation of outer- and inner-directed knowledge;
  Respect for others is based on material achievement and chronological old age;
- Sense of empathy and kinship with other forms of life;
  Sense of separateness from and superiority over other forms of life;
- View proper human relationship with nature as a continuous two-way, transactional dialogue;
  View relationship of humans to nature as a one-way, hierarchical imperative.

The specialization, standardization, compartmentalization, and systematicity that are inherent features of Western bureaucratic forms of organization are often in direct conflict with social structures and practices in indigenous societies, which tend toward collective decision making, extended kinship structures, ascribed authority vested in elders, flexible notions of time, and traditions of informality in everyday affairs. It is little wonder then that formal education structures, which often epitomize Western bureaucratic forms, have been found wanting in addressing the educational needs of traditional societies.

This picture is not as bleak as it once was, however, as indigenous people themselves have begun to rethink their role and seek to blend old and new practices in ways that are more likely to fit contemporary conditions. The actions currently being taken by indigenous people themselves in communities throughout the world clearly demonstrate that a significant "paradigm shift" toward the integration of indigenous knowledge systems and ways of knowing is already well underway, with the educational orientation moving consistently toward an emphasis on the use of local knowledge and people in the educational process. As this transition evolves, it is not only indigenous people who will be the beneficiaries, however, since many of the issues that are being addressed are of equal significance in nonindigenous contexts (Nader 1996). Many of the problems that originated under conditions of marginalization have gravitated from the periphery to the center of industrial societies, so the pedagogical solutions that are emerging in indigenous societies may be of equal benefit to the broader educational community. With that in mind, let us take a closer look at how these issues are played out in a particular situation.

LIFE IN THE MARGINS: WESTERN SCIENCE MEETS INDIGENOUS REALITY

Each summer since 1989, the University of Alaska-Fairbanks has been offering a cross-cultural orientation course for educators in which we take students out to a remote abandoned village site that now serves as a cultural camp thirty miles down the Tanana River from the community of Nenana. When we first began exploring the idea for the camp, we went out to the village of Minto to meet with a group of about a dozen local elders to inquire if they would be willing to work with us to put together a program in which we would take a group of educators to the Old Minto camp to work with the elders and learn a bit about the Athabascan world and the role of education from their perspective.

By chance, when we arrived in Minto and went to the Elder's Hall, they were just beginning a meeting with a group of State Department of Fish and Game and Department of Natural Resources representatives from Fairbanks. The agency personnel had gone to Minto to explain what they were going to be doing in the way of research in the Minto Flats that summer, so that if people were out and about fishing or hunting in the Flats and ran across some of the monitoring equipment, they would know what was happening. Old Minto (*Men-tee*) is on the south end of Minto Flats on the Tanana River, and the new village of Minto, established in 1970, is on the north end of the Flats on the Tolovana River. The people of Minto are the permanent residents of the 500 square miles of lakes, streams, and forest that lie between the old and new village sites. Regardless of where the village is, Minto Flats is their home, and they know the area like they know the palm of their hand.

From the very beginning, it was obvious that the researchers regarded the meeting as a one-way event in which they were going to provide information to the people of Minto; the elders, in contrast, saw the meeting as an opportunity to provide input on issues they felt the State should be attending to on their behalf. Before they even started there was a communication problem because of the different impressions of why they were meeting, but that turned out to be the least of the difficulties. As they introduced themselves, each of the agency representatives noted his area of specialization. Present were a beaver specialist, two fisheries specialists (one on whitefish and one on pike), a moose specialist, and a hydrology specialist who knew something about mining sedimentation. Each had a fairly clear notion of what they wanted to convey, so they set about explaining what they were going to be doing in Minto Flats to help the people of Minto.

One of the concerns of the fisheries biologists was to find out more about pike migration patterns in the Minto Flats area because of a serious decline in the number of pike in recent years. One of the fisheries biologists brought along a small radio transmitter that could be inserted into the pike so the signal could be used to track their movements. As he went through his explanation he passed around one of the transmitters, which was about the size of a thumb. He started to explain that these were inserted into an incision in the bottom of the pike, but he had barely gotten the words out of his mouth when one of the elders spoke up and said: "Oh sure! We see those all the time. But you ruin the fish with them! We can't eat the fish after that!" The biologist objected: "No, we are very careful to put them in the gut sack so we don't mess with the meat of the fish. We make a small incision and put it in the gut sack." At this the elder pointed out, "But that is the problem. The gut sack is the best part of the pike. The meat has so many bones. The gut sack is what we like, but we can't eat it anymore." It was apparent that the elder's comment didn't register with the biologist, who went on to explain how the data were transmitted to a satellite and eventually placed on a map to track the movement of the pike, all of which only added to, rather than reduced the trepidation of the people of Minto toward the work of these outside researchers.

Another issue that the hydrology specialist was concerned about had to do with the impact of mining from the area near Fairbanks that drains into the Chatanika River, that feeds into the Tolovana River, that meanders through various sloughs in the Minto Flats and eventually into the Tanana River. The Minto people had been complaining about the amount of sediment that was coming down the river and covering over the spawning beds for various species in the area. To show that the State was responding to the concern, the sedimentation specialist demonstrated a piece of equipment he had brought along which would be placed on the side of a streambed with a hose going into the water. Several times a day, it would automatically suck up a sample of water and do a sediment analysis and then enter the results on a chart. At the end of the summer, he would have a graph of the varying levels of sediment in the water. When the sedimentation specialist finished his presentation, one of the elders raised the question: "What are you going to do about the burn policy?" After a brief pause with a quizzical look from the specialist, another elder repeated: "The problem is with the burn policy!" But the quizzical look remained. Finally, one of the elders said: "The BLM policy for controlling fires. They just let fires in the Flats burn until they get close to a man-made structure. That is what is creating a lot of the problems out here." One of the agency representatives eventually responded: "Well, there's no one from BLM here, and we can't speak for them. We don't have anything to do with their policies, so we can't deal with that issue. But, here is what happens when the sediment level builds up in the river. . . ." The meeting went on with the Minto people showing considerable patience, but the frustration level on both sides was growing.

Finally, ninety-year-old Peter John, an elder with very little formal schooling who has been the traditional chief of Minto for quite some time, got up and gave a fifteen-minute exposition on the ecology of Minto Flats connecting all of the different elements that make up the area, including the Minto people, and how they influence one another. Eventually, he got around to pointing out that because of recent changes in BLM's burn policy, which was to let fires burn unless they endangered man-made structures, the beaver habitat in the Flats was being impacted, so the beaver were moving upriver into the sloughs and building dams that were filling with sedimentation from mining, which destroyed the pike's spawning beds. He pointed out that just because the Minto people didn't build permanent structures out in the Flats, like the white man's cabins up along the rivers, didn't mean that they weren't using the area.

Referring to radio tracking of the pike, the Chief chided the biologists, "If you want to know where pike spend the winter, come and ask me. How do you think I lived to be this old? I can tell you exactly where we go to get the biggest pike and where the pike spend the winter. But I don't want to let those snowmachiners in Fairbanks know." In the course of Peter John's presentation, he pointed out that the fish and game people had referred to statistics that went back only thirty years to determine how many pike there had been in the past. "You are talking about thirty years. Our record goes back three hundred years. We know how many pike were around three hundred years ago, and how many it took to feed our families and dogs," at which point he proceeded to explain the seasonal fluctuations that were recorded in their knowledge base going back more than ten generations.

He described how, in the old days when families moved from camp to camp on the Flats they couldn't carry much food with them, so they needed to know exactly where they could expect to find the next supply. People shared this information whenever they met, and it was passed on from generation to generation as a matter of survival. The only difference was, it wasn't written down in a logbook the way the scientists do, but it was just as reliable and was accumulated over a longer period of time than is available to the scientists. He pointed out that the biggest change occurred about twenty years earlier when the State opened an access road to the Minto Flats for snow machines and four-wheel drive vehicles, which brought in a large influx of fishermen from Fairbanks, who took more fish than the rivers and lakes could handle. The Minto people were no longer able to obtain their food from the most accessible places and were having to travel farther out into the Flats to find adequate supplies.

What Peter John and the other elders were pointing out was an enormous gap between the way the Western-trained scientists and the people of Minto viewed the various elements that make up the Minto Flats area. While the scientists with their specialized knowledge and elaborate tools were well intentioned, the gulf between their compartmentalized, limited-time-frame view of the world and the holistic, multigenerational perspective of Peter John appeared insurmountable. The fish and game people couldn't see beyond their constituent areas of expertise to connect with what the elders were trying to tell them, though the Minto people had a quite sophisticated understanding of what the fish and game specialists were talking about. They had seen fish and game biologists and many other Western researchers come and go hundreds of times, and they knew what they did, how they did it, and why they did it. They knew all the issues and many of the answers before the specialists even began to collect their data. But the fish and game people didn't have any way to respond to the long-accumulated detailed information about Minto Flats as a complex interconnected ecosystem that Peter John had given them. Thus, one of the fundamental challenges before us is to figure out how to make connections between the view of the world that Peter John is talking about and what the fish and game people are trying to do, so that we can enter into joint ventures that are mutually respectful and recognize the validity of diverse sets of knowledge, as well as the benefits to be gained if they are pooled together in complementary ways.

The Minto elders did agree to work with us to implement a cultural immersion program for teachers, so for the past eight summers we have been taking about thirty educators out to Old Minto to spend a week to ten days (in the middle of a three-week session) with the elders as the instructors. We make no prior stipulations about what is to go on at the camp—no lectures, no seminars, none of the formal teaching we would normally do. Instead, we participate in whatever activities the elders arrange at the camp. It isn't until about halfway through the week that teachers start recognizing that we are in a different realm. Until then they process the activities through the filters they bring with them, applying what they already know from previous outdoor "camping" experiences to make sense out of the new circumstances. It's when they begin to notice the discrepancies between what they think is happening and what actually happens that they realize there is more going on than they initially recognized. It is at that point, when people start questioning their own presuppositions, that new insights begin to emerge. The elders and the other people from Minto who work with us have a remarkable capacity to open themselves up and draw people into their lives. Even teachers who are initially skeptical when they enter the program come out of it with a new set of lenses through which to view the world.

There are ways to break out of the mold in which we are oftentimes stuck, though it takes some effort. There are ways to develop linkages that connect different worldviews, at least for a few people under the right conditions. The kinds of insights that Peter John was trying to convey in the meeting with the fish and game biologists open up as many questions as answers. Each time we seek an answer to any one of the questions, more questions pop up. The exciting part of it is that more people are beginning to take these questions seriously. We have learned a tremendous amount from the experience at Old Minto, and we find each year that the more we learn the less we know, in terms of having penetrated through another layer of understanding of what life in that context is all about, only to recognize the existence of many additional layers that lie beyond what we currently grasp.

The tendency in most of the literature on Native education is to focus on how to get Native people to understand the Western/scientific view of the world. There is very little literature that addresses how to get Western scientists and educators to understand Native worldviews. We have to come at these issues on a two-way street, rather than view the problem as a one-way challenge to get Native people to buy into the Western system. Native people may need to understand Western science, but not at the expense of what they already know. Non-Native people, too, need to recognize the existence of multiple worldviews and knowledge systems, and find ways to understand and relate to the world in its multiple dimensions and varied perspectives.

SEEKING COMMON GROUND ACROSS WORLDVIEWS

For Alaska Native people, culture, knowing, and living are intricately interrelated. Living in a harsh environment requires a vast array of precise empirical knowledge to survive the many risks of unpredictable weather and marginal food availability. To avoid starvation they must employ a variety of survival strategies, including appropriate storage of foodstuffs that they can fall back on during times of need. Food gathering and storage must be energy efficient as well as effective. If this were not so, how could they possibly hope to survive? To help achieve this balance, they have developed an outlook of nature as metaphysic, from which are derived the "laws" that govern all aspects of the relationships between the seen and unseen worlds.

Alaska Native worldviews and technologies are conducive to living in harmony with the universe. Their lifestyles, including subsistence methods and technologies, exemplify their worldview. After all, the Creator for many Native people is the Raven, so how could the human being be superior to the creatures of Mother Earth? Harmony is the key idea behind Native subsistence practices. How could their hunting and trapping implements and practices not be respectful to animals that they have to kill in order to live? They believe all plants, winds, mountains, rivers, lakes, and creatures of the earth possess a spirit, and therefore have consciousness and life. Everything is alive and aware, requiring that relationships be maintained in a respectful way so as not to upset the balance.

Time-honored values of respect, reciprocity, and cooperation are conducive to adaptation, survival, and harmony. Native people honor the integrity of the universe as a whole living being—an interconnected system. Since it is alive, all things of the earth must be respected because they also have life. Native people have a reciprocal relationship with all things of the universe. The importance of maintaining the integrity of this relationship is captured by Harold Napoleon (1991) in his description of the foundation of the Yupiaq belief system.

At the core of the spiritual belief system of the Yupiaq people was the principle that all creation was spirit: alive, conscious, and very dynamic. The foundation and the chief characteristic of this spiritual Universe was balance and harmony *(qin'nuee'jaa'raq)*, with all in the Universe bound to preserving and maintaining it. In this spiritual Universe all creatures had their place, their roles to fulfill, whether it was the *I'rra'luq* (Moon), where the spirits of mammals and fish dwelt till sent to the *Nuna* (Earth) to replenish it, or the humble *ang'ya'ya'raq* (shrew), who, while physically tiny, was not inferior to human beings and other spirits, and had to be respected. Humans were not superior to other beings but were an equal to some, inferior to others; they were thus bound by the laws of the Universe to maintaining a harmonious relationship with all spirits if they were to survive.

This explains the Yupiaq preoccupation with maintaining a harmonious relationship with the spirits of the sea, the land, the rivers, the

Ellaa (the Universe, also weather); with keeping appeased the mammal and fish on whose beneficence they depended for food, clothing, and shelter. This spiritual reality is reflected in Yupiaq art and ceremonials. It is also the foundation of Yupiaq law (*Qaa'ner'ya'raat*). The basic principle of Yupiaq law is best stated in the phrase, "*Qin'nuee'-na'ne Yuuyaraq*"—to live in peace, harmony, which becomes the law, "*Qin'nuee'na'je Yuu'ge'je*"—you shall live in peace and harmony (Napoleon 1997).

From observing nature, Native people learned that the earth and the universe are built upon the premise of cooperation and interdependence. Western researchers, too, must respect these values to advance knowledge and expand our consciousness. The constructs and understandings of Alaska Native people need to be honored for their integrity on the same level as the modern scientific notion of the holographic image.

The holographic image does not lend itself to reduction or fragmentation. Reductionism seeks to break reality into parts to understand the whole, without realizing that the parts are merely patterns extant in a total web of relationships (Capra 1996). The Native worldview does not allow separation of its parts, as each part must be understood in its relationship to the whole. Respect for the Native people who formalized this view should be practiced. Native people have transcended quantifying and sensory-constricted studies of nature practiced by the modern world. Thus, it is to everyone's benefit that there be cooperation between the researcher and Native people. The researchers need to set aside notions of human superiority to things of the universe, and their own superiority to people considered primitive and backward. Native people should be treated as equal human beings with heightened powers of observation, critical analysis, and a gift of intuition.

To Alaska Native people there are many things in this universe that are cyclical and describe a spiral or a circle. Examples of these include the seasons, the solar system, the timepiece of the Big Dipper going around the North Star, the Raven's path across the sky visible at certain times (as the Milky Way spiral), an eddy in the river, a whirlwind, and many other cyclical patterns reflected in nature. In each instance there is a drawing force in the center. In the Native worldview, this can be thought of as the circle of life. In each Native person's life the central drawing force is the self. The self is grounded in the profound silence of the universe—its sustenance is spiritual, it is love, it is a sense of belonging to a tribe, belonging to the universe, belonging to something greater than one's self. Despite the impact of change in Native worldviews, many of these values have remained intact and are very applicable today.

While they can be quite useful in producing insights and solutions to particular kinds of problems, mathematical and scientific disciplines and their offspring, the engineered technologies, are often one-dimensional. These tools have the wonderful capacity for opening new discoveries in our world, but because of the Western tendency to want to control nature, they can also lead to confusion and a feeling of detachment from the life force and the attendant sense of connectedness. They are bereft of the values extant in the indigenous societies, which also have the power to open doors to new discoveries. Western mathematics, sciences, and technologies do reflect inherent values, some very beneficial to human well-being; however, they are too often usurped by the economic imperatives of a market-driven society in which short-term expediency, efficiency, and cost-effectiveness tend to take precedence over local considerations related to long-term sustainability, adaptability, and self-sufficiency. Indigenous societies, on the other hand, have continued to rely heavily on the latter qualities to survive in the contemporary world, as they did in traditional times.

Nature thrives on diversity. Look at the permutations of weather during a day, much less a month or year. The climates differ from one part of the earth to another. Flora and the fauna exhibit great variety and differ markedly from one region to another. Continents and their geographies differ. No two snowflakes are exactly alike. Stars, constellations, and other heavenly bodies appear to be unchanging, yet our learned astronomers tell us that many changes are constantly taking place. Novae, supernovae, black holes, stars dying and being born are indicators of a continuously changing universe. New sciences of chaos and complexity reveal patterns we never thought existed in nature. These all point to diversity, and it is the balance in all of these patterns and forces that helps nature thrive. Alaska Native people have recognized this diversity all along and have striven for harmony with all of life, even as their lives were torn asunder by forces beyond their control (Napoleon 1991). They have now come full circle and are seeking to heal the breaches that have put their life in jeopardy. As the Yupiaq people say: "*Seggangukut*"—"We are awakening, we are being energized!" They have adopted nature as their guiding force and have drawn energy from the earth.

Native people have long understood the forces of energy around us. An example of energy exchange is reflected in the story of a man out on the ocean. He gets caught on an iceberg that gets cut off from shore and drifts out. He has no choice but to try to keep warm and survive the night. The next day, he finds that the iceberg is stationary but is not attached to the shore ice. New ice has formed overnight in the water between. He remembers the advice of his elders that to test the newly formed ice and its ability to hold up a person, he must raise his ice pick about two feet above the ice and let it drop. If the weight of the ice pick allows the point to penetrate, but stops where it is attached to the wooden handle, he can try crossing on the ice. If, on the other hand, it does not stop at the point of intersection, then it will not hold up the man. In this case, the pick does not penetrate beyond the point. The man looks around him at the beauty and the might of Nature, and realizing the energies that abound, he gets onto the ice. He has to maintain a steady pace for if he stops or begins to run he will fall through as a result of breaking his rhythm and concentration. The story goes that when he begins his journey across the ice, there is a lightness and buoyancy in his mind. This feeling is conveyed to his physical being. Although the ice crackles and waves, he draws energy from nature by being in rhythm with the sea and ice; maintaining a lightness and buoyancy of mind, he makes it safely to the other side.

Western physics with its quantum and relativity theories suggests that matter is mostly condensed energy and that the world is made up of many interacting forces. If so, then Alaska Native people may be able to draw energy from earth because they are a part of it. All life comes from the earth. Alaska Native peoples' reliance on nature as a guiding force becomes corroborated by the Western theories. This also strengthens the argument that the laboratory for teaching and learning should be embedded in the place where one lives. Young people can be energized by being outdoors in nature, enjoying its beauty and becoming part of it. This can encourage self-respect and respect for others, as well as for the seen and unseen forces that dwell in and amongst all things of nature. Students in the outdoors are able to whet their observational skills while learning from nature and drawing energy for themselves. There is a vast difference in learning about the tundra in the classroom and being out in it. Being in and with the environment the whole year round, students can experience the vicissitudes of seasons, flora, fauna, sunlight, freezing, thawing, wind, weather permutations, gaining intimate knowledge about place—using their five senses and intuition to learn about themselves and the world around them.

Drawing energy from nature will allow the indigenous self to again become strong so that the breaks in the circle of life can be repaired. Then the individual and community can allow selected outside values and traditions that they think will strengthen their minds, bodies, and spirits to filter in. Alaska Native people will again become whole people and know what to be and what to do to make a life and a living. They will have reached into the profound silence of self to attain happiness and harmony in a world of their own making.

INDIGENOUS IMPLICATIONS FOR A PEDAGOGY OF PLACE

Indigenous societies study that which is invisible to temper the development of technology and guide its association with nature. Alaska Native worldviews deal with trying to understand the irregularities of nature, which are underlain with patterns of order. Many unseen forces are in action in the elements of the universe, so it is necessary to seek out the patterns and relationships that can be recognized through detailed observations over long periods of time. Such observations and reflections embody the processes on which all education depends.

To help students begin to understand these phenomena, indigenous education should begin with the five basic elements of the universe—earth, air, fire, water, and spirit (Kawagley 1996). The sacred gifts of each must be understood, as well as the human activities that contribute to the sustainability or destruction of these life-giving gifts. In order to be holistic, the curricular activities must include indigenous language and culture, language arts, mathematics, social studies, arts and crafts, and sciences. All must be interrelated as all of earth is interrelated.

For example, in dealing with the element "air," the teacher can focus on the sacred gift of weather. And what an unpredictable choice! Like many Native myths, weather is so very dynamic, ever changing, and, like the myth, very mystical. The wind has irregularities of constantly varying velocity, humidity, temperature, and direction due to topography and other factors. There are nonlinear dimensions to clouds, irregularities of cloud formations, anomalous cloud luminosity, and different forms of precipitation at different levels. There are patterns, however tenuous, such as the path of a jet stream or fronts to be studied. The Native students' visual acuity and memory for detail can be used to advantage. The weather's dynamic is such that each part is part of a part which is a part of another part and so on. The local Native elders can explain how they are able to predict weather based upon subtle messages given to them by the wind and sun twenty-four hours earlier. This involves the language of feelings from the inner world coupled with the language of reason.

Being inclined toward the spiritual, the Native person is able to understand and accept unpredictable permutations of weather. Native people have learned certain general patterns of weather connected to the seasons and moons, yet the Native student can also get acquainted with the now-predominant tools of the meteorologist, such as the thermometer, barometer, anemometer, hydrometer, satellite pictures, and other tools that give the elders' knowledge depth, detail, and a broader view. Introducing students to the notion of irregularities and anomalies of form and force (chaos and fractals) necessarily introduces them to holism. The key idea is for the students to understand the interconnectedness of all things in the universe.

In using the five elements of life to teach, it is of utmost importance to emphasize that each element is a gift to the life-giving forces of the living earth. The teacher must be careful to explain that those gifts are absolutely necessary for life on earth to continue. Yupiaq people honor and respect these gifts in their rituals and ceremonies, incorporating all five elements in mutually reinforcing ways.

Take for example, the *Nakaciuq*, or the "Blessing of the Bladders." The Yupiaq people believed that when the seal or some other sea mammal gave itself to the hunter, the spirit of the seal entered its bladder upon giving up its life. This required that the people take care to remove the bladder, inflate it to dry, and save it for the winter Bladder Festival to honor the sacred gift of the element, "spirit." In this way the Yupiaq people honored and showed respect to animals, upon which they depended for survival, as a gift of the element, "earth." During the festival, the bladders were reinflated with life-giving air and hung on poles for the duration of the activities. In the *qasgiq* (community house) were placed two three-to-four-foot stout poles in front of the place of honor for the elders. Two earthen lamps with wicks filled with seal oil were put on the flattened upper end of the poles. The wicks were lit and the lamps kept burning during the entire festival. One or two people were given the responsibility of keeping the lamps going. The gift of the element, "fire," was used to light and give warmth to the community house. To purify the air and the participants in the house, wild parsnips were burned. Another gift of the element, "earth," the parsnip plant was used to create purifying smoke with the transforming gift of the element, "fire." At the conclusion of the Bladder Festival, the bladders were taken down, deflated, and carried to the ocean or river where an opening in the ice had been made. With collective mindfulness of all the Yupiaq participants that the spirits of the animals were happy and satisfied with the care and careful execution of the required rituals and ceremonies, and that they would come back and give themselves to the hunters, the bladders were returned to the sacred gift of the element, "water," the womb of creation.

To give such a curriculum real meaning for Native students, a multidisciplinary and multisensory study of the elements should be undertaken for the entire school year. The students would begin to understand that the experience of knowing and making intimate acquaintance with a place takes time. The students can be helped to finetune their endosomatic sense-makers through carefully planned and executed lessons of observation that incorporate their language of feeling with the language of reason. The ultimate gift is that of the element, "spirit," which, through the Native language, mythology, rituals, and ceremonies, introduces students to "a lifeway appropriate to place" (Mills 1990).

Modern schools are not teaching students how to live a life that is fulfilling. Rather, the schools are giving information to students without showing them how they can transform that information into useful knowledge for making a living, not to mention preparing them to individually and collectively understand how the usable knowledge can be transformed into the wisdom needed to live meaningful lives. Instead, students now look at an innovative teacher who refuses to use existing curricula, syllabi, textbooks, lessons plans, media presentations, photocopied materials and so on, as not really "teaching." They expect to be given a lot of information and to be entertained. The many machines, modern tools, and the vaunted computers, however, are not enough to teach a lifeway that meets the inner needs of the students.

Teachers and teachers-to-be must understand that the world is nonlinear and that science will never fully understand everything about the universe. They must realize and appreciate that in modern scientific and educational endeavors, mathematics, science, and technology are interrelated with all other disciplines. We must make sure that education becomes realigned with the common philosophical thread, or the "distant memory" of the ecological perspective. All peoples of the earth began from this vista, and therefore such a perspective makes it more possible to attain a new consciousness for a sustainable life.

INDIGENOUS CONTRIBUTIONS TO ECOLOGICAL AND EDUCATIONAL UNDERSTANDING

Indigenous people have much to offer in guiding education back to a grounding in the ecology of place. Four areas in which significant benefits can be derived by reconnecting educational practice to indigenous ecological understandings may be summarized as follows:

Indigenous View	**Educational Application**
Long-term perspective	Education must be understood (and carried out) across generations
Interconnectedness of all things	Knowledge is bound to the context in which it is to be used (and learned), and all elements are interrelated
Adaptation to change	Education must continuously be adapted to fit the times and place
Commitment to the commons	The whole is greater than the sum of its parts

One of the most important contributions that indigenous people are bringing to the scientific and educational arenas is a temporal dimension, that is, a long-term perspective spanning many generations of observation and experimentation, which enriches the relatively short-term, time-bound observations of itinerant Western-oriented scientists and educators. The indigenous perspective adds breadth to the scientists' depth (Kawagley 1995). As a result, patterns and cycles that are not evident in the Western scientists' data base of detailed in-depth short-term observations can be factored into the equation for educational purposes. For example, a Yupiaq hunter triggered research linking industrial pollution from factories as far away as Central Europe and China to "acid snow" affecting changes in the coloration of tundra plants in Western Alaska, which he had observed over a period of forty years. As a result, he was invited to participate in an international conference at Cambridge University on "Arctic haze" to provide a dimension that was not readily available through conventional tools of scientific observation.

Likewise, in education we tend to look for immediate solutions to problems that are often the product of long-term generational shifts, for which the solutions, too, must be understood at a multigenerational level. The observations of a Peter John can span up to four generations, out of which patterns can be discerned that are not obvious to the itinerant educator, yet it is the latter whose actions will directly impact the succeeding generation's ability to participate in a rapidly changing world. For everyone's benefit, it is essential that we recognize the contributions that can be derived from a multigenerational perspective.

Coupled closely with this long-term temporal dimension is another important contribution that indigenous ways of knowing provide—that of pointing out the interconnectedness of all the elements that make up an ecosystem, including the human element (as Peter John indicated). While Western scientists tend to specialize and conduct research in one component of an ecosystem at a time, the Native observer is immersed in the system and thus is more likely to recognize how the various components relate to and depend on one another over time and across species. An Aleut observer, Larry Merculieff, made this point forcefully at an Alaska Marine Mammal Conference in 1991, which he helped organize to deal with issues associated with the sustainability of the ecosystem and economy of the Pribilof Islands:

> Western scientific research systems are too specialized. Bird scientists study birds. Marine mammal scientists study marine mammals. Fishery scientists study fish. They specialize even within a single category. For example, bird scientists study reproductivity by counting breeding birds on cliffs, as one project. Another project may study just murres and kittiwakes, but not cormorants or puffins or least auklets, or fulmars or sea gulls. Another project may study cliff nesting birds at sea. Very few studies are done on how each species interacts with each other and under what environmental conditions.
>
> Because of how different scientists are funded and because scientists do not want to step on another scientist's territory, there is little if any coordination between research on different species. Marine mammal scientists do not closely coordinate with oceanographers and climatologists. Everything is placed in specialized, separate boxes, even though we know that everything is connected. Some Soviet scientists researching the Bering Sea call American scientists "anti-ecologistic" because of American emphasis on studying single species. We will never understand the Bering Sea unless we understand the connections of all things affecting it. The Western scientific system is unable to do this.
>
> We [Alaska Natives] see everything in terms of connections. When we hunt, we know weather, temperature, wind direction, presence of sea ice, how the ice is packed, time of day, type of season, human activity—all affect the behavior and survival of wildlife. We observe all these things all our lives.
>
> We must act to use our knowledge to re-direct how everything we depend on is being managed by over- specialized scientific systems. Scientists wonder what is happening to seals, sea lions, and birds. In the Pribilofs, we watch sea lions eating seal pups with greater frequency than ever in memory. We see chicks on bird cliffs dropping to the rocks below because they are too weak. We notice how seal pelts are thinner than ever in memory. We notice how mature

bull seals are smaller than just ten years ago. This tells us that all these species are having food problems. But no scientist or manager is interested in these observations. Every coastal village where there is strong dependency on the sea for a livelihood and way of life have their own observations. We should share this information among ourselves and then act on it. (3–4)

Since 1991, through actions of people like Larry Merculieff, including the formation of the Indigenous People's Council for Marine Mammals, Aleut practitioners and Western scientists have become collaborators in looking at the Bering Sea as an ecosystem. As a result of the input of Aleut observers, many new hypotheses have been put forward to be tested with the arsenal of specialized techniques and technology provided by Western science.

In addition, Merculieff has been instrumental in the establishment of a "Stewardship Camp" for young people on the Pribilof Islands, in which future generations learn about their place in the fragile ecosystem they occupy and the responsibility they carry as the stewards of that ecosystem. The instructors for the camp include local elders as well as visiting scientists, who learn from each other while they share their knowledge with the students. Through such educational programs connected to peoples' everyday lives, students learn that every action they take, from the careers they choose to what they do with a piece of trash, is part of an interconnected web of values and behaviors that shape who they are as a people—in this case the Aleut people. The surrounding environment can provide a rich laboratory for students to learn about the many interconnected forces that impact their lives and make a contribution to the well-being of their community, utilizing tools from both the indigenous and Western knowledge systems.

Another important contribution that indigenous people are making to our understanding of sustainable lifestyles is the relationship between human adaptation and the dynamic nature of cultural systems. In contrast to the Western observer's tendency to freeze indigenous cultural systems in time, as though they existed in some kind of idealized static state destined never to change, indigenous people themselves have been quick as a matter of survival to adapt new technologies and to grasp the "new world order." While retaining a keen sense of place and rootedness in the land they occupy, they have not hesitated to take advantage of new opportunities (as well as create a few of their own) to improve their quality of life and the efficacy of their lifestyles. This is done, however, within their own framework of values, priorities, and worldview, so that the development trajectory they choose is not always the same as what outsiders might choose for them.

The recognition of cultural systems as being dynamic and ever changing in response to new conditions has enormous implications for the sustainability of indigenous communities, especially where demographic changes, development opportunities, and technological innovations have combined to put pressure on available subsistence resources beyond the carrying capacity of the host bioregion. Nowhere has this been more complicated than in the regulation of the Bowhead whale stock available to Inupiaq hunters along the northern and northwest coasts of Alaska. When Native people in northwest Alaska had to establish a priority between maximizing profits in their role as Native corporate shareholders and sustaining the subsistence whale hunt that could potentially be disrupted by ships bearing ore from their own world-class lead/zinc mine passing through the migration route of the whales, they chose to place the subsistence hunting of the whales as the top priority, and established a panel of hunters from nearby villages who had the power to shut down the mine if necessary while the communities dependent on the whales conducted their hunt. Their multinational partners in the mining venture were not necessarily in agreement with this decision, but in this case, the resource, and thus the decision, was in the hands of residents of the region (Barnhardt 1996).

Similar actions have been taken by Inupiaq people with regard to the education of their children. Not satisfied with the either/or forced-choice options often presented by the schools, whereby students are expected to select between learning to be a subsistence hunter or learning Western academic knowledge, students in the village of Kaktovik have drawn on their traditional Inupiaq base-twenty counting practices to create a unique numerical notation and computation system that is capable of performing high-level mathematical calculations. The system has been so successful that when they were challenged by a team of oil-field engineers with electronic calculators, the Inupiaq students were able to accurately perform the calculations faster than the engineers. They have demonstrated that it is possible to adapt to the imperatives of the Western educational system without sacrificing their own cultural traditions in the process.

Another important dimension that illustrates the contribution that indigenous people can make to our thinking and practice in our relationship to the world around us is a qualitative dimension placing a priority emphasis on the sustainability of family, community, and the cultural systems reflected therein. Whereas Western-derived practices tend to focus on individually oriented considerations and goals, indigenous people are more likely to seek a community-oriented approach, focusing on the commons as the basis for individual sustenance, and the individual as the basis for the strength of the commons. The educational practices associated with such an outlook are grounded in the same premises as the African proverb, "It takes a whole village to raise a child."

Along with the emphasis on sustainability of community, indigenous worldviews are more inclined to see humans as a subset of the natural world in which they are precariously situated, rather than to see nature as a repository of resources for human exploitation (Knudtson and Suzuki 1992). Though this orientation to the natural world is often misunderstood and misrepresented in nonindigenous contexts, its spiritual and tangible connotations are very much a continuing aspect of indigenous people's livelihood, and thus underlie indigenous perspectives on the sustainability of all life. The significance of this perspective is reflected in the following preamble to a statement on Indigenous Peoples and Conservation, prepared by Indigenous Survival International in 1991:

> The Earth is the foundation of Indigenous peoples. It is the well of their spirituality, knowledge, languages and cultures. It is not a commodity to be bartered to maximize profit; nor should it be damaged by scientific experimentation. The Earth is their historian, the cradle of their ancestors' bones. It provides them with nourishment, medicine and comfort. It is the source of their independence; it is their Mother. They do not dominate Her, but harmonize with Her. (41)

SUMMARY

When examining educational issues in indigenous settings, we must consider the cultural and historical context, particularly in terms of who is determining what the rules of engagement are to be, and how those rules are to be implemented. As indigenous people have begun to reassert their aboriginal rights to self-determination and self-government and assume control over various aspects of their lives, one of the first tasks they have faced has been to reorient the institutional infrastructures and practices that were established by their former overseers to make them more suitable to their needs as a people with their own worldview, identity, and history. In some instances, the initial response has been to accept the inherited structures without question and perpetuate the Western systems that were put in place before, including their implicit forms of decision making, social stratification, and control. In most cases, however, there have been deliberate efforts to modify the inherited institutions, or create new institutional and political structures, such that indigenous cultural forms and values are taken into account wherever possible (Barnhardt 1991). The tide has turned and the future of indigenous education is clearly shifting toward an emphasis on providing education in the culture, rather than education about the culture. From this we will all benefit.

It is recognized that the obstacles to change are many and the challenge is enormous, but no less than the survival of indigenous people as distinct societies is at stake, and with them the essential diversity that is vital to the survival of all humankind. The elemental nature of the work before us is succinctly captured by the following observation on the current state of Native education:

> In the past, Native people tended to view formal education as a hindrance to their traditional ways, but now they are beginning to look at it in a different light. They are seeking to gain control of their education and give it direction to accomplish the goals they set for it, strengthening their own culture while simultaneously embracing western science as a second force that can help them maintain themselves with as much self-reliance and self-sufficiency as possible. They have learned to thrive in a tough environment, and they can make it easier and less harsh, first as humans, secondly as scientists, with a carefully developed technology supported by an attuned educational system. (Kawagley 1995, 111)

Notes

We wish to acknowledge the support of the Alaska Federation of Natives, the University of Alaska-Fairbanks, the Annenberg Rural Challenge, and the National Science Foundation for the establishment of the Alaska Native Knowledge Network and the work that has contributed to the preparation of this article.

References

Barnhardt, Ray. (1991). Higher education in the Fourth World: Indigenous people take control. *Canadian Journal of Native Education* 18:2.

Barnhardt, Ray. (1996). Indigenous perspectives on marine mammals as a sustainable resource: The case of Alaska. *Marine Mammal Workshop Proceedings*. Iceland: University of Akureyri.

Bielawski, Ellen. (1990). *Cross-cultural epistemology: Cultural readaptation through the pursuit of knowledge*. Edmonton: Department of Anthropology, University of Alberta.

Capra, Fritjof. (1996). *The web of life: A new scientific understanding of living systems*. New York: Doubleday.

Indigenous Survival International. (1991). Statement on Indigenous peoples and conservation. *Arctic environment: Indigenous perspectives,* pp. 41–47. Copenhagen: International Work Group for Indigenous Affairs.

Inuit Circumpolar Conference. (1993). *Arctic environmental protection strategy*. Anchorage, Alaska: Author.

Kawagley, Angayuqaq Oscar. (1995). *A Yupiaq worldview: A pathway to ecology and spirit*. Prospect Heights, Illinois: Waveland Press.

Kawagley, Angayuqaq Oscar. (1996). Earth, air, fire, water and spirit as a foundation for education. *Sharing Our Pathways,* 1:1–3. Fairbanks: Alaska Native Knowledge Network, University of Alaska Fairbanks.

Knudtson, Peter, and David Suzuki. (1992). *Wisdom of the elders*. Toronto: Stoddart Publishing, Limited.

Madison, Curt, and Yvonne Yarber. (1986). *Peter John Minto*. Fairbanks, Alaska: Spirit Mountain Press.

Merculieff, Larry. (1991). *An Indigenous people's position paper on the management and use of the Bering Sea*. Anchorage, Alaska: Marine Mammal Conference.

Mills, Stephanie. (1990). *In praise of nature*. Washington, D. C.: Island Press.

Nader, Laura. (1996). *Naked science*. New York: Routledge.

Napoleon, Harold. (1991). *Yuuyaraq: The way of the human being*. Fairbanks: Alaska Native Knowledge Network, University of Alaska Fairbanks.

Napoleon, Harold. (1997). *A glimpse at the Yupiq spiritual universe*. Anchorage, Alaska: Personal Communication.

Orr, David W. (1994). *Earth in mind: On education, environment and the human prospect*. Washington, D.C.: Island Press.

Part Two
Higher Education and Nonformal Settings

7 Liberation and Compassion in Environmental Studies

Stephanie Kaza

Two circles of students sit cross-legged on the carpet in the classroom. Those in the inner circle speak, those in the outer circle listen. The conversation is intimate, intense, riveting; the topic is environmental racism. But they are not talking about toxic waste sites in Louisiana or uranium mines on Indian lands. They are grappling with their own environmental racism. The fish bowl brings the conversation close to home. A student of color has challenged the group to see the impact of white privilege on the environment; the others struggle to escape the guilt of collective history. I stay back to let them face the issues from their own perspectives. This is not a time for explanation or lecture. This learning is about the struggle itself, the struggle to be liberated from oppressive social conditioning and its consequences.

These students are undergraduates at the University of Vermont, a land grant university supported 15 percent by state funds, 85 percent by tuition. Half the students come from around Vermont, a mostly rural state; the other half migrate north to the Green Mountains from urban New York, New Jersey, and Massachusetts. They are drawn to the beauty of the environment, the skiing, the partying; the students are mostly white and some are very affluent. Blatant lack of racial diversity has spurred student protests and concerns about racism. Environmental studies students are often on the front lines in discussions of racism, sexism, colonialism, classism. Since I teach classes examining environmental values and ethics, I hear the students' concerns in class. For many, the topics generate a sense of being overwhelmed and powerless. I try to imagine their experience, the world viewed from an undergraduate perspective in the late 1990s. Development, strip malls, suburbia, television, divorce, drugs, and perhaps only each other to hang on to—it is not the same as the 1960s.

To teach these students I must continually try to understand the values they carry and the sources of these values. Who is "Generation X"? What do they stand for? I wonder, is this really the "Lost Generation"? The students drawn to the Environmental Program at the University of Vermont are already a cut apart from many others on campus for they share a common urgency and a desire to care for the planet they call home. Very quickly, in the introductory courses including International Environmental Studies, which I teach in rotation with other faculty members, the students come to see our program's emphasis on global systems perspectives and the role of human values in determining the direction of environmental health. Each student must mature enough to take responsibility for planning his or her own self-designed course of study through the major, built from a broad range of university and department offerings. Those who want to explore environmental values in depth come to my courses in Ecofeminism, Radical Environmentalism, and Religion and Ecology.

I think it is important to begin by describing the students I work with since they are my co-learners in the process of transformational education. Also, I can't be certain how much of my experience generalizes to students on other campuses. But perhaps some of these observations are relevant where others teach environmental studies. One of my graduate student teaching assistants pointed out that this generation holds a particularly ambivalent relationship to liberation movements of their forebears (DeBoer 1995). Some have lived with parents who chose to homestead and live off the grid or who have fought for women's rights. Some have struggled to find their own "Third Wave" forms of earlier movements. They have been taught that the feminist movement liberated women and yet women, including their own classmates, are still raped every day. At the same time their own peers, reflecting the backlash of the '90s, mock young women who stand up for women's issues. Civil rights is similar: Black history month is well established on college campuses, yet there is still inner-city violence, and racist stereotyping is rampant in the dorms. The environmental movement is likewise subject to question—if so many laws were passed and environmental awareness has steadily increased, how can the world be in such bad shape? Overall, it seems the movements have been inadequate to the overwhelming scale of current issues. The students observe the fragmentation of effort caused by differing agendas; they yearn for some more integrated and effective approach.

In the face of such apparently unsolvable problems, these young people in Vermont turn to their own inner lives. Some feel this is the only place for genuine environmental work—the realm of the spiritual or psychological. If they can't understand racism, sexism, and consumerism from within themselves, how can they ask others to change? This turn toward the subjective is further reinforced by the overwhelming deluge of information available to this generation. Environmental data from almost every corner of the world can be accessed with a few clicks on the computer screen. Nonprofits working for every possible cause are up on the Web with the latest rainforest or human rights bulletin. This generation can learn in a year what it took my generation ten to twenty years to find out about the environmental crisis. But to do this so quickly is a painful coming of age.

As a teacher I feel both compassion for their struggle and need for inner solace, and also frustration with their seemingly extreme individualism. At times their favoring of the subjective can feel overly self-referential, almost indulgent, ahistoric in a way. In my courses I work with the power and tension of this subjectivity, using it as a base for liberation work. I sense that at the core of their self-absorption is a yearning for wholeness, a desire to free themselves from the relentless assault of fragmenting, soul-stealing influences—television, advertising, consumerism, urban development. In order to feel they can make a useful contribution to the environment, they want to first gain some sense of internal strength and self-knowledge.

One consequence of this subjectivism is a kind of political paralysis among my students which is based on accepting everyone's experience and position as valid. In defining the particular nuances of their own perspectives, they balk at consensus and group organizing. Relativism reigns. The context for their efforts in self-definition is less than supportive. Every semester I hear how environmental studies students are marginalized or belittled by their peers as "crunchies," "enviro-geeks," "tree-huggers." They don't want to take a position for fear of losing the comfort of friends, so critical in their passage to adulthood.

In many ways today's students mirror the despair, denial, and self-absorption in the culture around them. It has been my experience as an environmental educator that exposure to facts alone is not enough to turn people toward environmental action. The facts can actually turn people away from meaningful engagement with the issues. They say the situation is too complex, too all-encompassing, too demanding, too scary, too big to tackle. If I don't address these feelings with my classes, I find myself looking out on a room of blank faces.

I have been very fortunate to be exposed to two liberatory models of education which I have adopted in teaching environmental studies classes. Together they provide a philosophical foundation and pedagogical method for working with social and internal blocks to environmental understanding. The first of these is the "despair work" developed by Joanna Macy and her colleagues at Interhelp (Macy 1983). The second model I draw on comes from the work of Gerard

Fourez (1982) in liberation ethics. Macy's work evolved to break through the psychic numbing around nuclear threats described by Robert Lifton (1968). Macy and others, motivated by their own concerns for the serious dangers of both nuclear warfare and nuclear power, pioneered a series of workshops across the United States which gave people of all walks and professions a forum for addressing their fears and denial. They developed experiential exercises, group sharing, and a collective process based in systems philosophy as the primary mode of learning. By leading people through a process of waking up to their own feelings for their world, the work releases bound energy which can then be engaged in positive effort. The aim of despair and empowerment work is to overcome patterns of avoidance and psychic numbing while generating compassion and commitment to act. Like Paulo Freire's work, despair work takes place in community and helps to build community through authentic exchange.

Macy begins by validating as natural the feelings of distress, grief, and anxiety that arise when people consider the present conditions and future prospects for the world. These various forms of emotional pain are seen as indicators of a wider interconnectedness with the web of life. Dread, rage, guilt come up—it can hurt to think about the state of the world, to listen to the endless litany of losses. It is natural to want to block out that pain. But, as Macy points out, this cuts people off from a flow of information and connection that is central to human vitality. The work invites people to contact their own authentic, experience-based responses to the deteriorating condition of the environment. In the group learning framework they are able to share the causes of repressing such awareness—fear of the pain itself, fear of being morbid, fear of appearing too emotional, fear of feeling powerless—and then go on to experience the supportive power of acting in community (Macy 1983, 6–12).

The philosophy of Macy's model directly challenges most Western higher education, which assumes that emotions interfere with objective learning. Subjectivity has traditionally been an anathema to the university classroom except perhaps in creative writing or art courses. For our students at the University of Vermont, emotional response to the environment is often what has brought them to the Environmental Program; it is obvious from the stories they tell us. They speak frequently of their devotion to specific places or their sadness at losing childhood woods to new housing. Macy's work has given me a way to start with this emotional response and build on it. By validating student feelings, I invite them to bring their whole lives and personal motivation to their environmental stories.

At the core of Macy's work is an emphasis on learning in community. Perhaps the most debilitating aspect of painful feelings for the environment is the resulting isolation. Cut off from genuine contact with each other, people fall further into despair. Through exploring these arenas together and releasing blocked feelings, participants in the work find new surges of energy for tackling difficult issues. They also develop compassion for each other and their own struggles in the complex web of causes and conditions. Many of Macy's exercises are designed to foster compassion as a heart-opening antidote to pain for the world.[1] This too is hardly a common element in the traditional Western curriculum which emphasizes competition and self-will as the road to mastery. Even among many Environmental Studies programs, objective science and legalistic policy courses carry far greater weight than philosophy or values-based humanities approaches (Strauss 1996).

Pedagogically, Macy's model is based in experiential learning. The workshops are guided by a facilitator rather than taught by a teacher. The facilitator's role is to maintain a safe setting for depth of authentic contact and help participants acknowledge their own feelings as signals of interconnectedness. The facilitator also helps structure the turning from despair to empowerment through sensitivity to timing and group process. In a classroom setting this process is stretched out over the semester, drawing on specific assignments and class projects to address the elements of the work. I have led this work in both weekend and 10- to 12-day adult sessions for the Institute for Deep Ecology; adapting it to the undergraduate classroom presents new challenges—the constraints of instructional periods, the self-conscious shyness of college students, the high status and power of the professor. In this chapter I share some of the methods I've developed for implementing Macy's work for awakening and transformation.

I encountered the work of Gerard Fourez, the source of the second model, in a course on Christian social ethics for my seminary degree. Shaped by his training as a physicist and Catholic priest, Fourez's ideas evolved through contact with liberation theology and Marxism. In teaching ethics to science students, he developed analytical tools for evaluating issues in the context of social conditioning, particularly patterns of oppression and domination. Fourez believes "the task of ethics must begin with analyzing the established power relationships, laying bare a given society's inner institutional relationships and decoding its legitimating myths" (1982, viii).

The first step in this process is evaluating dominant social norms and values and identifying the agents that promulgate these values. For my students this was most dramatic in looking at consumerism. They know all too well the social pressures to buy more things; they are more assaulted by media advertising harassment than any generation before them. The next step is to see how these social values make up an ideology that serves those in power and whose rhetoric skillfully hides dominating relationships. When such values have been deeply internalized, they contribute to the formation of "conscience." Fourez suggests that the moral reasoning capacity of one's conscience is more strongly influenced by dominant ideologies and less by absolute moral codes. Social ethics tend to mirror the social structure. Free trade, private property rights, and economic gain are all justified as ethical by those who profit from them. Thus in Fourez's model, questions of environmental ethics necessarily raise issues of relationships of domination.

Fourez's method for investigating these patterns of internalized norms and power relationships is what he calls "conscientization"—waking up the conditioned conscience to see the ideological forces at work. In this process the student recognizes the possibility for deeper moral choice. The work is closely related to Paolo Friere's methods, but is more ethical rather than behavioral in nature. Fourez suggests that people act out of a relational ethic built on actual experience and the stories of others far more than they act according to normative absolutes. People are "called" to respond to others and make meaning out of their lives based on these calls. From this relational point of view, Fourez (1982) considers "the intersubjective world . . . as a field in which [human] beings make calls upon each other and communicate the meaning of their actions" (70). To take an ethical position is to stand in solidarity with those who have called you.

Like Macy's work, this liberatory method offers both philosophical foundation and pedagogical method for environmental studies courses. By examining the production of values and ideologies, students can be freed from the constraints of current environmentally destructive rhetoric and consider other alternatives. In deconstructing their own conditioning, they become liberated from the dominating relationships that restrict their expression of power and ecological self-interest. The pedagogical method of naming these values and relationships and questioning moral absolutes leads to more authentic recognition of calling relationships.

One more piece of Fourez's work is useful for environmental analysis. He points out that most of our ethical principles evolved to handle situations of individual one-to-one human social relations. They do not necessarily address structural situations that maintain overall patterns of oppression. For environmental studies students, structural ethics are critical, for it is all too clear that most environmental destruction is directly tied to the interests of big corporations, national governments, and even major religious and academic organizations. Individual choices to recycle or reduce consumption have only small impact if the system-wide incentives favor production of more virgin materials. Fourez's model provides both a way to liberate students from dominating relationships that perpetuate environmental deterioration and a method for distinguishing social change from individual guilt. This analytical tool combined with Macy's experiential exercises can generate both awakening and empowerment, freeing students to act responsibly in a relational world.

APPLYING THE MODELS

How then to use these models as a basis for liberatory environmental education? What experiential learning activities could I design to engage students in this empowerment process? In my elective courses as well as the large-group introductory lecture class, I have tried several experiments with these objectives in mind. I oriented the three elective courses around values analysis and environmental action, using student assignments to structure the inquiry. In Ecofeminism we look at parallel patterns of domination between women and nature, reviewing literature in ecofeminist philosophy, activism, and spirituality.[2] In Radical Environmentalism we start with Fourez's work and then examine five radical environmental movements and philosophies for their liberatory agendas: animal rights, deep ecology, social ecology, ecofeminism, and environmental racism.[3] This work evolved to break through the psychic numbing described by Robert Lifton around nuclear and other environmental threats. In Religion and Ecology, we review major world religious traditions for both traditional and revisionist green perspectives.[4] In International Environmental Studies, the second semester of our introductory majors course, we take a close look at North/South political and economic relations as they drive global environmental degradation.

In the Ecofeminism course, students undertake two projects beyond their open-book, take-home exams. The first is an ongoing journal of subjective responses to class discussion. This assignment not only allows students to release some of their despair, it allows me to validate their feelings by serving as a witness through their writing. This sort of response was not uncommon at some point or another in many students' journals:

> Sometimes I feel that the problems are too large and too deeply rooted to be changed and I feel frustrated, angry, and helpless. . . . It is tempting to give up by saying that nothing will ever change, the problems are too embedded, and my effort won't make a difference. (DeBoer, 3)

Because many of the students were reluctant to voice their strongest feelings in class, the journal provided an outlet and a place to integrate the principles they were learning with their personal lives. Sometimes I asked the students to read to each other from their journals as a way to move the despair into connection and out of isolation.

The second assignment is a group activism project designed by the group to address a relevant topic of common concern. The project is an opportunity to apply ecofeminist principles to real ecological and social problems and a deliberate exposure to the joys and frustrations of political activism with a community of peers. As I wrote on the assignment sheet, "this project is your chance to change the world in some small and immediate way, . . . to take action and change the way we think or act about women, oppressed peoples, and the environment." To come up with topics, we brainstormed a blackboard list of many possibilities and gave everyone first three votes, then one, until the less interesting choices were eliminated. Though I provided some outside assistance, the groups were more or less on their own to find methods that best addressed their topics. By working in groups of four to six, the students together overcame their individual uncertainty and reluctance to engage an issue. Though some groups suffered from weak group process or poor "chemistry," most focused on their goals and made significant contributions.

One group developed a campus awareness program with tabling, leaflets, and campus lectures on breast cancer and the environment. Another group investigated the toxic chemicals in tampons (dioxin, rayon, chlorine bleach) and mounted warning stickers in all the women's restrooms. This fall a group took on Halloween and the negative stereotyping of witches; they built a shrine to those who'd been burned in earlier witch hunts and leafletted by it outside the library. On Halloween night they designed a pagan ritual for the class and supportive friends to honor the time of year as part of the seasonal cycle. Another group became outraged at sweatshop labor conditions for women and the direct connection for women consumers in the United States. Realizing that many of their clothes were most likely produced by sweatshop labor, they undertook the necessary research to prepare educational literature and petitions of support. Perhaps the most evocative action was a slide show on parallel dominations of women and animals. The students found very disturbing ad images and photos of women that portrayed them as animals, sex objects, and hunted game. Their moving and insightful script left many in the audience alert and upset in a newly "conscientized" way.

In this class the liberatory work came first through studying ecofeminist theory about the logic of domination. While they wrestled with subjective implications privately, in class they put together the reinforcing dualisms of man/woman, human/nature, reason/emotion, spirit/matter, etc. (Griffin 1975; Plumwood 1993). Seeing through the values and norms produced by the dominant patriarchal society gave them new insights into some of their previously unquestioned behaviors. This mental liberation opened the way for experiential learning through the activism project, in which they responded to a call and actively took a position of solidarity. One student wrote in her course evaluation, "the activism project was great—both a great learning experience and a great way to make friends in the class." By working together in groups, the students built community and support for each other as they took their work out into the wider campus arena.

In the Radical Environmentalism course I assigned a similar activism project, but preceded it with an exercise in exposing values and ideologies related to common everyday products. For this "Life Cycle Analysis" I asked students to investigate a specific product and all the various implications of its use—energy costs, groundwater pollution, shipping distances, volume consumed in Burlington, labor policies in the production place, associated environmental hazards, and alternative, less environmentally destructive options. My students were naturally drawn toward items they held some stake in using: last year the groups investigated coffee, beer, soy milk, tampons, and paper. This year they are investigating products used in quantity at UVM, as part of the new Environmental Council's efforts to "green up" the campus. These groups are looking at locally produced food purchased by campus food operations, the degree of pesticide use, water waste in the dorms, paper procurement policies, and campus investments.[5]

This assignment requires "action research"—going beyond the library to the people responsible for a company's policies and choices. Students inevitably hit some brick walls and begin to see why it serves a producer to keep certain information out of sight. Their frustration points them toward Fourez's power relations analysis; they begin to see the ideological values promoted by producers to ensure consumers will buy their product. Students also begin to glimpse the scale of environmental impact generated from Northern patterns of overconsumption. The soy milk group, for example, found out that EdenSoy milk was produced in Hong Kong from organic soy beans shipped across the Pacific from the United States; the milk was then sent back across the Pacific to California for packaging and distribution.

In dealing with campus products, this year's class will inevitably be faced with structural issues that require structural solutions. The paper group already knows that the best environmental interests of the central purchasing department are undercut when virgin paper prices drop below recycled paper costs. Although the state of Vermont has mandated that all internal correspondence and reports be printed on recycled paper (a structural solution), no such mandate has been issued from the university administration. The campus investments group wants to know what environmental misdeeds the university might be supporting through its stockholdings in Monsanto and Mitsubishi. Enforcement of a socially responsible investing policy would also require structural change based on structural or social ethics. The university might want to consider whether its investments are consistent with its emphasis on environmental education programs, energy efficiency, and campus stewardship through recycling.

The activism projects for Radical Environmentalism are purposely grounded in the liberation agenda of one of the movements we study. We spend time in class brainstorming about campus ecology issues that would be of concern to deep ecologists (pesticide use, natural areas management), to ecofeminists (proportion of women professors in the sciences, inclusion of ecofeminist perspectives in environmental and natural resources courses), to social ecologists (bioregional planning on campus), to animal rights activists (treatment of experimental lab animals), to environmental justice advocates (custodial staff exposure to chemical hazards). I ask the students to identify who their action strategy for social change will affect and how it will produce conscientization. By applying Fourez's model in their own student-motivated projects, they try out the liberatory praxis for themselves. By presenting the results of their efforts in class, they come to articulate the values and process linked to the conscientization.

In the Religion and Ecology course it seemed clear that many environmental studies students needed to reflect on their religious and spiritual upbringing or the lack of it. Many came to the course convinced that Christianity was the root of all environmental evil. Very few had been exposed to any concepts of stewardship or respect for nature through traditional religious practices. Readings and class discussions offered the opportunity to delve into some of these arenas, but I thought they might leave the students still distant from their own personal anguish about the topic. Thus, based on Macy's despair principles, I assigned a first self-assessment paper which would allow students to encounter their own denial and frustration with the absence of connection between religion and the environment. They were asked to explore ways in which their attitudes toward religion and nature were shaped by experience, institutions, and influential people in their lives. I also wanted them to identify specific religious or spiritual "messages" from their culture and personal history that they carry with them in their orientation toward the environment. The autobiographical nature of the paper allowed for full expression of their subjective experience; for many this was deeply satisfying and illuminating. It was striking how many students felt their spirituality was unique to them, an internal knowing based almost entirely in individual experience.

The second part of the assignment addressed Fourez's work in another form. Often religious messages are closely associated with the development of "conscience" and moral values. It can be difficult to distinguish between religious rhetoric that supports an institutional view and true moral response to a situation. Most Judeo-Christian traditions emphasize an absolute set of moral guidelines as expressed in the Hebrew Bible and New Testament. In Fourez's model it is important to identify the sources of influential values and understand how they represent a dominant group's position. This leads to questioning the absolute nature of normative moral commands. This, in turn, can generate the possibility for a more relational ethic based on taking personal responsibility for one's own actions. In order for students to find a constructive green path, they had to be able to see their religious training for what it was—and then go on to make it meaningful in a new way. The most striking comments were from those raised Catholic who had been actively taught to hate their bodies and anything that remotely suggested sensuality (and by association, paganism). The students could see that such anti-body positions not only contradicted their own personal experience in nature (skiing, swimming, hiking, etc.) but suggested by inference that the Earth as body was also to be repulsed (Spretnak 1991).

Following Macy's empowerment model, I knew that it was important for students to keep moving with their insights, that it would not work to leave them struggling and bitter about their religious inheritance. I should acknowledge here that a small proportion of the group did in fact have very strong religious upbringings that encouraged love and respect for the natural world and people. But this gift, too, needed to be put in the perspective of the majority's experience. Thus the second paper I assigned offered a chance to try some new religious practices from various world traditions which could foster a greener ecospirituality. Students were asked to choose five different religious practices and undertake one each week over a period of five weeks. Some were able to do this with more discipline and rigor than others, but in general, the results were tangible and profound. Some of the practices were:

vegetarianism	Jainism (ahimsa or nonharming)
sun salutation yoga	Hinduism
walking meditation	Buddhism
meal prayers	Christianity, others
eco-kosher eating	Judaism
relations with a special animal	Native American
daily visit to a sacred place	Native American
five daily prayers for life	Islam

Though students confessed their unfamiliarity with the traditions they "tried on," they could plainly see the difference the practices made in their awareness and relationship to the natural world. The discipline itself was the point of empowerment, held by the students, nudged along by the teacher. By releasing some of the disparaging energy in the first paper, students could move forward to find more authentic engagement with the environment. As one student summed up in her course evaluation, "I came to class with a negative view of organized religion being brought up in what I feel was a repressive Catholic tradition, but now I see the inspiration and values that religion can provide."

Though the papers did provide safety and privacy for students in their exploration, they did not accomplish the community-building aspect of Joanna Macy's work. To include this critical piece, I assigned three group projects. The first was to design a short opening for each day's class based on the principles and practices of the religion we were studying that week. Groups of three to five students shared readings, poems, songs, drumming, tai chi, yoga, and guided meditations to set an inspirational tone for the class. Though these required relatively little preparation, they opened a window for a less teacher-dominated form of interaction. The second project was to investigate ecospiritual activism in response to particular environmental issues. I wanted students to realize there were religiously based organizations engaged in addressing population concerns, forest issues, biotechnology, sustainable development, etc. Working in groups they uncovered inspirational efforts by the National Religious Partnership for Life, the EcoJustice Committees of the Presbyterian and Congregational churches, the "redwood rabbis" leading Tu B' Shevat seders in the Headwaters ancient forest grove, among others. This exposed them to the wider green religious community, a community of like-minded people they could choose to join in their efforts.

The third group project was perhaps the riskiest. I didn't really know what would happen when I suggested it. I wanted students to actually try to build community by communicating with others some of their knowledge and experience in the realm of religion and ecology. For Earth Week, they were to design a "service" to "engage a wider circle of participants from beyond the class in questions in the domain of religion and ecology." One group did plan an entire Sunday service for a Unitarian-Universalist congregation where one student's father was the minister. Three others spent the afternoon as "eco-evangelists" at the student Earth Day fair, wearing animal costumes and handing out earth prayers. Two groups worked with children to raise environmental values in a class setting, another organized a cleanup of a nearby natural area, including poems and silent walking meditation as part of the experience. One hearty group waited until the full moon after Earth Day and held a midnight walk at a wooded lakeside park. There in the drizzle they shared poems from various religious traditions and gave themselves to the power of the night.

The last class, International Environmental Studies, was certainly the most difficult challenge in applying the principles of Macy's and Fourez's work. This was due primarily to the class size (200 students) and the class format (lecture). Some degree of intimacy, however, was afforded in the required discussion sections led by undergraduate teaching assistants. Traditionally the TAs had managed their groups somewhat independently, following general guidelines set at weekly meetings with the professor. When I was asked to fill in for someone on sabbatical, I seized the opportunity to orient the course around the upcoming 1992 Earth Summit in Rio. I myself was fascinated by how the event galvanized nongovernmental organizations (NGOs) and government to develop positions through both Agenda 21 and the Earth Charter. I thought we could hold a Model Earth Summit on our own campus, using discussion groups to represent various regions of the world (nineteen altogether). I really had no idea what I was getting into, but I was sure this would generate community in the class and compassion for the real world conversation taking place.

The course itself had a reputation for being "Gloom and Doom 101," a seemingly endless list of global problems, none of which was getting any better. It was hard to add humor to the lectures when the topics were so serious and all-encompassing—deforestation, desertification, fisheries decline, global warming, human rights, structural adjustment. The lectures generated a certain amount of despair and discouragement, especially as students began to develop a systems perspective and could see how many of the deteriorating influences worked synergistically in a negative way. I introduced some of Macy's exercises to the TAs who brought them to their small groups. This barely made a dent in the tsunami of emotional helplessness, so I turned to the empowerment aspects of the work, enjoining the students to help plan the Model Earth Summit.

Each regional discussion group sent a representative to the Earth Summit council which met several times in April before the two-day event following Earth Day. Together with my head teaching assistant (TA) and a research intern, the group figured out student keynote speakers, chairpeople, logistics, music, publicity, and food donations. We designed the agenda to allow each group to present its concerns and then for caucus groups to propose changes to the draft Earth Charter. I encouraged groups to be creative in finding ways to communicate their concerns and to organize to work together where helpful. We held a short dress rehearsal in the lecture hall, where students practiced using the mike to address the entire group formally. This alone was quite empowering for the formerly passive audience to my lectures.

On the day of the event, the television cameras and reporters turned out to cover the colorful scene. Central America's table was covered with tropical houseplants and brightly woven cloths; the Middle East delegation was dressed in veils and long robes. Southeast Asia had free curry and rice to give away; Oceania offered pineapples and papaya. The indigenous groups' delegation followed the lead of their TA, who shaved his head into a Mohawk for the occasion and wore a loincloth. Following the group presentations, we began to address the agenda. Then things got interesting, and I just watched from the back. The four African delegations banded together and insisted on deleting free trade from the Earth Charter, since it only drained their resources and kept them from sustainable independence. The women's caucus staged a sit-in after networking with all the groups to sign their statement recognizing the particular impacts of environmental deterioration on women and children. And the indigenous representatives completely blocked the proceedings, demanding they be given a voice and a vote at the Summit. The student chairs handled each event, doing their best to hear the needs of the delegates on the floor despite the consistent efforts of the United States (acted out by the teaching assistants in suits and ties) to block everything.

The Summit was exhausting in its endless logistics but extremely rewarding in its pedagogical effectiveness. The two-day combination theater event and international meeting was more than a role play. Based on in-depth preparation in the discussion sections, the entire class became one learning community, sharing its frustrations and creativity as part of the international conversation. We were the first such model Earth Summit to take place in the United States. Two of the TAs subsequently found grant support to travel to Brazil and attend the actual summit, where they organized with other students to represent the youth voice. One student wrote, "I think this was a terrific project for the class to do together. The entire class came together as one unit with a common goal. You don't see classes of this size do this. I learned *a lot* and I think that it was a great project."

I thought this experience had been a one-of-a-kind event, clearly linked to the Earth Summit timing. But four years later I was again asked to teach the course, and again, I felt it essential to do something that would bring the entire group together in a meaningful way. This time we organized around Human Rights and the Environment.[6] As we discussed the various biological and geophysical aspects of global environmental decline, we considered the impacts on specific groups of people in various regions and of various economic classes. The discussion sections researched human rights issues in their own regions, looking for environmental links where documented. Once more we organized a representative council to design the culminating event. This time it was a one-day Human Rights Tribunal, a set of testimonies from the regions of the world, designed to bring attention to human and environmental suffering.

Regional tables held maps, petitions, handouts, individual stories, and of course, the ever-popular regional food. Again we invited the television stations to cover the event, both to raise the issues and to show that students could do something creative and compassionate in response to global issues. The testimonies were moving and well prepared. The Central American section read actual statements from prisoners; the West African section told the story of Ken Saro-Wiwa, recently executed for his environmental work in Nigeria. The Middle Eastern group demonstrated the gulf between white American perspectives and Islamic citizens. Perhaps the most touching moment was a tribute to all those who had suffered from nuclear testing in the Pacific Islands; the students passed out lit candles to the entire group as a symbol of hope in the darkness. One student expressed these feelings: "The Human Rights Tribunal was definitely the culmination of the whole semester. Not only did it unite our class and empower us to speak out, it left me with a feeling of hope that we *can* make change and we will, after a semester of incredibly depressing material."

Both large group events were driven by my desire to engage students at the feeling level and to empower them to speak out and give voice to their concerns. The shyness and timidity of first- and second-year students would have been almost impossible to overcome in a smaller-scale event. By generating such a complex and highly choreographed event, with students organizing and TAs helping, many were swept along in the process of the larger learning community. The sharing of testimonies in a public forum reduced the despair of such stories held in isolation. The horrors were laid bare for all to see; the links between environmental degradation and human suffering were unmistakable. In this forum at least, environmental concern was not mocked or marginalized. The students could take their own feelings seriously and be motivated to raise awareness and compassion in others for the unfolding environmental tragedies. They had the support of those who had been through the empowerment process with them. Now, I hoped, this compassion would serve as a foundation for future engagement with environmental issues, whether local or global.

CLOSING

I am nervous each time I begin another one of these explorations into conscientization. What will come up this time? Will I have the courage to let the students struggle into their own insights? Will I have the strength to engage my own conditioned thinking as part of our process together? Will I be able to face my own ongoing environmental despair as I invite the students to be authentic with theirs?

The conversation accelerates in the student circle on environmental racism. They are not likely to come to any satisfactory conclusions in this round. The subjects are too rich, too controversial, and too far-reaching to penetrate in a single session. Like the experimental assignments and group projects, the fishbowl offers a taste of another way of working. Like the Earth Summit and Human Rights Tribunal, the group discussion provides a forum for sharing feelings and concerns. My courses are popular among students; they seem to want the chance to engage both subjectively and in community. The material is challenging and often unresolvable; the realms for awakening seem infinite.

I am well aware that these experiments in environmental education go against the grain of current academic culture steeped as it is in scientific "objectivity" and individual competition. Academic values such as these may not be the most helpful in generating environmental change. They may, in fact, be a big part of the problem. I believe the most effective response to the global environmental crisis is first a moral response. Emotional connection in a supportive community can strengthen the callings that arise naturally in environmental studies courses. Raising awareness through dialogue can mitigate the unfortunate loneliness of many student journeys toward environmental conscientization.

Though outcomes of this kind of work may not be easily measurable, I am convinced by my students' experience that this work is essential for long-term environmental change. With this exposure to despair, empowerment, liberation, and compassion I hope my students will carry the seeds of empowerment to others and help turn this world toward sustainable, healthy, and responsible relations with all beings.

Notes

1 These include the following: guided meditations on the web of life and overcoming obstacles; a truth-telling mandala for expressing grief, rage, and fear; the Council of All Beings; and various shorter exercises in pairs and small groups. For the Council of All Beings see John Seed, Joanna Macy, Pat Fleming, and Arne Naess, *Thinking like a mountain: Towards a council of all beings.* (Philadelphia: New Society Publishers, 1988).

2. Textbooks have included: Diamond and Orenstein (1990); Griffin (1978); Merchant (1980); Mies and Shiva (1993); Plumwood (1993).

3. Textbooks have included: Bullard (1993); Fourez (1982); List (1993); Merchant (1994); Singer (1990); Taylor (1995); and Zimmerman et al. (1993).

4. Textbooks have included: Gottlieb (1996); Hallman (1994); Reynolds and Tanner (1995); and Tucker and Grim (1993).

5. For a guide to campus eco-audits see April Smith, *Campus ecology*. (Los Angeles: Living Planet Press, 1993). For sample life cycle stories of everyday items, see John Ryan and Alan Thein Durning, *Stuff: The secret lives of everyday things*. (Seattle: Northwest Environment Watch, 1997).

6. For sample case studies, see Barbara Rose Johnston, ed., *Who pays the price? The sociocultural context of environmental crisis.* (Washington, D.C.: Island Press, 1994).

Textbooks

Bullard, Robert O., (Ed.). (1993). *Confronting environmental racism*. Boston: South End Press.

Diamond, Irene, and Gloria Orenstein, (Eds). (1990). *Reweaving the world: The emergence of ecofeminism*. San Francisco: Sierra Club Books.

Fourez, Gerard. (1982). *Liberation ethics*. Philadelphia: Temple University Press.

Gottlieb, Roger S., (Ed.). (1996). *This sacred earth. Religion, nature, environment.* New York: Routledge.

Griffin, Susan. (1978). *Woman and nature*. New York: Harper and Row.

Hallman, David, (Ed.). (1994). *Ecotheology: Voices from South and North.* Mary Knoll, New York: Orbis.

List, Peter C. (1993). *Radical environmentalism: Philosophy and tactics*. Belmont, California: Wadsworth.

Merchant, Carolyn. (1980). *The death of nature: Women, ecology, and the scientific revolution*. San Francisco: Harper and Row.

Merchant, Carolyn, (Ed.). (1994). *Ecology*. New Jersey: Humanities Press.

Mies, Maria, and Vandana Shiva. (1993). *Ecofeminism.* London: Zed Books.

Plumwood, Val. (1993). *Feminism and the mastery of nature*. New York: Routledge.

Reynolds, Vernon, and Ralph Tanner. (1995). *The social ecology of religion*. New York: Oxford University Press.

Singer, Peter. (1990). *Animal liberation*. New York: Aron Books.

Taylor, Bron R., (Ed.). (1995). *Ecological resistance movements*. Albany: State University of New York Press.

Tucker, Mary E., and John Grim, (Eds). (1993). *Worldviews and ecology.* Lewisburg, Pennsylvania: Bucknell University Press.

Zimmerman, Michael E., J. Baird Caldicott, George Sessions, Karen J. Warren, and John Clark. (1993). *Environmental philosophy*. Englewood Cliffs, New Jersey: Prentice Hall.

References

DeBoer, Kristin A. (1995, January). *Teaching ecofeminism*. Paper presented at the 22nd Annual Richard R. Baker Philosophy Colloquium on Ecofeminist Perspectives, Ohio.

Fourez, Gerard. (1982). *Liberation ethics*. Philadelphia: Temple University Press.

Griffin, Susan. (1978). *Woman and nature*. New York: Harper and Row.

Lifton, Robert J. (1968). *Death in life: Survivors of Hiroshima*. New York: Random House.

Macy, Joanna Rogers. (1983). *Despair and personal power in the nuclear age*. Philadelphia: New Society Publishers.

Plumwood, Val. (1993). *Feminism and the mastery of nature*. New York: Routledge.

Spretnak, Charlene. (1991). *States of grace*. San Francisco: Harper Collins.

Strauss, Benjamin H. (1996). *The class of 2000 report: Environmental education, practices, and activism on campus*. New York: Nathan Cummings Foundation.

8 Changing the Dominant Cultural Perspective in Education

C.A. Bowers

Like early childhood education and educational administration, environmental education has become another area of specialized study within many colleges of education, and it has further become identified as a branch of science education. The effect of this categorization is that the other areas of teacher education and graduate studies in education continue to ignore the connections between the values and ideas they promote and the cultural behaviors now overwhelming the viability of natural systems. In addition, the association of environmental education with the sciences helps to perpetuate the modern myth that science and technology provide the most effective means of restoring the environment. This, in turn, makes it more difficult to recognize that the ways in which humans interact with environment (including their ameliorative uses of science and technology) are influenced by generally unconsciously held cultural assumptions. To state the challenge facing colleges of education in its most succinct form: the aspects of the ecological crisis that can be attributed to human behavior are cultural in nature and are directly related to the modern ideas and values that are the basis of the knowledge learned in teacher education programs and in other areas of graduate studies in education.

The failure of education faculty to recognize the truth in David Orr's insight that "All education is [some form of] environmental education" (1992, 90) can be attributed, in part, to the taken-for-granted view that modern and, now, postmodern culture have progressed beyond the environmentally disruptive technologies of the Industrial Revolution. While certain sectors of society are moving to paperless forms of communication, and computer-driven machines are replacing both workers and old-style factories and offices, the deep cultural assumptions that served as the basis of political, economic, and technological changes associated with the Industrial Revolution continue to be the foundation of the high-status knowledge promoted by multinational corporations, the media, and in all areas of the university curricula—

including colleges of education. These modern assumptions include viewing change as progressive in nature, intelligence and creativity as attributes of the autonomous individual, science and technology as the source of empowerment, and the commodification of all areas of community life as the highest expression of human development. These assumptions are also responsible for the introduction of more than 60,000 chemicals into the environment, the depletion of fisheries and forests, changes in the carbon cycle in ways that contribute to global warming, and the loss of both species and cultural diversity. Although the connections between these assumptions and the Industrial Revolution are generally not acknowledged, they are basic to the ethos of universities: rewarding new (and ecologically experimental) ideas and values, representing intelligence as an attribute of a form of individualism that is assumed to be free of cultural influence, associating scientific and technological development with the cutting edge of progress, and promoting (through the use of computers) the further commodification of knowledge and relationships as the next step in educational progress. Indeed, their taken-for-granted status within the university (including colleges of education) makes it impossible to recognize the legitimacy of alternative cultural assumptions—even when they are shown to be the basis of ecologically sustainable cultures.

In addition to the linkages between the cultural epistemology of the Industrial Revolution and the different genres of educational liberalism (technocratic, emancipatory, and neo-romantic) that continue to frame how education faculty socialize the next generation of classroom teachers and professors of education, students coming into the field of education bring a self-identity and way of thinking that is based on these same assumptions, which are also essential to the elite groups who determine which forms of community knowledge and relationships will be brought under the influence of scientific, technological, and market forces. In effect, there is a direct connection between the liberal assumptions professors and students take for granted and the process of commodification that Karl Polanyi describes in his classic study, *The Great Transformation* (1957). In addition, many students enrolled in teacher education programs bring another concern that makes them even more resistant to rethinking the connections between the cultural assumptions underlying both the explicit and implicit curriculum and the ecological crisis. This concern is based on a deep fear of losing control in the classroom, which leads to their feeling that discussions of how the languages of a culture reproduce pre-ecological forms of intelligence are unrelated to their need to learn teaching and behavioral management strategies. This fear of the liminality that is part of every teaching/learning situation adds a further level of difficulty in reforming teacher education in ways that take account of the culture/ecological crisis connection.

CHARACTERISTICS OF ECOLOGICALLY SUSTAINABLE CULTURES THAT ARE RELEVANT TO THE REFORM OF COLLEGES OF EDUCATION

The general misunderstanding of how traditions are unconsciously reenacted and carried forward, even in the most innovative areas of scientific thought and technological development, has contributed to the failure to recognize that radical educational reform requires basic changes in our guiding cultural assumptions. One way, I would suggest, for breaking the hold of modern assumptions is to consider the implications for educational reform of what are now being increasingly recognized as common characteristics of ecologically centered cultures that have developed profoundly different approaches to living within the limits of natural systems. When I suggest to various audiences that we can learn from traditional, ecologically centered cultures, the near-universal response is that I am being both impractical and romantic because "we cannot go back to a more primitive form of existence." This response, which reflects a modern evolutionary pattern of thinking deeply rooted in racism, fails to take account of the fact that traditional, ecologically centered cultures are part of the contemporary world. That many of these cultures have resisted embracing modern technology and the other aspects of the modern epistemology that would enable them to participate in the globalized economy leads to viewing them as backward and "primitive." However, if we can set aside these prejudices, it may become possible to recognize alternative pathways of culture development that are essential to living within the limits of the Earth's ecosystems and to a viable and just form of community existence. Again, I want to emphasize that I am not suggesting that we borrow the traditions of other cultures. Rather, the focus here is on identifying the traditional areas of cultural development (what Gary Snyder refers to as the mainstream of human development) that can serve as guidelines for reforming teacher education and graduate studies in education.

Recovering the Traditions of Noncommodified Forms of Knowledge and Community

Karl Polanyi's book, *The Great Transformation*, examines how the Industrial Revolution undermined the self-sufficiency of communities by turning both nature and labor into commodities to be bought and sold. Today, we are witnessing how science and technology are being used to transform nearly every aspect of community life—including the healing arts, play, ceremony, nurturing, mentoring, and convivial activities—into market relationships. Megastores such as Toys 'R' Us have replaced the transgenerational sharing of children's' play and stories, the preparation of food and recreational activities have been turned into huge economic markets, and knowledge of self and relationships have become the domains of impersonal experts whose primary motivation is to sell either chemically based or trendy psychological healing strategies. Even such basic aspects of community life as education, human reproduction, and care of the elderly have become commodified.

The transformation of community, where reciprocal relationships and knowledge that sustains everyday life are dominated by technological and economic concerns, into exploitable markets of opportunity for multinational corporations and small entrepreneurs, has a number of implications that are relevant to the reform of teacher education and graduate studies in education. First, the commodification of all aspects of individual and community life, while justified as contributing to continued economic growth, contributes directly to the amount of toxic waste that disrupts the biological processes of reproduction and development throughout the environment (Colborn, Dumanoski, Myers 1996), the misuse of nature's varied sources of energy, and exploitation and degradation of bioregions that other cultures depend upon. Second, the commodification process fosters a form of moral education that contributes to anomic individualism and relativistic values, and thus undermines the values essential to the moral ecology of the community and of human/nature relationships. Third, as Jeremy Rifkin points out in *The End of Work* (1996), the current approach to technological development, which is also being globalized as the model for modern development, involves displacing humans with computer-driven machines which can be operated in countries that have the lowest wages and weakest environmental restrictions. This approach to technology continues to undermine what remains of the traditions that made communities relatively self-sufficient. Increasingly, the loss of traditional forms of knowledge that were the basis of many forms of reciprocity that sustained self-reliant communities has led to the cruel paradox of large numbers of unemployed now being dependent upon buying the essentials of daily life that previously were shared through a variety of noneconomic community relationships.

Efforts to reform teacher education and graduate studies in education need to be based on careful consideration of the many ways in which current approaches, from the theory learned in graduate classes to guiding student teachers, contribute to the further commodification of culture that began as a primary strategy of the Industrial Revolution. This will require a critical examination of how current educational ideas and values contribute to maintaining the distinction between high- and low-status knowledge that serve the economic and political interests of elite groups. It will also require clarifying the connections between low-status knowledge (what is not part of the curriculum of universities and public schools) and the noncommodified relationships and traditions of community life—both in the dominant and minority cultures. The ability of education professors to recognize forms of community relationships, traditions, and norms of reciprocity and civic responsibility that are not dependent upon consumerism carries over to helping classroom teachers understand how to clarify for their students the connections between high-status knowledge and the ecological crisis. They also help educators recognize the complexity of low-status (generally noncommodified) knowledge and its importance to community relationships and activities. The ability to bring the study of community, the historical process of commodification, and the connections between high-status knowledge and economic globalization into the curriculum of the public school are essential for challenging the mesmerizing power of the dominant consumer-oriented culture. One of the great ironies is that the so-called "primitive" cultures that kept their marketplace activities as essential yet peripheral parts of community life (Sachs 1992 70–87) developed forms of symbolic complexity that met the need for meaning, community participation, and, most importantly, a land ethic. In the years ahead teachers need to be able to provide students with examples of noncommodified community activities, traditions, and moral norms that do not have an adverse impact on the environment.

Knowledge of Place

Ecologically sustainable cultures co-evolve in ways that take account of the changing characteristics of the bioregion. That is, the narratives, technologies, foods, medicines, and clothes encode a deep knowledge of place that is passed on from generation to generation. The emphasis on a knowledge of place, which characterizes current approaches to science-based environmental education, tends to focus on monitoring natural systems. It may even include biodiversity mapping and the documentation of cultural heritage. While important, the scientific study of changes occurring in the bioregion, including changes caused by cultural practices, is profoundly different from the way in which indigenous cultures frame their understanding of the nutritional and medicinal characteristics of plants and the life cycles of animals, as part of a coherent spiritual universe. By way of contrast, our scientific approach relies on the instrumental form of thinking that was basic to the Industrial Revolution; but in recognizing that our fate is tied to the fate of natural systems, the current approaches to environmental education represent a positive step beyond the exploitive mindset that is present in the efforts to turn the commons into market relationships.

The taken-for-granted attitude that represents natural systems as part of the same spiritual universe that requires both a holistic way of understanding and respect cannot be addressed in a meaningful way until there is a radical transformation in what is regarded as high-status knowledge—which is currently being influenced by developments in the sciences and computer technology. But teacher education and graduate studies in education can make important contributions to undermining the double bind by addressing other aspects of indigenous knowledge. Classroom teachers need to be able to help students recover the community of memory stored in the stories told by previous generations—stories that embody what they learned about human/nature relationships as well as cultural expectations that did not take account of local conditions. Learning the stories and mythopoetic narratives of earlier cultures that inhabited the land is also important to acquiring a knowledge of place.

In addition to re-storying the land, classroom teachers need to help students understand how economic and political forces influence the sustainable characteristics of natural systems: for example, the effect of policies that promote an industrial approach to farming, forests, and fisheries. Also needed is an understanding of how policies can be formulated in ways that contribute to greater community self-reliance. For instance, in the area of technology (which is the most prominent aspect of the dominant culture) teachers need to possess the background knowledge that will enable them to clarify for students the differences between modern technologies that are now being globalized, and technologies that incorporate the principles of ecological design. The five principles of ecological design, as articulated by Sim Van Der Ryn and Stuart Cowan (1996), involve making aesthetic, moral, functional, and economic decisions that require a deep knowledge of place. Indeed, each of the following principles—(1) Solutions Grow from Place, (2) Ecological Accounting Informs Design, (3) Design with Nature, (4) Everyone Is a Designer, and (5) Make Nature Visible (1996, 54–56)—foreground the importance of sustainable cultural practices within the context of sustainable natural systems. If teachers are not introducing students to this ecological way of understanding relationships, then they are socializing students to the current reformulations of the Industrial Revolution agenda of using technology to exploit and control the environment.

Tradition and Elder Knowledge

A generalization that will hold up to critical scrutiny is that there are no historical examples of ecologically sustainable cultures that relied on the myth of unending progress to justify making an experimental approach to ideas, values, and technologies the basis of their high-status knowledge. Indeed, the conceptual and moral orientation of the dominant technologically and scientifically based culture, which creates the mix of nihilism and myth essential to the growth of corporate capitalism, is unique in the history of humankind—and its record of ecological devastation is equally unique. A study of diverse indigenous cultures, as well as marginalized cultures within American society, reveals an important characteristic that is universally shared. In various ways, they all developed traditions for storing and renewing knowledge of essential community relationships. In addition to the storage and renewal function of ceremony (including song, dance, and narrative), elders play an important role in the transgenerational renewal of knowledge that is, over generations of experience, raised to the level of wisdom. To make this point in another way, ecologically sustainable cultures, and even cultures that have a more anthropocentric orientation but have retained a viable noncommodified commons, have not placed responsibility on each generation to discover through their own immediate and supposedly individually determined experience the ideas, values, and technology that are to be the basis of the community. Even though the dominant culture promotes this approach as a guiding ideology, its innovations are based on traditions that have been refined over generations—even in such leading areas of technological development as the aircraft and computer industries. The problem is that the further development of technological knowledge that is rooted in the past is not guided by wisdom about the nature of just and viable human communities, and human/nature relationships.

Before I recommend that teacher education and graduate studies in education be based on a more sophisticated and less ideological understanding of the complexity of tradition (a word that really stands for the historical aspect of culture), and of the unique responsibilities that separate elders from older people, I want to anticipate the possibility that the conceptual categories of many readers will lead them to misinterpret my argument as suggesting that all traditions and forms of elder knowledge should be uncritically accepted—and thus made part of the curriculum. Not all traditions were properly constituted in the first place. Some traditions that seemed an advance in earlier times have changed too slowly. And other traditions have been lost without general awareness of the long-term consequences—such as the loss of privacy rights that has accompanied developments in computer technology. Nor am I proposing that we borrow the forms of elder knowledge of cultures that have developed symbolically along less destructive pathways. But I am suggesting that traditions are an exceedingly complex and important aspect of cultural life, and that an educational system that fails to present students a critical and balanced understanding of the many ways they reenact the patterns and technologies handed down from the past, is contributing to a nihilistic form of consciousness that is more receptive to being manipulated by the media and other promoters of consumerism. I am also suggesting that students need to learn to recognize the difference between elder knowledge and the advice of older people who are passing on the dream of modernity. In addition, students need to learn how to interact with elders in ways that renew cultural wisdom within the current context—which is also the initial phase of being mentored by elders. Students should also be able to recognize the many ways that the dominant culture undermines the moral authority of elder knowledge by making the logic of technology and the marketplace fashionable and exciting.

A Cultural/Ecological View of Intelligence

As I have written extensively on why intelligence (even seven forms of intelligence) should not be considered an attribute of the individual (1990, 1993a, 1993b, 1995, 1997), I shall summarize the evidence and identify only a few of the many reasons that the orthodox view of intelligence that underlies the subfields of graduate studies in education (including teacher education) needs to be radically reconstituted. The long-held myth that intelligence is an attribute of the individual (and now being argued as reflecting the genetic endowment of the individual) only makes sense when the encoding, storage, and reproduction characteristics of language are *entirely* ignored. The myth of the rational and creative individual also requires ignoring the profound differences that exist between cultural epistemologies, as well as the epistemic patterns and values shared within a cultural/linguistic community. Building on the insights of George Lakoff (1987), Mark Johnson (1987), and Richard Brown (1978), I have argued that earlier forms of cultural intelligence were based on the prevailing root metaphors, and that the process of analogic thinking (which is framed by these root metaphors) that prevails over time become encoded in the iconic metaphors used at the taken-for-granted level of thought and communication. For example, the iconic metaphors that encode earlier root metaphors include "data," "intelligence," "creativity," "community," "tradition," and so forth. These iconic metaphors can be traced back to earlier processes of analogic thinking, and the taken-for-granted deep assumptions of the time.

When culture, in all its semiotic forms of expression, is taken into account, it also becomes clear that the traditions (technologies, norms governing metacommunication, and conceptual patterns) that are reenacted at a taken-for-granted level represent a cultural form of intelligence. Even the design elements of a culture, which range from buildings and the layout of communities to household implements, embody earlier forms of cultural intelligence that both shape our sense of reality and enable us to attend to issues related more to our individualized perspectives and needs. The purposive rational, reflective, and "creative" aspects of intelligence, which philosophers, psychologists, and educators have overly emphasized, is deeply influenced by the metaphorical languages that sustain cultural life. These various expressions of explicit and intentional thought can be seen as a third and more individualized expression of intelligence.

Also, as I have pointed out elsewhere (1993b, 1995, 1997), intelligence or the ability to respond to a "difference which makes a difference" (to use Gregory Bateson's phrase) is always part of a larger set of interacting patterns and relationships—which as a whole can be understood as an ecology of human/nature relationships. A form of cultural intelligence that ignores how toxins introduced into the environment disrupt the reproductive patterns of different forms of life jeopardizes its immediate members as well as future generations. Technologies that put lead and PCBs into the environment, require sources of energy that contribute to global warming, and contribute to the commodification of health care should be viewed as a pathological form of cultural intelligence. Thinking of intelligence as ecological, where the shift is from viewing the individual as thinking about an external world to viewing intelligence as an integral aspect of all relationships (the "patterns that connect," as Bateson puts it) is even more radical than thinking of intelligence as part of a shared cultural epistemology. The diverging trendlines between the increasing demand of humans on natural systems, and the rapidly decreasing viability of natural systems to reproduce themselves, makes it imperative that we learn how to understand intelligence in terms of an ecology.

As I will later explain more fully, a cultural/ecological view of intelligence requires a radical shift away from basing educational theory, technologies, and classroom strategies on the modern assumptions about the culture-free nature of technology, the individual's ability to construct his or her own version of reality on the basis of data and direct experience, and empowering students to discover new ideas and values. As the implications of a cultural/ecological view of intelligence becomes more fully understood, the importance of integrating into teacher education and graduate studies in education a more complex understanding of community (in all its commodified and noncommodified dimensions), place, tradition, and culture/ecology relationships will be recognized. The challenge will be for education professors, as well as their colleagues in other departments, to recognize how the patterns of thinking they now equate with progress and enlightenment contribute to the ecological crisis, and to make the radical shift in consciousness that is now required.

The fact that environmentally oriented courses and programs have an add-on status that leaves largely intact the modern (and postmodern) conceptual and moral orthodoxies that underlie academic disciplines, and that environmental awareness is largely limited in public schools to recycling, classroom eco-tourism projects, and science education, does not make me particularly optimistic. But given the current national priorities for allocating resources to computer technology and for aligning education with economic development, the example of the two graduate programs based on a deep cultural and ecological perspective that have been started in the School of Education at Portland State University, is evidence that ecologically oriented reforms can be achieved even in limited circumstances. It is estimated that since 1991 $9.5 billion have been spent bringing computer technology into the nation's classrooms. By comparison, the efforts of environmentally oriented professors and classroom teachers are generally undertaken as part of their work overload. While the modest success at Portland State University should not be viewed as representing a national trend in education, efforts here may be useful for other education professors who now recognize the need for radical change.

FROM THEORY INTO PRACTICE: INTRODUCING A CULTURAL AND ECOLOGICAL PERSPECTIVE INTO GRADUATE STUDIES IN EDUCATION AT PORTLAND STATE UNIVERSITY

As the other chapters in this book indicate, there are many important examples of how to integrate environmental education with community renewal. Leadership in these pioneering efforts is centered in the efforts of university faculty and classroom teachers who combine tenacity, knowledge of how to integrate environmental issues into the curriculum, and an awareness that the ecological crisis is the starting point for addressing other social justice issues. At the same time, it is important to recognize that colleges of education are not providing leadership in developing approaches to environmental education in the same way they have promoted multicultural education, and school-to-work educational goals—including computer-mediated learning. It is also necessary to recognize that the environmental education courses offered in colleges of education too often combine scientific knowledge of natural systems, liberal assumptions about progress and individualism, and other important parts of the epistemological legacy of the Industrial Revolution that we now call "modernization." While there were several education professors who taught courses that touched on the social and educational implications of the ecological crisis when I joined the faculty at Portland State University in 1993, there were no programs that provided the opportunity for systematic and in-depth study of educational issues and processes from a deep cultural and ecological perspective. The graduate specializations in Education, Culture, and Ecology (at the master's degree level), and Community and Environmental Renewal (at the doctoral level), that have since gained faculty support and now survive because of their willingness to devote time and energy beyond their regular assignments, represent models that faculty in other colleges of education may find helpful.

How the Specializations Were Developed in the Context of Budget Reductions

When I moved from the University of Oregon to Portland State University (PSU), I found the climate in the PSU School of Education completely different from the behaviorist and technicist orientation that had frustrated my earlier efforts to base teacher education on a cultural/ecological model of understanding. The PSU faculty already had thought through and articulated the social justice principles that were to guide the development of all new programs. Thus there was a receptiveness to the proposal for "greening" existing courses in the different categories required for the master's degree. As the School of Education was (and still is) facing budget cuts, the strategy of updating the content of existing courses, with such traditional titles as Curriculum Materials, Advanced Educational Psychology, Philosophy of Education, and so forth, in ways that took into account cultural issues relating to the ecological crisis was absolutely essential. If the approach had been that of adding new courses and hiring additional faculty, the entire effort would have failed. By taking existing courses and demonstrating how the issues and theoretical foundations in such areas as learning theory, curriculum, and classroom communication could be based on understanding how individuals are nested in culture, and culture is nested in natural systems, we demonstrated that a cultural approach to environmental education must start with the reconceptualization of the dominant paradigm that underlies the mainstream education. Because initially only a few faculty felt ready to teach these revised courses, most of the program was offered during the summer session when financial resources were made available to bring Gregory Smith, Joe Sheridan, Joseph Kiefer, and Gregory Cajete as visiting faculty. Today, graduate students can put together a program of study where all of the education courses either address issues raised by the cultural dimensions of the ecological crisis or involve thinking about educational issues and processes from within a cultural/ecological paradigm.

The effort to develop the theme of "Community and Environmental Renewal" began with a memorandum sent to all faculty in the School of Education that announced a meeting for faculty interested in the connections between the problems facing communities and the forces contributing to the degradation of the environment. Seven faculty from different departments attended the first meeting, and following subsequent planning meetings the group submitted a proposal for doctoral level study within the existing degree program offered by the Department of Curriculum and Instruction. The purpose or theme, as approved by the departmental faculty, includes:

> The doctoral theme of Community and Environmental Renewal offers an opportunity for interdisciplinary study of the relationships between educational practices and policies and the challenges facing communities and the environment. Included among the challenges are institutionalized class privilege, racism, sexism, and anthropocentrism—which will be addressed as enduring cultural constructions. To accomplish these goals this theme calls on the expertise of faculty in all departments of the School of Education. The areas of study have three foci: (1) to understand the nature of the cultural and structural changes that are influencing the viability of communities in the areas of

work, family, food cycles, gender, ethnicity, recreation, mental and physical health, and transgenerational communication; (2) to understand the nature of the ecological crises, how they are part of a crisis in cultural ways of knowing, values, and practices, and how educational policies and curricular decisions contribute to ecologically problematic cultural practices; (3) to develop the skills, strategies and ability to articulate reform-oriented educational policies and classroom practices necessary for working with groups which are addressing environmental and social justice issues in their communities.

Again, budget restrictions forced faculty to change the content of existing courses rather than add new courses. These restrictions also forced them to attend additional meetings to discuss issues related to the shift from the modern paradigm for thinking about educational reform, as well as take on additional responsibility for advising doctoral students without any reductions in their other departmental work. It is important to mention this because it demonstrates the deep concern that some faculty have about the future, and their willingness to take on additional work when they learn that other faculty share similar concerns. What I learned from this is that it was not until I began to explore the degree of shared interest among the faculty that I discovered that I did not have to work alone in introducing students to a combined culture and ecological way of thinking that was, with few exceptions, overwhelmed by the modern orthodoxies they encountered in their other education and liberal arts courses. The collaborative effort also led to the awareness that while existing degree requirements would force compromises, it was still possible to cobble together programs of study that could provide students in-depth exposure to ecologically and community oriented faculty both within education and other departments on campus.

Reflections on the Content of a Cultural Approach to Environmental Education

Since the publication of *Cultural Literacy for Freedom* (1974), I have been teaching courses that address different cultural dimensions of the ecological crisis. Many of the courses became the core area of study for doctoral students working with me at the University of Oregon. And two of the courses (Cultural Ecology of the Classroom and Reflective Practitioner) were developed specifically for students going into the fifth-year teacher education program. Over this period of time I used what became highly predictable patterns of student reaction to the combined deep cultural and ecological perspective as a basis for adjusting course content. A problem that continues to arise, even today, is connected with what can be described as culture shock for many students who encounter a way of thinking about education that is not based on the modern view of individual agency, the neutrality of language and technology, and the assumption that education should foster *new* ideas and values in order to promote progress. The second problem is connected to a phenomenon identified in the sociology of knowledge a number of years ago: namely, that as people move into different language environments their sense of paramount reality changes. Thus, a cultural/ecological interpretation of educational issues and processes has cogency while students are engaged in their first class with me, but as they sit in classes taught from the perspective of the modern epistemology, and as they later work in school settings, the sense of what is important shifts in ways that marginalize both the cultural mediating role of teachers and the importance of attending to cultural ways of thinking in the curriculum that are ecologically problematic. After students have taken several graduate-level classes based on a cultural/ecological perspective, they begin to challenge the deep assumptions that are the basis of their other classes—at least this is what I hear back from colleagues. I mention these issues here because of the need to be realistic about the limited influence of a single course that addresses the culture/ecology connection.

The reality of having students' attention for a minor part of their teacher education program or graduate studies has led to certain insights about the most effective way of ensuring that students will later be able to relate a culturally and ecologically based interpretative framework to their classroom practice. When I first began to introduce a cultural/ecological perspective into my courses I was still under the influence of the modern assumption that the best way of contributing to the students' powers of critical reflection was to expose them to a wide range of educational and social theorists. Thus, my philosophy of education courses covered the ideas of Buber, Skinner, Marx, Dewey, Freire, Nietzsche, Berry, and Leopold. Over the years, as I became more grounded in the literature of cultural anthropology, social linguistics, phenomenology, the sociology of knowledge, and the thinking of Bateson, it became increasingly apparent that there was a basic problem with this smorgasbord approach.

The first and most important problem was that the survey of important thinkers did not allow for the in-depth study of the culture/language connection that is so vital to understanding how the curriculum reproduces the earlier forms of cultural intelligence connected with the Industrial Revolution. Nor did this approach allow for any consideration of the characteristics of ecologically sustainable cultures. With the exception of Berry and Leopold, the other philosophers on the list totally ignored environmental issues, including the need to transform the symbolic foundations of modern culture in ways that would put it on a more sustainable pathway. It would not be inaccurate to say that the most influential of these theorists (Dewey and Freire) uncritically accepted both an anthropocentric way of thinking as well as the modern assumption about the progressive nature of critical reflection. Combining a superficial introduction to the theory that explains how teachers mediate the way students encounter the culture represented in the explicit and implicit curriculum with an introduction to philosophers who were part of the problem, was simply adding to the student's intellectual and moral confusion. It did not take too many years to realize that they would be encountering the same survey-type introduction to Dewey, Freire, Piaget, Gardner, and so forth in their other education classes and that my challenge was to provide an in-depth understanding of the cultural coding and reproduction processes that are at the core of teaching and learning. In addition, my increasing focus on a comparative study of cultural epistemologies, as well as the metaphorical nature of the language/thought process, led to the further awareness that the idea of the critically autonomous thinker is itself part of the modern myth that was, among other things, essential to globalizing the latest manifestations of the Industrial Revolution.

These insights led to the development of a course that takes students from the state of initial shock and disorientation to being able to recognize ecologically problematic cultural assumptions in educational theory, curriculum materials, and current justifications of new technologies that previously would have been accepted on a taken-for-granted basis. The course also establishes the theoretical framework for recognizing how to incorporate into classroom curricula both a critical discussion of cultural and environmental relationships, and what might be called an inventory of ecologically sustainable cultural traditions (i.e., the noncommodified relationships and activities of different cultural groups in society). The title of the course is Curriculum and Culture, and it focuses entirely on the different forms and layers of cultural coding and reproduction that occur in teaching/learning situations. The course begins with an examination of the different ways in which culture is tacitly learned and becomes part of the students' interpretive framework of understanding, as well as how culture becomes reified. It then devotes considerable attention to how the cultural ways of knowing and valuing are encoded and reproduced in the metaphorical language that everyday life is built upon, and which plays such an important constitutive role in the process of primary socialization that teachers mediate. The understanding of how language reproduces earlier forms of intelligence (metaphorical constructions) sets the stage for an in-depth examination of the complexity of tradition, including how this temporal aspect of culture is oversimplified and grossly misunderstood by modern theorists—including educators. The differences in cultural reproduction (including patterns of community interaction, and forms of knowledge that are privileged and marginalized) between orality and literacy are also considered. Particular emphasis is given to the connections between literacy-based forms of consciousness and the modern proclivity for context-free thinking—including theories and technologies. Considering the differences between orality and literacy leads, in turn, to an examination of the culturally mediating characteristics of computer-based learning—including the connections between the forms of cultural knowledge amplified by computers and the globalizing of the modern monoculture that has such an adverse impact on the environment.

Since culture is the symbolic medium that influences every aspect of student/teacher relationships, each of these aspects of culture—how it becomes part of the student's natural attitude, its metaphorical languages, traditions, spoken and written patterns of discourse, and now computer-based learning—is essential to the professional knowledge of teachers. By examining how the different characteristics of culture are related to commodification, time, and a sense of place, a conceptual basis is established for a more critical awareness of the form of culture (as well as whose culture) that is being reproduced through the curriculum. Indeed, without this understanding of the multiple forms of cultural encoding, storage, and reproduction, teachers will not be able to recognize how to bring a critical awareness to the form of environmental education that is part of the curriculum.

As every aspect of curriculum, use of technologies, and pedagogy involve cultural patterns, this course provides the necessary basis for the other ecologically oriented courses that address learning theory, classroom management (what I prefer to view as the ecology of the classroom), and policy issues in education. This background understanding of culture also enables students to recognize what is ecologically problematic about the theories of Dewey, Freire, Piaget, and other ethnocentric and anthropocentric theorists. Students who have not taken this course have more difficulty recognizing what is culturally and ecologically problematic about representing intelligence and creativity as attributes of the individual. They also have more difficulty recognizing how the thinking of Dewey and Freire is based on the same deep cultural assumptions that were the basis of the Industrial Revolution.

While each of the faculty involved in the master and doctoral level specializations has taken different approaches to integrating the themes of ecology, culture, and community into their courses, the changes made in two traditional courses may serve as further examples of how to "green" educational reform. In the course in the philosophy of education, students address the educational issues framed by thinkers who have been primarily concerned with community and environmental relationships. These include Gandhi, Berry, Orr, Dewey, and Leopold. As several of these thinkers do not address the cultural dimensions of ecological sustainability, the writings of the more ecologically oriented thinkers (Berry, Orr, and Leopold) provide an important perspective for building upon the more community-oriented insights of the other thinkers.

The course on advanced psychology might seem, given its long history of individually based theory and research, particularly difficult to change. But a cultural and ecological perspective is clearly visible in the course objectives, which include: (1) to understand the individualistic orientation of traditional educational psychology; (2) to apply the basic tenets of ecopsychology to education; (3) to understand the fundamental connection of the learner to the sustainability of the planet; and (4) to write and talk about the various connections of learning and self-identity with experiences with the natural world. Readings from ecofeminists such as Charlene Spretnak and Riane Eisler, as well as contributors to *Ecopsychology: Restoring Earth, Healing the Mind* (1995) are used as a basis of understanding how a nature/community-centered view of self-identity and learning contrast with the more modern learning theories of constructivism and behaviorism. A strength of both courses is the introduction of a comparative perspective that is lacking in education courses that ignore how individuals are nested in cultural systems, and how cultural systems are nested in natural systems.

If I were to again find myself as the lone culturally and environmentally oriented faculty member in a college of education, the content and sequence of the course on curriculum and culture would be used as the introductory conceptual framework for enabling teachers to recognize how their curriculum reproduces the modern mindset that has proven so environmentally destructive, as well as how to help students recognize the noncommodified and more ecologically sustainable cultural patterns in their communities. But witnessing how each new fad that sweeps through colleges of education seems to represent even more extreme expressions of modernity can also lead to skepticism about whether the dominant perspective can be changed. Identifying and then regularly meeting with interested faculty may prove to be far more constructive. From this would emerge collaborative reform efforts and the faculty development needed to make this an ongoing endeavor.

References

Bowers, C.A. (1993a). *Education, cultural myths, and the ecological crisis: Toward deep changes*. Albany: State University of New York Press.

——— (1993b). *Critical essays on education, modernity, and the recovery of the ecological imperative*. New York: Teachers College Press.

——— (1995). *Educating for an ecologically sustainable culture: Rethinking moral education, creativity, intelligence, and other modern orthodoxies*. Albany: State University of New York Press.

——— (1997). *The culture of denial: Why the environmental movement needs a strategy for reforming universities and public schools*. Albany: State University of New York Press.

Bowers, C.A. and David Flinders. (1990). *Responsive teaching: An ecological approach to classroom patterns of language, culture, and thought*. New York: Teachers College Press.

Brown, Richard H. (1978). *A poetic of sociology*. Cambridge, England: Cambridge University Press.

Colborn, Theo, Dianne Dumanoski, and John Peterson Myers. (1996). *Our stolen future: Are we threatening our fertility, intelligence, and survival?—A scientific detective story*. New York: Dutton.

Johnson, Mark. (1987). *The body in the mind: The bodily basis of meaning, imagination, and reason*. Chicago: University of Chicago Press.

Lakoff, George. (1987). *Women, fire, and dangerous things: What categories reveal about the mind*. Chicago: University of Chicago Press.

Orr, David. (1992). *Ecological literacy: Education and the transition to a postmodern world.* Albany: State University of New York Press.

Polanyi, Karl. (1957). *The great transformation*. Boston: Beacon Press.

Rifkin, Jeremy. (1996). *The end of work: The decline of the global labor force and the dawn of the post market era*. New York: G. P. Putnam's Sons.

Sachs, Wolfgang, (Ed.). (1992). *The development dictionary: A guide to knowledge as power.* London: Zed Books.

Van Der Ryn, Sim, and Stuart Cowan. (1996). *Ecological design*. Washington, D.C.: Island Press.

9 Environmental Autobiography in Undergraduate Educational Studies

Peter Blaze Corcoran

> The role of environmental education in the care of the environment is crucial. What of the role of the teacher in environmental education? Is it not, arguably, the priority of educational and, certainly, environmental priorities, as experience increasingly teaches us?
>
> —Daniella Tilbury

In order to put ecological education into action, teachers at all levels need education, training, and materials. I agree with Tilbury that environmental education in teacher education is the "priority of priorities." There is widespread agreement internationally regarding the crucial role that teachers will need to play in bringing about behaviors consistent with the ethic of sustainability (World Commission on Environment and Development 1987; UNCED 1992). At the heart of this ethic is the mitigation of the impact of humans on the earth and the management of resources and wastes. This in turn affects what political scientists define as the essential issue of politics: "Who gets what, when, and how?" (after Orr 1992, 145). Issues of social justice are integrally connected to issues of ecological literacy.

One of the challenges of the coming decade will be reshaping teacher education to acknowledge the far-reaching changes that must be made if our culture is to become ecologically sustainable. If environmental education is to become the "priority of priorities" in teacher education as current conditions demand, we must consider the goals of such education and the activities likely to promote their realization. If we are to fulfill the need for education for ecologically sustainable action, we must prepare undergraduate preservice teachers through environmental education courses in their educational studies program. The course and teaching approaches described in this chapter are my response to this urgent need.

Environmental philosopher Arne Naess (1973) has argued that a desire to protect the natural world arises from a deep sense of affinity with the land and nonhuman beings that surround us. He speaks of the need to extend our sense of self beyond the limited scope of our bodies and self-centered consciousness to the environment in which we live. The kind of energy and dedication that will be necessary to transform our schools and cultivate values that support the integrity, stability, and beauty of the biotic communities of which we are a part (Leopold 1949) will arise from this profound connection to the world. E. O. Wilson (1984) and others now argue that central to our nature as humans is the experience of biophilia, of our love for other living beings. Such a love is the ground from which emerges a desire to know the world beyond the built environment. This sense of connection needs to be the starting point for the preparation of environmental educators.

In this chapter, I make a case for the use of environmental autobiography in a course on environmental education as a powerful tool to stimulate personal responsibility for a student's own education about relationship to the environment. Throughout the course in which this autobiography is written, I encourage students to think for themselves about the field and what their contribution might be. The course often becomes a personal quest for knowledge and meaning. The autobiography helps make the course personally significant. This assignment tells students that stories are important, and that their story is important. It gives voice to each student. It allows for a critical analysis of the disempowering quality of much education and its failure to teach responsibility to the environment. It invites students to reconceptualize their relationship to their education, to their environments, and to each other.

What texts and methods might assist with this process of reflection and reminiscence? How can adults be helped to enter their childhood memories? How can environmental autobiography be used effectively with undergraduates? The activity itself is nested within the following course goals:

- to achieve a broad perspective of the field of contemporary environmental education—its theory, practice, research, and relationship to other fields;
- to develop a historical perspective and a futures perspective of the field—its roots in nature study and science education and its prospects for future development;
- to extend one's individual teaching skills in environmental education;
- to broaden and enrich one's own experience of nature.

In order to accomplish these goals I ask students to keep an ongoing journal that is a combination of a naturalist's journal and a reflective practitioner's journal on retrospection and environmental education. To begin the phase of autobiographical reflections, I encourage students to recollect childhood experiences in nature that were of significance to them and to consider their sense of place recalled in adult reflections. I ask them to reflect on several questions: Recollecting your own experiences in natural and human-made environments, what kinds of places held importance for you? At what ages? Did you have a favorite place? Who were your environmental educators? In a letter sent in the summer, I suggest that students, if possible, return to places of childhood that were meaningful to them. I also invite students to reflect on the goals of the course. I welcome their early engagement, forewarn them that the course will be rigorous on several levels, and, in particular, initiate the first major topic, childhood experience in nature. The visit to childhood places is possible for many students; invariably they find it powerful. Whether the wild places have been developed into malls and housing or left undisturbed, the return to childhood places, whether rural, suburban, or urban, evokes thought and feeling.

The first readings in the course allow us to consider this thought and feeling more deeply. Rachel Carson's *The Sense of Wonder* (1965) helps students begin to explore the relationship between cognition and emotion in ecological education. Carson writes: "It is not half so important to know as to feel." Carson's sensitive explanation of her educative relationship with her young nephew opens much discussion of the importance of an adult interpreter of nature for the child. Through Edith Cobb's essay, "The Ecology of Imagination in Childhood" (1969), we begin to think developmentally about childhood experience. Louise Chawla's essay, "Ecstatic Pieces" (1987), points to the power of environments in shaping the world view of the child. After investigating more of Chawla's Cobb-inspired research, we move to Nabhan and Trimble's *The Geography of Childhood: Why Children Need Wild Places* (1994), always drawing on the power of students' own recollected experience as children. We review research on significant life experiences (Tanner 1990); doing so allows students to compare their formative experiences with those reported in the literature. We also critique the methodologies and narrow cultural focus of much of the research.

These readings allow us to consider the rich themes of nature as teacher, of the value of childhood memory, of the child's continuity and discontinuity with natural processes. We mine Louise Chawla's work for the impact of environmental memory, of belonging, of identification. Her research and conclusion as to what makes places memorable lead to stimulating discussions about what this might mean for environmental education. Nabhan and Trimble introduce the question of gender and how the experience of nature may be different for females and males. Students' personal exploration of these questions helps them frame research questions of value. We look at how little research has been done. We consider and critique Joy Palmer's (1993) work in the formative experiences of environmental educators. Her research indicates the significance of various stages of life upon attitudes toward the environment and of influential heroines and heroes; this opens up many possibilities. We discuss new directions research might take and what the field might learn.

These early discussions are invariably engaging because the authors evoke the magic and power of the influence of place. Carson's book in particular seems beloved. I try to have students draw out the key concepts and the ways Carson speaks explicitly to environmental education. Consistently over the years, I find students return throughout the course to Carson's environmental philosophy. The purpose of these readings is to consider significant environmental influences in childhood and their formative impact upon later life. I vary the readings (but for Carson) in different years—sometimes using more literature such as Sandra Cisneros' *The House on Mango Street* (1991) or Barbara Cooney's *Miss Rumphius* (1982), sometimes using more research. Students respond to these readings in their journals and continue with their environmental autobiographies, thinking beyond informal childhood experience to the formal educational experiences of adolescence. Reading fictional stories aloud in class also helps to create focus, to share important messages, and to bring engagement to the learning process.

Building community in the classroom is a major element of the course. Sitting in a circle in the classroom has importance in terms of community building, and so does students' learning the names of fellow classmates. This is a way of saying that this is a place where all voices will be heard and all faces will be seen; and nonverbal communication and engagement will also be valued. In taking into consideration the importance of an ethos of caring for one another, students are encouraged to be mindful and to attend to what can be learned from one another's autobiographies. A number of class sessions are held outdoors. Since the assignments require students to delve deeply into their own environmental experiences and values, such a setting is important for the stimulation of memories. Another aspect of learning from each other and about each other in order to build community involves inviting students to write for an audience of the class and make their papers available for others to read. Along with my comments, students are invited to provide feedback, sometimes informally. Student papers themselves turn out to be rich resources for thought and for teaching. Autobiographical sketches from students are presented below with the intent of illustrating certain themes that emerge when students are reflective about their childhood experience in particular environments.

STUDENT AUTOBIOGRAPHICAL SKETCHES

In his environmental autobiography, Jay related the following stories:

> Earliest memories were of the jungle-like garden in our backyard. The tomatoes were red suns that towered above my impressionable eyes. I dug for the carrot's hidden orange treasure. The year my dad let me plant the cucumbers was special. After the summer had raced by I ate the results of a single miraculous seed. One day near the garden I was scurrying over the cap of an immersed boulder. As I peeked over the top I was suddenly eye to eye with the most astounding face. The ancient eyes flickered, set like gems in a scaly armor. The snake's ancient gaze returned me to the age of the dinosaurs. I was frozen with awe. Suddenly the dragon's tongue flared out and whipped my eye. Pain and fear sent me screaming for Mom. Later, I would smile, knowing I had been forever marked with the touch of my fascinating legless friend.
>
> My young mind and body craved the outdoors. Feeling the tickling prick of a caterpillar or the slippery skin of a frog instilled me with so much excitement. . . . At that age I was also very unaware. I thought everyone in the world was seeing nature with the same eyes. Soon, I realized not everyone had the chance, like some kids I knew in the city. Then, slowly, I realized what people were doing to my world. As I began to explore deeper into the woods I found it scarred by people like me. Piles of trash stained the gurgling streams with red. The trails were tainted by discarded metal and plastic shells.

Here we notice the joys and miracle of gardening and the permanent impact that Jay's experiences with nature have had; his memories of connection to place also evoke grief at the loss of what is no longer there. This contrast is alluded to by a number of students, either between the way a place once was and now is, or between a rural and urban environment; it can be seen in stories recollected by Jesse and William below. Jesse's memories vividly capture various sensory images even as the reader is presented a picture of stillness and magic intertwined with a child's attraction to mysteries:

> I am eight years old, a little boy standing at the edge of a stream. I have a fishing rod in my hand. I can smell the purity of the air and taste it as it blows off the water and across my face. I am entranced and amazed by what I see. As an in-

sect glides effortlessly across the surface of the stream, I realize how many mysteries of the world surround me. In my attempt to mimic the insect, I try to place my foot on top of the water and immediately end up with a soaked sneaker. How is this creature doing this and why doesn't it sink? Why can't I walk on the water?

As I walk out of my [current] front door, I am greeted by the briny smell coming out of the Hudson River. A man with matted hair and layers of tattered clothes rifles through the garbage to add cans and bottles to his plastic sack. A waft of sizzling souflaki assaults me as I turn onto Broadway. I pass a woman engaged in an intense conversation with herself, while a silent group awaits the bus under a clear shelter. This is my everyday life in New York. It is a far cry from the stream in Franklin County that I fished in as a little boy. I love living in the busy urban metropolis of Manhattan, but I have always valued and treasured those times spent out on the water in nature. I still feel the same sense of excitement that I felt in childhood. That delicate space between mystery and knowledge is still enticing me.

William, too, shares memories of place experienced with friends. Remembrances of such experiences of nature often sustain individuals like William when living in urban areas:

We had gone to a wetland preserve of the Audubon Society and had already spent the first day waist deep in mud exploring a marsh and a bog. The three of us got into a canoe and we drifted off into the pond next to our campsite. As we glided through the cool mist rising off the pond, Steve told us to be very quiet, and then whispered: "Look over there . . ." We looked over to where he was pointing to see two beavers working on their lodge. It was, far and away, one of the most wonderful things I have ever seen. I was only nine years old that morning on the pond, but I knew at that moment that I wanted to give other kids those kinds of experiences. At the end of the summer I would return to the concrete of New York City, learn how to survive as a child in that environment, and dream of summers, ponds, and beavers.

Like Carson (1965), Erin paints a poetic picture of her experiences with the natural environment—water, snowflakes, grass, birds, sunsets—all become meaningful as she evokes the five senses to present her recollection of the past:

She held hands with nature. She tasted flowers. She climbed trees. She swung on vines. She danced with birches. She found fairy houses. She caught snowflakes on her tongue. She spoke with jack-in-the-pulpits. She made sculptures of clay. She sat in waterfalls. She followed deer paths. She gently touched jewelweed. She held bees.

Every summer she went on vacation for two weeks to the Atlantic Coast.

There she felt the pull of the moon and the tides. She learned the vast vocabulary of the ocean—sometimes whispering, sometimes raging, sometimes speaking of centuries ago, sometimes hinting at things she could not yet comprehend, yet always happening in the present. She felt sand between her toes, in her hair, in her mouth. She felt her skin pulled taut by salt and breathed the sea air in hungrily. She heard the rustling of grasses and watched each evening while herons and egrets flew home to the marsh. She marvelled at their wings and their long, graceful legs. She put her face in marshmallows and ran her fingers through phragmites and searched the jetties for sea stars and watched the endless kicking of barnacle "feet" and popped seaweed. She watched the water in the salt pans of the estuary grow and recede. She raced with sandpipers and she rode the waves.

When she returned home, a bit older, she drove to the lake and waded the shores to see sun fall into water and sky slathered with color. She listened to the quaking of poplar and followed beaver in her canoe. She watched lazy turtles and frolicking kits and inquisitive does. She lay in silence late at night under the stars on the sand, liberated from the world. She held driftwood and pearly clams and minuscule snail shells and heard the lazy lapping of water.

And then there is Eric, for whom care and attachment to place are so strong that he is compelled to become an activist to protect the place he cherishes:

My home since I was one week old has been a tiny clearing on the shore of a small pond in the shadow of White Cap Mountain. In the Maine Atlas you can find me on page 42 and the official name of my home is Township A, Range 12 WELS. On the north shore of First West Branch Pond is a small cluster of little black squares. Those are my parents' camps which we run for what old timers call "sports." Nowadays we call them "people from away" or simply "guests," but occasionally I still catch my grandfather asking Mom how many sports we have in camp.

But anyway, it was one of these sports whom I would say had the greatest impact on my appreciation for and knowledge of my natural environment. Former State Representative Maria Holt has been making an annual spring pilgrimage to Cabin #1 for as far back as my memory takes me. . . . Together we walked the trails around the pond and through woods, seeing, touching, and listening to the world unfold and renew itself after a long cold winter. . . . Eventually, I outgrew mud-dabbling and moved to fight battles beside Maria to stop the Department of Energy from locating a high level nuclear waste dump in our Katahdin granite. All the while the trees in our township were falling faster and faster. Clearcutting had become the method of choice for realizing high rates of return on paper company stock, and the woods all around my home were reduced to shelter strips and the open ground planted to neat little rows of red pine. One special place in particular really hurt me when its trees fell to the chainsaw; a small hill near a camp that we call Maple Ridge had been a source of maple syrup for several generations of my family.

Certain themes emerge from these five autobiographical sketches. The power of the natural as compared to human-made environments is evident in all the stories. Whatever the environments of growing up, it is the "wild" places that emerge as memorable, be they city lots or backyards. Recollections of nature are often accompanied by appreciation of the privilege of knowing such a place. It is quite common for students to report the destruction of favorite childhood places.

There is a sense of drama as students mine their past and recollect their experiences. These autobiographies collectively present multisensory experiences that are memorable to the students: the preciousness of undeveloped land; the expanse of time; a sense of adventure; a sense of comfort; experiencing nature without a specific purpose; a sense of wonder, magic, and mystery, associated with natural things incomprehensible to the inexperienced; and a sense of service. Thoughts and emotions intermingle in their voices. The autobiographies capture how students cherish what is alive at a particular moment in their lives. Often, the memories also bring to the surface a sense of loss and grief for what is no longer there. In their recollections, students occasionally mention an older person who has served as a guide or mentor in showing the beauty or meaning of place. Affection for these lovers of nature is deep and abiding and is often accompanied by a desire to emulate their efforts to preserve it, as shared by Eric.

CONCLUSION

The stimulation of memories that vivify these autobiographies is possible because of a combination of things. The readings, which include novels and poetry, studies and research, contribute by triggering and bringing to the surface memories of childhood places. The classroom setting creates a community wherein students can freely share their stories and their past experiences. And the outdoor classes help students to reconnect with nature.

During and immediately after the course, students express great enthusiasm for the study of environmental education and for the learning and awakening they have experienced. I wondered what they thought years later; so I surveyed students who had earlier participated in the course over fifteen years at three different liberal arts colleges.

What became clear in their comments is the importance of integrating the cognitive and the affective as we consider the content of environmental education. One student valued the "truly integrative, holistic educational experience" provided by the course. Another noted that "The out-of-door experience (as children) greatly influenced our lives (as adults) but it was in your class [that] those childhood voices were allowed to be heard, and valued. . . . It is becoming apparent that fewer people are growing up near access to the great outdoors and I believe that as cohabitants of planet Earth we need this experience in and of itself. If *Environmental Education* as a course brings just one more person closer to the natural world, it is worthwhile. As teachers or anyone working with future generations it is therefore even more important that these connections be made." A third student observed that ". . . a fantastic 'tool' used in the course was the prompting to examine our own experiences and memories for authentic and significant testimony which might have other remained forgotten." Environmental autobiographies provide a vehicle for tapping these experiences and memories. By reacquainting future teachers with the powerful impact that encounters with the natural world have had in developing their own sense of themselves, they become more likely to seek ways to provide their own students with experiences that will instill a love for that world in the next generation. Their words assure me that the setting of even a single course, if thoughtfully and carefully constructed, can provide students with the opportunity to examine the purpose and meaning of their education and their capacity to put it in the service of their environmental concerns. Students need to know how to take effective action based on these concerns. In addition, they must be motivated to do so. It is my belief that such commitment is born of affinity for the earth and its people.

References

Carson, Rachel. (1965). *The sense of wonder.* New York: Harper and Row.

Chawla, Louise. (1987). *Ecstatic places.* Unpublished manuscript.

Cisneros, Sandra. (1991). *The house on Mango Street.* New York: Vintage.

Cobb, Edith. (1977). *The ecology of imagination in childhood.* New York: Columbia University Press.

Cooney, Barbara. (1982). *Miss Rumphius.* New York: Viking.

Fien, John, and Peter Blaze Corcoran. (1996). Learning for a sustainable environment: Professional development and teacher education in environmental education. *Environmental Education Research 2*(2): 227–236.

Corcoran, Peter Blaze, and Eric Sievers. (1995). Reconceptualizing environmental education: Five possibilities. *The Journal of Environmental Education* 25(4): 4–8.

Gabriel, Nancy. (1990). *Teach our teachers well: Strategies to integrate environmental education in teacher education programs*. Cambridge, Mass.: Second Nature.

Leopold, Aldo. (1949/1963). *A Sand County almanac*. New York: Ballantine Books.

Nabhan, Gary P., and Stephen Trimble. (1994). *The geography of childhood: Why children need wild places*. Boston: Beacon.

Naess, Arne. (1973). The shallow and the deep, long-range ecology movements. *Inquiry* 16: 95–100.

Orr, David. (1992). *Ecological literacy: Education and the transition to a postmodern world*. Albany: State University of New York Press.

Palmer, Joy A. (1993). Development of concern for the environment and formative experiences of educators. *Journal of Environmental education*, 24:3, 26–30.

Tanner, Thomas. (1980). Significant life experiences: A new research area in environmental education. *Journal of Environmental Education* 11(4): 20–24.

Tilbury, Daniella. (1996). Environmentally educating teachers: The priority of priorities. *Connect* 15(1): 1.

United Nations Conference on Environment and Development. (1992). Promoting education and public awareness and training: *Agenda 21*, Chapter 36.

Wilson, Edward O. (1984). *Biophilia*. Cambridge: Harvard University Press.

World Commission on Environmental Development. (1987). *Our common future*. Oxford: Oxford University Press.

10 Reclaiming Biophilia

Lessons from Indigenous Peoples

Gregory Cajete

The perspectives of small-scale, regionally based indigenous peoples of North America reflect long-term relationships to place. These perspectives can provide an important conceptual base for the development of a new genus of environmental curriculum capable of addressing the ecological challenges of the twenty-first century. "Indigenous" may be defined as belonging to a locality or originating in a place in reference to races and species that have not been introduced from elsewhere. For indigenous peoples the word indigenous is more than a descriptive adjective: it is a way of being; it is a verb! Indigenous also refers to the perspective that, historically speaking, all people originate from some "place," and that place is ultimately both a natural and soulful place. This chapter explores selected views and ways of knowing of indigenous peoples as it describes what it means to be "indigenous," to be connected to land, community, and traditions of reverence for nature.

By touching upon the "deeper" dimensions of environmental education and the ways "coming to know" and to feel deeply linked to one's place are expressed in indigenous life, the chapter seeks to recover a quality and context for contemporary education that is about and for sustainable ecological relationships to place. It presents an approach to environmental education that parallels the kind of environmental teaching and learning indigenous peoples around the world have been applying for thousands of years. Indigenous education is an education that focuses on the core aspects of human biophilia. It is an education about community and spirit whose components include: the recognition of interdependence; the use of linguistic metaphors, art, and myth; a focus on local knowledge and direct experience with nature; orientation to place; and the discovery of "face, heart, and foundation" in the context of key social and environmental relationships. As such, the serious exploration of indigenous education by designers of environmental curricula can bring important insights into the nature of "biophilia" and its connection to learning in contemporary education.

"Biophilia" is a term first used by Harvard zoologist E. O. Wilson (1984) to describe what he perceives as "the innate human urge to affiliate with other forms of life" (85). This biophilic sensibility appears to be a primal and innate dimension of our humanity. It also appears that the development and nurturance of this sensibility play a very important role in maintaining our physical, mental, and psychological health. Biophilia, however, also seems to have an aberrant and counteracting sensibility called "biophobia," a fear of nature reflected in the culturally conditioned tendency to affiliate with technology and human artifacts and to concentrate primarily on human interests when relating to the natural world. The biophobic tendency is associated with a kind of "urbanity of the mind" that seems to be learned and internalized as a result of living a life largely disconnected from nature and propagated by the advent and development of cities. Because biophobia underlies aspects of the prevailing mindset of modernism, it influences the "hidden curriculum" of modern Western education. Indeed, the evolution of biophobia as expressed in the attempt to control and subdue nature has its own unique historical progression in Western religious, philosophical, artistic, and academic traditions. Biophobia also underpins the epistemological orientation of most Western governmental, economic, religious, and educational institutions. Although largely unconscious, this orientation contributes to the dysfunction of modern relationships to the natural world.

Implicit in this chapter is the importance of moving beyond the idealization and patronization of indigenous knowledge, something that inadvertently can lead to marginalization of the most profound indigenous epistemologies regarding the interaction of human beings and nature. Indigenous people must be supported in their collective attempts to restore their traditions while also revitalizing themselves in ways they feel are appropriate in contemporary society. One of the places where this can happen is in the area of indigenous-based environmental education. As indigenous peoples around the world assert themselves politically and economically, they are also beginning to explore and revisit their ancient educational practices in conjunction with contemporary educational priorities—a point demonstrated by Angayuqaq Oscar Kawagley and Ray Barnhardt also in this volume.

Indigenous people have been touted as the spiritual leaders of the environmental movement. Such a designation is more symbolic than actual since most environmental education is still primarily founded upon mainstream Western education models. Still, many environmental educators, writers, and philosophers advocate getting back to the basics of relationship to the environment and to each other within communities. These ways of getting back to basics parallel the traditional practices of indigenous societies. Recognition of these parallels is appropriate since indigenous peoples around the world have much to share. However, recognition must also be given to the fact that indigenous peoples still struggle against exploitation, oppression, and usually suffer the greatest loss of self-identity and culture when dealing with various development and educational schemes. In spite of this, indigenous groups around the world have a very important message, a message that is related to the message of evolving disciplines such as ecopsychology and ecophilosophy. This chapter relates the connection between the rise of interest in "biophilia" and the process of indigenous education as "a curriculum of place." Such curricula of place are continuing to evolve among indigenous peoples and hold great promise for new models of ecological education.

INDIGENOUS EDUCATION AND THE CULTIVATION OF BIOPHILIA

What are the origins of biophilia? What does biophilia have to do with education? What does biophilia have to do with indigenous orientations? As it turns out, the origins of biophilia have much to do with human evolution and the way our brains have developed through interaction with natural environments. The myriad ways humans have interacted with the places where they have lived and their awareness of these relationships are encoded in their myths, religions, art, rituals, songs, and dances. The most representative expressions of these forms convey the deep emotive feelings a tribal people have for the places in which they live. Indeed, the biophilic sensibility has long been the guiding paradigm of indigenous forms of education found throughout the world. Biophilia forms a foundation upon which humans construct meaning from their relational existence. Indeed, humans as a biological species derive their meaning from interaction with other forms of life, and it is our biophilic programming that motivates us to explore these meanings. Biophilic inspired motivation tends to be most evident in the way very young children naturally express themselves. When left to themselves, young children attempt to establish direct relationships with the living things they encounter in their first explorations of the natural world. Although the biophilic sensibility makes its most basic expression in childhood, it continues to evolve, passing through many cultural, social, and educational filters at different stages of life (Orr 1994, 131–153).

Our biophilic sensibility, then, provides the makings for one of the most basic and potentially powerful foundations for a true educational revolution because it is rooted in the deep levels of our biological nature and psyche. It is up to us to learn about this innate human sense after years of repressing its presence in our modern psyche. It is up to us to reintroduce it in every form of education in ways that will allow its inherently creative energy to assist us in facing the ecological crisis we have wrought upon ourselves. David Orr in his eloquent exposition *Earth in Mind* states:

> The biophilic revolution is about the combination of reverence for life and purely rational calculation by which we will want to be efficient and live sufficiently. It is about finding our rightful place on earth and in the community of life, and it is about citizenship, duties, obligations, and celebrations. . . . The biophilic revolution must come as an ecological enlightenment that sweeps out the "modern superstition" that we are knowledgeable enough to manage the earth and direct evolution. (Orr 1994, 146)

In Orr's view there are two major barriers of consciousness that block grasping the magnitude of the environmental crisis and the blindness of current ways of thinking. The first barrier is modern society's psychology of denial and its unwillingness to admit that science and technology cannot solve the ecological crisis. The second barrier is modern society's pathological lack of biophilic imagination. Current trends toward thinking in terms of technological utopias, continued material progress, and our faith that science will improve human life are not only simplistic and wholly inadequate, but they continue to enable the denial of our innate biophilia and our essential humanity.

Modern schooling in this context is simultaneously a major part of the problem and potentially a major part of the solution. Contemporary education must shift its attention from what in reality is essentially a myopic focus on the workplace to a focus on the "eco-place." As Orr advocates, the first step is a rededication of education to the rediscovery and facilitation of the formational power of the experience of innate biophilia naturally present in children. Children and young adolescents must be provided with an educational context and tools that perpetuate this kind of discovery. The whole enterprise of school must undergo a fundamental transformation to accommodate the development of biophilic sensibility. We must redesign curricula and school environments as ecological learning communities. Biophilic curriculum must be designed to allow children to make a lasting affective connection, a connection rooted to a "home-place." This includes the home-place of the urban neighborhood as well as the rural hometown. Schools must learn how to enable children to preserve their naturally arising biophilia.

This education would take place outside the boundaries and limitations of the traditional classroom. It would be contextualized in local communities or neighborhoods. It would be a comprehensive curriculum that would educate not only for traditional academic literacy but would also educate people, as advocated by David Orr (1994), in the "ecological design arts," which are a combination of perceptions, understandings, and skills founded upon ecological wisdom (148). Orr's orientation closely parallels traditional indigenous education, which was based on immersion in a larger community of relationships, nature, and the unique character of each child. Serious study of the biophilic orientation of indigenous education is essential to the development of such a new and contemporary expression of biophilic education.

Central Characteristics of Indigenous Education

The basic framework for indigenous education is an intimate and complex set of inner and outer environmental relationships. It is this relationship to a place "that Indian people talk about" which forms the backdrop for the development of biophilia. This is not only a physical place with sun, wind, rain, water, lakes, rivers, and streams, but a spiritual place, a place of being and understanding. This place is ever evolving and transforming through the life and relationship of all its participants. Humans naturally have a geographic sensibility and geographic imagination borne of millions of years of our species' interaction with places. Humans have always oriented themselves by establishing direct and personal relationship to places in the landscapes with which they have interacted. These places have also created us since this sort of relationship building is really the result of processes of co-creation.

Teaching about place in this way is not the intent of contemporary mainstream curricula, most of which are designed to condition students to view the natural world as a collection of objects that can be manipulated through science, technology, and human economic interests. Essentially, modern education conditions us for "consumer consciousness" which in turn supports the notion that land without modern human habitation is devoid of real value and is therefore "empty" territory that becomes valuable only when it is bought, sold, developed, and inhabited. In contrast, indigenous education is based on a recognition that human interactions with places give rise to and define cultures and community. The relationship of indigenous peoples to sources of their life and the natural world is reflected in stories, metaphors, and images, and expressed in multiple ways through their arts, through their dance, and through their ways of community. These expressions present a window into a whole context of community, with people, plants, animals, and nature being mutually supportive and reciprocally dependent. Indigenous orientations to place, to "that place that the people talk about," anticipate the evolution of a biophilic orientation to education. For indeed, it is true that, as some indigenous elders may be heard to say, "In sacred place we dwell." The story of indigenous peoples is about the place of nature in the soul of each of us.

There is an ideal that all indigenous people strive for in the process of their teaching and their way of transferring the essence of who they are to each generation. This process is most often exemplified in the life of the elders. In indigenous societies, elders are venerated, not simply because they are old, but because they are embodiments of an indigenous way of learning and understanding. This understanding is reflected in the ways that they carry themselves, in the ways that they speak, and in their ways of being who they are. Indigenous elders reflect an indigenous way of being biophilic.

Indigenous education thus is rooted not only in place but also in the development of a whole sense of being human. The Aztecs have a beautiful metaphor that describes the essential qualities of a "true" education. They say that a true educational process must do four things within concentric rings of broader contexts of relationship. First, they believe that a true education should help individuals "find their face." That is simply to say that each individual should be transformed through the process of education and find that special "place" where reside one's unique qualities of self. For the Aztec, a key purpose of education is to help find one's character, to help find one's identity, to help find one's true relationship with oneself, with one's community, and with the natural world. It is this process of searching for innate and important relationships that helps us define our "authentic" face. A second goal of Aztec education is to help people "find their heart," that is, to help individuals find that particular place within themselves where desire and motivation reside. Simply said, it is about searching for the passion that allows us to energize those things we feel are important. For the Aztecs, "heart" is equivalent to the song of the soul. The third goal is to help individuals find that kind of work, that kind of foundation, that kind of vocation, that thing that would enable them to express most fully who they are. It is an education that helps them to express their face, express their heart, and express the authentic truthfulness of their being. All this is aimed at achieving a fourth goal of "becoming complete" as a man or as a woman (Portillo 1964). It is the interaction and the harmony of these ways of being human that give human life its special quality and balance.

So, this relative state of "completedness" is the ultimate goal of indigenous education. The expression of such "completedness" is personified by indigenous elders and what they represent in the context of a tribal tradition. It is this manifestation of biophilic sensibility that is respectfully acknowledged by indigenous people in their deference to the elderly. Tied to this deference to elders is the emphasis that many indigenous societies place on children as a vital part of the community. It is really a concern for children that motivates indigenous education since the ultimate purpose of education is the transfer of culture and an accompanying worldview to the next generation.

Sources of Indigenous Understanding

What are the sources of indigenous understanding? How do these sources facilitate indigenous understanding? What is the relationship between these sources of understanding and education? These are essential questions whose answers are needed to revitalize the biophilic sensibility through contemporary education. Orientation to place, recognition of interdependence, and symbolic representations in indigenous material technology, art, dance, song, story, and ritual all provide windows through which we may glimpse the sources of indigenous understanding and gain insights into the nature of indigenous relationships and biophilia. This relational education, as it turns out, is among the oldest educational processes, as the paintings from the cave of Lasceaux in France testify. The paintings portray primal relationships. Among the first relationships humans attempted to symbolize were those they had with the animals they hunted. Indeed, all human cultures began as hunting cultures. The first precepts of religion, the first mythologies, the first sense of ecological relationship expressed by indigenous peoples were a direct result of their interpretations of relationship they shared with the animal world. Forty thousand years ago, human beings had come to terms with this mutual-reciprocal relationship and honored and understood their direct ties to the animals that gave them life. Likewise, in that world of forty thousand years ago, men and women understood their relationship to the earth, itself. They came to see the earth as a feminine energy and as a procreative being, a being that was alive. They transmitted their understanding to each succeeding generation through elaborate complexes of myth, ritual, and ceremony. These relational understandings inspired the creation of the first religions, which grew out of shamanistic practices that occurred in the caves and sacred places of paleolithic man. Some of those traditions still continue in almost unbroken continuity in contemporary indigenous societies.

Joseph Campbell (1988) differentiates cultures that relied on hunting from those that relied on planting as representing two different strains of mythic expression. In many indigenous cultures both orientations are represented in the evolution of traditional symbols, mythic themes, ways of dance, and ritual. Ecological transformation, the "hunter of good heart," hunting rituals, and indigenous gardening, each have spiritual foundations that reflect the essence of indigenous biophilia.

The understanding gained from animals about ecological transformation is portrayed in many forms among indigenous people. Each tribe reflects these understandings in its own unique ways; yet, core understandings are similar. The essential focus is relationship; the guiding sentiment is respect. The central intent revolves around honoring those entities that give life to a tribe. Whether it is hunting in the Southwest or in the far North, an intimate bond is established between the hunter and the hunted. There is an ecological understanding that animals transform themselves. Animals eat other animals, and those animals that are eaten become a part of the substance of the life of the animal kingdom. Humans eat animals and are at times eaten by animals, so humans also participate in this primal process of energy transformation. Indigenous peoples understood that animals can teach us something about the essence of transformation.

Indigenous people create many symbolic ideals to reflect their relationship to animals. The essence of one such ideal is captured in the symbol of the "hunter of good heart." Hunting is simultaneously a spiritual, ecological, and educational act. The hunter of good heart is really another kind of representation of the complete man. Indeed, the hunter of good heart is a bringer of life to his people. Indigenous hunters have intimate knowledge not only of the animals they hunt, but also a deep and abiding respect for their nature, for their procreation, for their continuance as species. The indigenous hunter tracks animals physically to feed himself and his family. Metaphorically, he also tracks the source of his life and that of his people. Through the act of hunting he comes to understand on a deeper level his relationship with the animals he hunts. The hunted animal becomes one of the symbolic guides of relationship and community in indigenous education.

In an indigenous community and in the whole process of hunting, there is always a time for teaching. That time is often directly expressed when the hunter brings back his catch. A typical scene in many indigenous communities takes place when a hunter returns from the hunt, says prayers of thanksgiving to the animals he has killed, and then gathers his extended family around him. He then tells the story of the animal which has been slain. He talks about the importance of maintaining the proper relationship to the animal which has given its life to perpetuate the life of the family and community. He expresses to his family why it is so important to continue to understand that life is sacred, and that animal life also begets human life through the sacrifice of its flesh to feed and clothe humans. He reminds all that one day we as human beings will provide the repayment of life through our own flesh for the purpose of perpetuating animal life. The necessity of sharing is also symbolically emphasized through the hunter sharing his catch with his extended family. These symbolic acts of respect and remembrance reinforce the communal relationship to animals that have given their lives for the community's benefit. It is a way of remembering to remember relationship!

Dance, ceremonies, and art provide additional vehicles for "remembering to remember" relationship. Animal dances are a commemoration of our continued relationship with the animal world. Indigenous dances not only renew opportunities for remembering to remember, they are also used by indigenous people to help maintain the balance of all essential relationships in the world. Such is the case with the Yurok White Deer Skin dance, which is performed to ensure the balance of the world from one year to the next. Indigenous people feel responsibility not only for themselves, but also for the cosmos around them. The world renewal ceremonies conducted by indigenous tribal people reflect this deep ecological sensibility and sense of responsibility.

Indigenous people created annual ceremonial cycles based on the belief that acknowledgment of the sources of a community's life must be made year in and year out. Once people break those cycles of remembering, they begin to forget and start doing the kinds of things that have led to the crisis we see today ecologically. And so indigenous people dance the relationship of people to animals as reflected in their guiding stories. They represent the symbols of their life in their art forms, and in the things they use in their daily life. These symbols help them to maintain their indigenous identity and continue to honor their essential life-affirming relationships.

In the Southwest, plants and gardening became part of the way that Pueblo people express these essential relationships. Puebloan peoples learned how to cultivate corn in many different kinds of environments and developed many strains that were drought resistant and grew under a variety of conditions. Corn, for Pueblo people, became a sacrament of life, a representation of life and the connection they feel toward the plant world. It is reflected in Pueblo art forms and in Pueblo ways of understanding themselves as a people. In many Hopi cottonwood carvings, First Man and First Woman are represented as perfect ears of corn shrouded and guided by the Corn Mother who is a representation of the earth mother. Pueblo people express this understanding and relationship by dancing for the corn. During the months of July and August grand corn dances occur among many Pueblo peoples in the Southwest. These are the dances that Pueblo people continue today, representing themselves and their reflections of each other as a community. We are indeed related to one another in many, many different ways.

Another primal symbol related to gardening is the Pueblo cloud motif. This motif reflects the importance of water, water's various states and cycles, and the ecological understanding of how water circulates in a semi-arid environment. Pueblo elders recognized at least six different kinds of rain. They understood that in their arid environment rain was the state of water essential to the maintenance of life and their survival. Pueblo elders would watch the clouds day in and day out. After centuries of such observation they came to recognize the kinds of rain that would be possible from particular kinds of clouds. And they prayed for the kinds of clouds that brought the qualities of rain they needed, whether it was snow, sleet, wind with rain, "baby" rain, grandfather rain, or mother rain. It is these coded understandings that may be found in many Pueblo design motifs and traditional indigenous art forms.

Finally, spiritual orientation to place is a key source of indigenous education. Indigenous peoples honor their place and understand that they are situated in the center of a sacred space, and that sacred space has very distinct natural orientations. They recognize and name the directions in terms of the relational qualities associated with them. For instance, they name North by describing the way they orient themselves to this direction when facing the sun, "to the left side of the sun rising," South "to the right side of the sun rising," East "to the sun rising," and West "to the sun setting." Similar qualities are included when describing colors, plants, animals, winds, kinds of thought, and features of the landscape associated with each direction. Orientation is essential for indigenous people because each is a person of a place. Understanding orientation to place is essential in understanding what it is to be related. Indigenous people recognize basically seven directions, not only the four cardinal directions but also the above, the center, and the below. This way of viewing orientation creates a sphere of relationship founded on place that evolves through time. It is a rich and meaningful reflection of relational orientation.

INTEGRATING THE BIOPHILIC APPROACH IN CONTEMPORARY EDUCATION

There has always been a special relationship between Native American people and their gardens. They cared for their gardens as they would care for their family and community. Their gardens received such attention because they literally were the foundation for their life and well-being. In tending and nurturing their gardens they also nurtured their own life. This is the essential lesson of indigenous gardening. Although much has been lost, Indian people still continue to garden and remember the importance of gardening as a way to come to know what is important in individual and community life. As indicated earlier, plants such as corn, beans, and squash have been given a special place in American Indian mythology. Stories of the origin of corn abound among the many tribes who have cultivated it. American Indians not only have dozens of preparations for corn, but there are equally numerous corn songs, dances, and stories. Indeed, it can be said that for American Indians, corn was a metaphor for human life, relationship to nature, and the expression of a deeply embedded sense of caring for life (Caduto and Bruchac 1996).

Traditions of farming are still strong in many indigenous communities. In many others, traditions lay dormant or forgotten as a result of the interplay of certain historical, economic, and sociocultural factors whose cumulative effect has been to disconnect a whole generation of indigenous people from their gardening roots. A natural place to begin re-engendering the gardening tradition is through the creation of Native gardens. There is a natural inclination on the part of many young people to bring forward their best qualities when gardening, caring for animals, or just being in nature. The garden becomes not only a place to watch plants grow but a direct way for young people to participate in a greater circle of life. As young people work the soil, plant seeds, pull weeds, nurture seedlings, and harvest crops they experience the fuller development of their "natural connections" and participate in an age-old indigenous way of becoming related to place.

The Indigenous Garden Curriculum

The Indigenous Garden Curriculum is based on giving indigenous students from tribal communities with a tradition of farming a context in which they may reconnect to community, ancestral traditions, and the earth. Through the garden curriculum they are able to rekindle the experience of biophilia by exploring the nature of their relationship to water, soil, air, plants, and the inherent meaning of a cultural tradition tied to agriculture. Through their exploration they are able to begin to understand the importance of land-related issues such as water rights and the importance of the wisdom of older generations of farmers in their community. They begin to understand the rich heritage of community, language, stories, traditions, and practical technology that have sustained their tribes through time. They come to understand the important role seeds, soils, insects, and animals play in maintaining the biodiversity of their immediate environment.

The garden curriculum draws upon the philosophical concept of "La Resolana," which has evolved from the work of Dr. Tomas Atencio, a northern New Mexico native, sociologist, and community activist. Dr. Atencio describes "resolana" in the following way:

> Resolana is a place, a metaphor, and a process. Resolana as a metaphor is a philosophy and method for men, women and children to uncover knowledge and learn in "a place of light and tranquility." The foundation of Resolana as a theory and method is the place itself. Resolana is a metaphor for learning and building knowledge. Resolana becomes a meaningful metaphor if one accepts and understands the idea that learning and knowledge-building can derive from everyday experience and imagination; that structured dialogue can uncover subjugated knowledge and add to existing knowledge and as a result those involved in the conversation or dialogue, learn. (1997, 2).

The Indigenous Garden Curriculum is a part of two broader cultural revitalization initiatives entitled the "Poeh Indigenous Garden Project" sponsored by the Pueblo of Pojoaque Poeh Cultural Museum, Pojoaque Pueblo, New Mexico, and the Siete Del Norte Americorp Project, Embudo, New Mexico. The implementation of the Indigenous Garden Curriculum unfolded over a three-month period from mid-May to mid-August in 1995. The curriculum evolved through a process of community-based education, gathering of stories, and work at the community garden site. After a preliminary orientation, participants first researched particular issues identified by the community. What community members mentioned most often was that they wanted to revitalize the traditions of farming that they had grown up with. They wanted to develop a stronger sense of health, self-reliance, and community. They felt strongly about safeguarding natural resources, providing more community-based employment opportunities for young people that would allow them to stay in the community, and caring in some way for the land and traditions of the community.

Participants then created strategies for practical problem solving or advocacy and shared what they had learned with community members and younger participants assigned to them as mentees. Various forms of indigenous gardening and plants were researched to find the best possible combination for the greatest natural yield. These included traditional Pueblo waffle gardens, permaculture gardens, and the incorporation of principles of organic gardening and insect management. Other spinoff activities included the holding of community forums, creation of newsletters, photography, video production, murals, and the cultivation of awareness regarding important issues facing Pueblo communities. The garden curriculum addresses the real challenges faced by many Indian communities to translate indigenous orientations into a new foundation for community renewal and environmental sustainabilty (Siete Del Norte Resolana 1995).

In the implementation of the curriculum, the garden site and community were used as the context for teaching and learning about indigenous gardening, community renewal, and environmental sustainability. This allowed for direct teaching and utilization of the knowledge of community members in a familiar context. Participants also visited other Pueblo communities to share ideas and discuss issues, problems, or solutions regarding the revitalization of farming traditions. As a result of such sharing and dialogue, participants' learning was significantly enhanced. Also, the opportunity to work with younger children in the community allowed older participants to teach what they were learning. Labor in the garden and community allowed for work, learning, and community to coexist side by side. Learning how to cultivate different plants, to manage the irrigation system, to make and use traditional tools, to identify wild plants, and to share in the overall care of the garden allowed all participants to experience the kind of direct learning and teaching that characterize traditional indigenous education (Siete Del Norte Resolana 1995).

Shared experience is the basis of indigenous teaching and precipitates learning that nourishes and reinforces natural connections to land and community. The Indigenous Garden Curriculum offers a context for participants to give back to their land and community. At the same time it provides an outlet for their collective and personal expressions of biophilia. The work with the garden instills in participants the need to preserve natural resources. Participants also experience first-hand the difficulty of raising their own food and the real connection of the tradition of gardening to the community. Learning how to care for and work with the land on its own terms is also an essential experience of the garden curriculum. Participants begin to understand that community is "constructed" through cultivating relationships and that these relationships must be kept up through time. They realize that community requires participation and work.

In summary, the garden curriculum unfolds through the process of exploring an aspect of a community's relationship to place. This exploration in turn leads to a dialogue to gather knowledge, understandings, and perspectives of the people of a community. Then the collected forms of knowledge are given back to the community in new ways. These ways will, hopefully, allow for a new synthesis and understanding to emerge regarding issues or situations that arise as a result of cultural conflict, culture loss, or a modern educational system that tends to educate people away from their communities and innate biophilic sensibilities.

The aim of the curriculum is the wholistic development of the participants along with service to and building of community. This development is reflected not only through the actual garden but also through research projects, art work, newsletters, and audio and video presentations produced by participants. In learning about the dimensions and expressions of our biophilia we are also relearning the connections we have to each other. "We are kernels on the same corn cob," is a Pueblo saying that characterizes the kind of empathy we must once again establish with each other and the web of life upon which we collectively depend. Added to this are two quintessential educational challenges that we must come to terms with in the twenty-first century. These are the challenges of the environmental crisis and living together in a multicultural global society. Both challenges revolve around issues of proper life-supporting relationships. They are both issues of ecology, one dealing with physical ecology and the other with social ecology. To this may be added a third challenge, that of creating new ecologically compatible forms of social, economic, philosophical, and spiritual consciousness. Biophilia underlies the expression of all of these forms of consciousness.

Biophilia lies at the heart of the Indigenous Garden Curriculum. As such, this curriculum may be said to be an expression of a new generation of "biophilic" education. If indigenous communities are able to revitalize agricultural practices, rituals, symbols, and the biophilic sensibility that historically characterized their traditional education then they may truly redirect the course of their future and create healthy communities and environments. Aspects of the biophilic curriculum also allow indigenous people to take advantage of information technology for their own betterment rather than demise. The Indigenous Garden Curriculum is a beginning which moves education in the direction of becoming a true ally in the development of indigenous communities. The Indigenous Garden Curriculum provides a vehicle for applying knowledge from all appropriate sources while revitalizing and applying knowledge that comes from the heart of the indigenous understanding of relationship.

Principles of Biophilic Education

The preceding example demonstrates a number of principles that might guide us in the shaping of environmental education grounded in biophilia. First, such an education would possess a community-based orientation. It would begin with a comprehensive exploration of where a community or tribe has been in terms of its relationship to place. This would form the basis for context and history and focus on community as a firm foundation upon which to build. Such an exploration would lead to a deeper understanding and reaffirmation of the indigenous way of biophilic education and "belonging to the Earth." This comprehensive orientation would firmly embed and legitimize the ways a people have become a part of the land and the land a part of them. It would also recount the way in which the biophilic sensibility has been reflected in the community activities of a people. This first stage would set the foundation for the school-community relationships that would be necessary for the evolution and sustainability of the biophilic curriculum at the community and family levels.

The second part of such a model would focus on the child. It would supply the necessary tools for self-exploration. This stage would also provide for the development of a community of learning. Such a community of learning would engender the development of bonding, caring, and sharing necessary for nurturing biophilic relationships and understanding at the communal and individual levels. The other essential parts of this curriculum of biophilic learning would allow students to turn inward to learn about themselves. This kind of introspective learning is both active and interpersonal in its traditional expression in indigenous communities in that the child learns through interaction with other members of a community and with plants, animals, and landscapes.

The third dimension in this curriculum involves active involvement in the cultural activities of one's community. It includes the exploration of one's cultural roots, which can take the form of making tools, planting gardens, creating art, building, hunting, fishing, or any other daily activity of "making a living" in a place. This dimension would also include a close look at traditions that bind the community through time. Shared traditions as related through story, song, dance, art, and practical applied technologies embody the indigenous foundation of life, history, and relationship. Traditions are the cornerstone expressions of indigenous art, science, and other forms of knowledge. They are the basis of an education for life and relationship in a place. An additional aspect of this dimension includes exploring the connections of one's own spirit to a place, a community, and a way of life grounded in relationship to nature. This is about seeking one's own soul through our relationship to place. It is about searching for, finding, sharing, and celebrating our essential humanity and relationship to all the world. It is the beginning of a journey to "ecospirituality."

The fourth aspect of this biophilic educational approach includes learning through direct encounters with natural places. This aspect of teaching/learning deals with exploring "place" at a micro- and macrolevel of living. It is about tuning into the dance of living process. It is about becoming aware of a natural place at all its levels with all of our senses. It is about connecting to the essence of its living process with body, mind, and soul. It is about interlocking one's being with the "being of a place." It is about communicating with all that a place is—its soil, its plants, its animals, its rocks, its trees, its mountains, its rivers, its lakes, its entire being. Finally at a practical level, it is about learning to sustain one's life in a natural community. This is the essential test of understanding ecological process, relationship, and responsibility. It involves the attainment of a truly mature expression of biophilia.

FINAL THOUGHTS: THE PLACE OF INDIGENOUS EDUCATION IN A POSTMODERN WORLD

Indigenous people around the world express their understanding of place and of relationship through their traditional ways of life. Today, indigenous people struggle with living in two worlds. Therefore, expressing their understanding of themselves as a traditional people through their symbols, art, and education while surviving in a modern context presents special challenges. The traditional designs found on

Pueblo pottery reflect not only an earth-based art form but also a relationship to those things in the environment that give Pueblo people their life. Similar to other indigenous people, Pueblos developed sustainable agriculture patterns and lived off the bounty of the land. They understood the whole concept of sustainability and what it means to maintain ourselves within an environment. These understandings contributed to healthy living because Puebloan peoples believe that health both at the individual and communal level is essential for maintaining a harmony and balance between themselves and the surrounding world. These relational traditions of reverence reflect the spiritual ecology that is the foundation of indigenous education.

Much of what I have discussed is an ideal image that in many cases is more representative of the past than the present. Indigenous people today are affected by a kind of cultural schizophrenia as they are required to adapt to a hostile social environment insensitive to their cultural orientations. It is a social environment that does not really validate or respect those life symbols, those perspectives, those understandings of being, those ways of "remembering to remember" that indigenous people hold dear. It is a social environment that does not respect "that place that Indian people talk about."

I am reminded of a sculpture of a former student of mine at the Institute of American Indian Arts. This student created a clay piece that symbolized her feelings as a young Native woman attempting to be an artist, living in two worlds, trying to be traditional and also modern. The clay sculpture was an androgynous figure sitting in a forlorn position with its arms folded and hands wrung around each other in such a way that the whole form expressed extreme anxiety. To extend this sculptural metaphor of anxiety, the head of the figure had been split in half. Half of the face was drawn up in a smile and the other half drawn down in a frown. The artist revealed a deeply felt sense of being split, torn between opposing views of the world. She captured the feeling of fragmentation and the dilemma that we all face as modern people living in an ecologically schizophrenic world. She tapped into the sense of "splittedness" many indigenous people feel and represented it in her sculpture. This sculpture is the counterpoint of the complete man and complete women who embody the ideal goal of indigenous education. My sense as a native educator is that education must now focus on the recovery of our biophilic sensibility and its nurturance in our children. The education of the twenty-first century must be about healing this cultural and ecological split. Healing this schizophrenia is not just the task of indigenous education but the task of all education. Our essential educational task is that of reconnecting with our innate biophilia. It is the task of each of us to "Look to the Mountain!" and engender a vision of a sustainable future for all children.

References

Atencio, Tomas. (1974). *Perspectives in contemporary Native American and Chicano thought*. Davis, California: DQ-U Press.

Atencio, Tomas. (1997). *Resolana, service learning and documentation center*. Unpublished manuscript, Albuquerque, New Mexico.

Caduto, Michael J., and Joseph Bruchac. (1996). *Native American gardening*. Golden: Fulcrum Press.

Cajete, Gregory A. (1994). *Look to the mountain: An ecology of indigenous education*. Durango: Kivaki Press.

Campbell, Joseph. (1988). *The power of myth*. New York: Doubleday.

Orr, David W. (1994). *Earth in mind: On education, environment and the human prospect*. Washington, D. C.: Island Press.

Portillo, Miguel Leon. (1964). *Aztec thought and culture*. Norman: University of Oklahoma Press.

Siete Del Norte Resolana. (1995). *Learning while serving Americorp*. [video]. Embudo, New Mexico.

Wilson, Edward O. (1984). *Biophilia*. Cambridge: Harvard University Press.

11 Creating a Public of Environmentalists

The Role of Nonformal Education

Gregory A. Smith

Among the most daunting challenges of our era is the task of bringing about the transformation of consciousness that will be required if we are to move away from a culture predicated on consumption and the values of the market toward one that strives to balance human activities with the requirements of the natural world. If we were not already beyond the limits, as Donella Meadows and her associates have so well documented (1991), it might be possible simply to wait for those who believe in the paradigm of industrial growth to pass away and the adherents of more ecologically centered beliefs to assume leadership of our institutions. This has been the history of shifts in scientific thinking (Kuhn 1966), and it seems plausible that a similar process may well take place in other human arenas as well. Much of the activity of environmental educators seems to be predicated on this faith. If we had more time than the forty or so years that Meadows (1991) and others such as Lester Brown (1990) at the Worldwatch Institute suggest may be all that remains before natural systems are set on a devastating downward spiral, we might be able to rely on a process that could be played out over two to three generations. Big changes, however, will need to take place more rapidly.

It therefore seems imperative that people concerned with these issues consider ways that nonformal educational experiences directed toward adults might contribute to the shift in thinking required to engender the new values and understandings needed to live more in harmony with the earth. By nonformal education, I am referring to learning settings and opportunities that are not tied into the acquisition of diplomas, degrees, or licenses. Such learning, for adults, has often been located in the less formal educational relationships found in families, neighborhoods, workplaces, and churches. Specific institutions have also been created to foster these ends. The Highlander Research and Education Center in New Market, Tennessee, for example, has for more than half a century offered leadership training seminars for community activists in the labor, civil rights, and now environmental movements, providing people with conceptual and organizing skills needed to address constraining and oppressive conditions in the South as well as other regions (Adams 1975). Rosa Parks had participated in a Highlander seminar just weeks before she decided not to sit in the back of the bus. Other approaches to adult education have not been located in specific places but have instead been based on a set of common understandings and principles. The liberation theology movement in Central and South America provides an example of this approach. So, too, does the Sarvodaya Shramadana Movement in Sri Lanka. Described at length in Joanna Macy's book, *Dharma and Development* (1985), the Sarvodaya Movement incorporates a systematic process aimed at enabling residents of rural villages to reclaim authority over their communities by developing organizational and social skills as well as value structures needed to accomplish different forms of collective action. In each of these examples, the transformation of consciousness has been a central educational aim. It has been achieved not through a certification process but through exposure to new ideas, dialogue, and in many instances, shared physical or organizational labor.

At the heart of these efforts lies either an attempt to revive indigenous or regional cultures weakened by colonialism and/or modernization or an evolution toward new interpretations and roles predicated on altered understandings of social reality. The educational work that has contributed to these changes is similar to the efforts of Paulo Freire (1973) to help illiterate Brazilian peasants and slum dwellers to grasp their role as creators of culture. Central to Freire's pedagogy is the incorporation of lessons and discussions that demonstrate to people commonly oppressed by traditional social relations that they possess a culture and have the capacity to alter it. Although Freire has been justifiably criticized for the way this process can potentially subject traditional cultures to the same kind of corrosive skepticism and change wrought by contemporary communications media and schooling (Bowers 1987), if citizens of industrial and postindustrial nations are to create an ecologically sustainable culture, they must go through a similar change of mind. The task for environmental educators is to determine how they might accomplish similar ends.

Moving away from an educational system largely driven by economic concerns to one aimed at preparing children to shape and sustain an ecologically beneficent society will require a constituency of adults willing to support a "green" curriculum and "green" values. This suggests that if ecological education is to become widespread, adults and children must learn how to interact differently with both the natural world and its human inhabitants. To some extent, mainstream environmental organizations have attempted to accomplish this end. By and large, however, the efforts of groups such as Greenpeace, the Sierra Club, the Audubon Society, or the Environmental Defense Fund have tended to speak primarily to their own members and to focus the majority of their educational efforts on the dissemination of information not easily available in the mainstream press. They have functioned more as special interest groups than as agents of cultural transformation. Educators concerned about the environmental crisis must find ways to move beyond enclaves of believers to a more ideologically diverse population. Two organizations that have attempted to do this are the Mattole Restoration Council located in the northern California community of Petrolia and the Northwest Earth Institute in Portland, Oregon. Both aim to stimulate the shift in thinking that must undergird movement toward ecological sustainability, and both attempt to achieve this end through broad-based educational experiences that reach out to a wide range of groups in their respective communities.

THE MATTOLE RESTORATION COUNCIL

The Mattole Valley is located in northwestern California just south of Cape Mendocino, the westernmost point of the state. The coastal highway that stretches between San Francisco and the Oregon border was built inland from this area, leaving it isolated from population pressures and development activities. Only a few thousand people are scattered over the 360 square miles of the Mattole watershed. Most live in or near a handful of small towns such as Petrolia, Honeydew, and Ettersburg. The economy has remained resource-based with cattle and sheep ranching and timber harvesting the primary sources of income. Between 1950 through the present more than ninety percent of the old growth forests that had once dominated three-quarters of the region were cut. As the Douglas firs and redwoods were removed from the watershed's steep hillsides, erosion increased dramatically. In two floods in 1955 and 1964, tons of silt filled deep pools and caused the Mattole River to overflow its banks, taking out extensive stands of riparian growth. The impact of this habitat destruction on the local salmon population was devastating. Runs of the indigenous species of King salmon which had numbered in the thousands were reduced to a handful of survivors.

This fact was obvious to everyone in the watershed, but it was a group of people who had migrated to the Petrolia area in the 1970s who decided to do something about it. In 1978, David Simpson, a writer, actor, and social activist who had moved to Petrolia from the Bay Area four years earlier, organized a meeting to address the issue. While in San Francisco, Simpson had worked with Peter Berg, one of the founders of the bioregional movement. During this time, he had become aware of the environmental crisis and the possibility that modern civilization, like any number of civilizations from the ancient world, was consuming its resource base at a pace that could not be sustained. Given these concerns, Simpson organized a meeting of "backwoods dropouts, conscious fishermen, natural scientists, and people involved in resource use" to explore ways they might be able to reverse the dramatic decline in the salmon population. Of particular importance was the participation of Nat Bingham, a salmon fisherman who later became the president of the Pacific Coast Fishermen's Association. Bingham's presence lent a level of credibility to Simpson's efforts. This attempt to reach out to a wide range of people in the Mattole watershed has characterized Simpson's work from the beginning. Rather than simply gathering individuals likely to agree with one another, he pulled together representatives of different interest groups in an attempt to develop a shared commitment to the solution of a common problem.

By 1980, Simpson and Freeman House, a San Francisco friend who had recently moved to Petrolia, formed the Mattole Watershed Support Group (now the Salmon Group). Initially, this organization sought to encourage people in the area to install hatchboxes—devices the size of pick-up toolboxes used to incubate fertilized salmon eggs in streams with heavy loads of silt—in an attempt to revive local salmon runs. In the process of working with salmon and locating hatchboxes in the river, however, it was not long before they realized that their efforts were not likely to make much difference unless they also became involved in landscape rehabilitation, watershed restoration planning, and water quality monitoring. This understanding led to the formation of a new organization, the Mattole Restoration Council, which took as its charge the reclamation of the health of the entire watershed. The Council chose four areas of activity as the primary focus of its efforts: habitat repair, erosion control, reforestation, and education. The breadth of the tasks they had chosen to address required the cooperation of all segments of the community.

Salmon enhancement continues to be the primary showcase activity for which the Council's Salmon Group has become known. The low technology and small-scale nature of this approach has been well suited to its aims. The use of hatchboxes requires members of the Salmon Group to catch spawning salmon and collect eggs and sperm, an activity that provides an important vehicle for community building and education. One December following a major storm, the phone at David Simpson's home rang regularly as volunteers called with the information about streamflow and salmon sightings needed to determine when and where to position that year's temporary salmon traps. The development of successful restoration projects is closely tied to such fine-tuned observations of local conditions. And the task of wading into fast-moving water to retrieve fighting fish can cultivate a deep sense of intimacy with this co-inhabitant species in the watershed. This kind of contact allows Council volunteers to become students of the salmon themselves. As Freeman House writes,

> To enter the river and attempt to bring this strong creature out of its own medium alive and uninjured is an opportunity to experience a momentary parity between human and salmon. Vivid experiences between species can put a crack in the resilient veneer of the perception of human dominance over other creatures. Information then begins to flow in both directions, and we gain the ability to learn: from salmon, from landscape, itself. (House 1990, 112)

From such learning has arisen the Council's effort to address specific problems that threaten the salmon habitat. From year to year, the Council seeks funding to repair a landslide, retire an unused road, or install a fish ladder on a culvert. Limited funding available from the state of California is augmented by local donations and foundation grants. Northern California mail order companies such as Smith and Hawkin, HearthSong, and Klutz Press have initiated a mitigation investment program that supports extensive tree-planting activities in riparian areas and on forestlands previously converted to pasture. Sometimes the land itself provides important information about natural processes. House recounts how after a careful review of aerial photographs taken three to four years earlier, the Mattole Restoration Council mapped a number of areas close to the river that showed virtually no vegetation. It was slated for a major tree planting operation, but when people went out to survey these areas on foot, they were unable to locate the sites. Initially, they thought that something was wrong with their maps. When they looked more closely, however, they realized that during a dry period in the late 1980s, ripe alder cones had been deposited on the scoured channels. While stream flows remained low, the young trees were able to establish themselves. By the time Council surveyors checked these areas, alder thickets four to twelve feet in height had become well enough established to withstand a flood year. House notes that

> The collective experience was so full of meaning that it still resonates years later. Our lives had become instilled with a new sense of time, the time scale dictated by the processes of natural succession. We were learning to pay attention not only systematically, but systemically, over time and space. Our ministrations might or might not be critical, but our watchfulness was an essential part of the healing process. Most importantly, we had received a shared experience of the systems which surrounded. (House 1995, 2)

Experiences like these provide a form of learning that can profoundly shape our understanding of the world, its capacity for healing, and the role of human beings in this process. For example, it was not uncommon for residents of the Mattole River to spear spawning salmon in pools near their homes with little if any thought about the implications their actions might have on the welfare of the species. If the salmon runs were to be restored, it was critical that this kind of behavior stop. David Simpson recounted a story about a young man who was the son of a rancher/poacher. After learning about the Mattole Restoration Council and sharing in its work, he now protects salmon in stretches of the river that flow close to his family's property. Loggers and road builders in the region needed to develop a similar understanding.[1]

To encourage more of this kind of transformation, the Council has taken on a number of educational efforts. At the outset, participants in restoration activities possessed more commitment to than knowledge about the work they had chosen. When they began to poll their friends and neighbors, however, they found a wellspring of local expertise. Nearby biologists, geologists, hydrologists, and natural historians came together with their neighbors to train one another to inventory the salmon habitat, the first of many tasks the group took on. After collecting these data and information about the status of salmon runs, disseminating findings to the broader public became the next task. To accomplish this end, the Council has been publishing the *Mattole Restoration Newsletter* since the early 1990s and issued a comprehensive study of a decade of restoration work entitled *Dynamics of Recovery: A Plan to Enhance the Mattole Estuary* (1995).

Members of the Council have also drawn upon drama as a vehicle for getting their message out to the broader public, both in their own watershed and up and down the West Coast. Two musical comedies,

Queen Salmon and *The Wolf at the Door*, written by David Simpson and choreographed by his wife, Jane Lapiner, have been taken on extensive road tours. *Queen Salmon* explores the challenge of bringing together loggers, fishermen, ranchers, and environmentalists in an effort to save the salmon. One of its most memorable scenes features a dysfunctional family of spotted owls who are told by a psychotherapist that they must go beyond their need for old growth forests. This scene is followed by another about a dysfunctional logging family told the same thing by the same therapist. At one of the productions, a fifth-generation logger was among the first people in the audience to join in a standing ovation. By translating to the stage the conflicts that have characterized their work to save the salmon, Simpson and his compatriots provide a way for potentially contentious stakeholders to laugh at themselves and recognize more important community needs that transcend their differences. *The Wolf at the Door* deals with the necessity to bring together the social justice and environmental movements. It tells the story about a mainstream environmentalist who realizes that his true allies are found among poor whites, blacks, and Latinos rather than corporate funders. In each of these plays, a potent message is delivered through jokes, songs, and dance. Both aim to educate and entertain at the same time. The woman who served as stage manager for the tours of *Queen Salmon* described the play as the most potent form of political action she had ever participated in. These experiences also serve to bring art into the realm of restoration work—allowing people to reclaim a sense of community and common purpose among themselves. From this standpoint, music and comedy are significant elements of the Mattole Restoration Council's broad-based educational effort.

Finally, some members of the Council have sought to influence the education of young people in the watershed in a more formal manner. At the public elementary school in Petrolia, watershed issues are integrated into the curriculum, and children have participated for many years in salmon restocking projects. Throughout the 1980s and early '90s, a number of residents of Petrolia also supported a private high school. Until 1994, the community had no public high school, so this school, in part, arose out of necessity. Its founders, one of whom was David Simpson, made environmental and regional issues a central part of the school's curriculum (Smith 1995). For several years, Simpson taught a course that focused on natural systems and agriculture. He would begin with a study of world and North American geography, eventually zeroing in on the local region. He would require students to memorize the tributaries of the Mattole River in the same way that children in other schools are asked to memorize the capitals of states and countries. In the course of studying the watershed, other academic subjects such as biology, geology, meteorology, and chemistry would come into play. Simpson would also include a study of cultural factors, moving from the subsistence practices of the indigenous residents of the Mattole valley to logging and ranching. As part of this course, students would be drawn into restoration work. During the first year of the school's existence, students participated in the planting of 20,000 trees in a fire-damaged area. Tree planting, in fact, became one of the defining features of the school. In many years, teachers' salaries came in part from money earned from the completion of restoration projects. Although Petrolia High School no longer exists in its original form, it will reopen in the spring of 1998 as a special junior-year program for students around the country who are interested in learning more about restoration ecology and living in place. Regeneration of damaged ecosystems is not something that can be accomplished quickly or done once and then forgotten, so drawing young people into a culture of restoration or reinhabitation is crucial.

In nearly all respects, the work of restoring damaged environments can be seen as educational and transformative. The direct involvement of human beings in efforts to reclaim the health and to bring back the wholeness of their own place has the potential of integrating people into surrounding ecosystems. In the modern world, we have come to think of culture as somehow being set apart from the natural world and of humans as elevated above the obligations and limits imposed by place. Until the past century, however, with its dramatic changes in the domains of communication and transportation, culture was very much a local phenomenon. Language, diet, clothing, architecture, and religion have traditionally been intimately related to particular locales. By centering the work of humans once more in the places where we live, it may be possible to reestablish the link between people and the natural world that has become so tenuous in industrial growth societies. This reconnection seems to lie at the heart of the concept of reinhabitation that undergirds the work of Freeman House and other bioregionalists such as Peter Berg. Berg and his associate, Raymond Dasmann, have written that:

> Reinhabitation means learning to live in place in an area that has been disrupted and injured through past exploitation. It involves becoming native to a place through becoming aware of the particular ecological relationships that operate within and around it. It means understanding activities and evolving social behavior that will enrich the life of that place, restore its life-supporting sys-

tems, and establish an ecologically and socially sustainable pattern of existence within it. Simply stated, it involves becoming fully alive in and with a place. It involves applying for membership in a biotic community and ceasing to be its exploiter. (Berg and Dasmann 1990, 35)

Through becoming alive to their place, humans could reestablish the feedback links that Gregory Bateson (1972) suggested form the basis of intelligence. For Bateson, it is in response to phenomena that intelligence is expressed. For example, when a person is splitting a piece of wood, his or her body responds to each blow of the ax with subtle changes in aim and force until the wood is split. These changes occur not in isolation from the wood but by attending to it and trusting the capacity of our body and mind to adjust to each moment's events. As long as we maintain our attention, the chances are good that we will split the wood without injuring ourselves or damaging the ax. For Bateson, the dangerous flaw in modern societies is that feedback loops between events in the natural world and human behavior have become disrupted and that as a result human decisions have become decreasingly intelligent and more dangerous. By reacquainting ourselves with the impact of our actions and decisions through involvement in restoration work, people may once more become participants in the broader form of intelligence that was the object of Bateson's concern. Freeman House (1995) draws on this tradition when he states that "Environmental restoration can be described variously as an emerging science, as a movement, and as a powerful tool for the re-invention of adaptive human cultures immersed once more in the ecosystem out of which they have risen" (1).

It is this adaptability that our species is in danger of losing as industrial growth societies become further removed from the limitations and opportunities that inhere in particular places. If other people, like the residents of the Mattole watershed, begin to carefully examine their own watersheds and the damage human beings have done to them, they, too, may come to develop daily practices that support a "fluid and flexible response to changing ecosystem conditions" (House 1994, 1). In this way, restoration work could contribute in a potentially profound manner to the shift in consciousness that must accompany the formation of an ecologically sustainable culture. From this interaction could develop the kind of ecological wisdom encountered in traditional societies where long engagement and experience have led people to become functioning, participating members of the land community.

THE NORTHWEST EARTH INSTITUTE

In contrast to the Mattole Restoration Council with its efforts to take people into their watersheds to restore damaged environments, the Northwest Earth Institute focuses much of its efforts on bringing the Earth into the workplace. Founded in 1993 by Dick and Jeanne Roy, NWEI has chosen as its primary goal the development of a group of leaders in the Pacific Northwest ". . . who are well grounded in the habits, values, and actions of living sustainably, and oriented to protecting the Earth" (in Motavalli 1996, 31). The Roys, native Oregonians, have spent much of their adult lives addressing such issues. Influenced by the nascent environmental movement in the 1960s while Dick was a law student at Harvard, the Roys made a commitment to live in ways that were less damaging to the planet. Although in many respects they appear to be solidly middle class in their value orientation, they say that ". . . we never needed very many material things to make us happy" (in Brant 1995, 99). Despite Dick's six-figure salary as a managing partner of the largest law firm in the Northwest, the Roys chose to live in a modest home not far from downtown Portland, drive a late-model Honda, and frequent thrift shops for their clothing.

When their frugality had brought them a modest level of financial independence in the early 1990s, Dick decided that it was time to devote either 100 percent of his income or 100 percent of his time to environmental causes. After watching his wife's more than two decades of work as an environmental activist, he chose the latter. Together they sought start-up funding for an organization aimed at creating "Citizens, united in their commitment to protect the Earth, leading the nation to a sustainable future" (masthead of the newsletter of the Northwest Earth Institute, *EarthMatters*). Dick would devote his time to this work until Earth Day 2000.

At the core of the Northwest Earth Institute's efforts is the facilitation of brown-bag lunch discussions at workplaces and other organizations throughout the region. The Institute has developed three curriculum packages that explore the topics of deep ecology, voluntary simplicity, and bioregionalism. The curriculum packages, developed by volunteers, offer a variety of accessible readings aimed at stimulating thinking and conversations about environmental concerns and lifestyle choices. The stance of NWEI and the readings it disseminates is pointedly nonpolitical. The Roys say that the most important thing they want to get across to people is that individuals can take actions that will reduce the negative impact of human beings upon the environment. When interviewed by Jim Motavalli of *E Magazine* in 1996, Dick said, "I believe that we're now in a window in time that began in 1962 when Rachel Carson's *Silent Spring* was published. By the late '60s, there was widespread environmental awareness, but that window will close when people lose hope. The opportunity won't last. We have to take advantage of the fact that we're human beings now, at this critical time" (in Motavalli 1996, 31). By focusing on understanding and personal decision making, the Roys have been able to gain invitations from a wide variety of organizations extending far beyond the special interest groups most clearly aligned with environmental causes.

Through 1997, NWEI courses have been held in more than 200 private sector, governmental, educational, religious, and nonprofit groups. Although most courses occur in Oregon and Washington, sessions have been sponsored in places as far away as the Stanford Business School, the University of Delaware Composite Materials Center, and Edinburgh University in Scotland. Especially striking is the list of business and government agencies that have considered the issues raised in NWEI courses. CH2MHill, a leading engineering firm in the Western states, has been an enthusiastic supporter of the Institute. Nike, Hewlett-Packard, Columbia Sportswear, Portland General Electric, and numerous law offices and architectural firms have been sites for lunchtime discussions. A wide range of public agencies have also opened their doors to the Roys and NWEI volunteers to initiate discussions around what are often controversial perspectives regarding resource use and management. The Environmental Protection Agency in Seattle has been the site of numerous discussion groups, and staff members of numerous state and federal resource agencies in Oregon, Washington, and Idaho have sponsored these nonformal educational gatherings. Regarding people's reactions to the readings, the Roys say that "It doesn't matter if they agree or disagree. What they are doing is confronting their own value systems and learning from each other. We hope the process helps them decide to take more personal responsibility for protecting the earth" (Thomas 1996, 7).

The curricula used in these courses are drawn from environmental authors such as Thomas Berry, Kirkpatrick Sale, Gary Snyder, or Wendell Berry who have gained a following among the general public. Articles from national periodicals such as the *Whole Earth Review, In Context,* and *YES!* are also frequently incorporated. The articles tend to raise important philosophical and ethical issues in a manner that is approachable to the lay public and do so in stimulating and provocative ways. Also notable in these readings is an effort to include local authors and perspectives that speak to conditions and challenges unique to the Pacific Northwest.

The curriculum packets provide a variety of aids to facilitate discussion. Following an introduction to the curriculum and an explanation about NWEI from a volunteer during the first session, the workplace participants are on their own until the final session of the course (generally seven to nine weeks in length), when a volunteer returns to get the group's feedback. Facilitation of subsequent sessions is rotated among discussion group members. To support this activity, an opening question is laid out aimed at encouraging people to discuss their feelings as well as their thoughts about the week's discussion topic. For example, during one of the first sessions about bioregionalism, participants are encouraged to name a place they feel connected to and describe the nature of that connection. During a later session, they are asked to consider the way mobility in contemporary society has affected their relationship to and sense of responsiblity toward the places where they have lived. For each set of readings, discussion questions, a list of practical applications, and titles of related books or articles are included. In addition, curriculum packets feature a set of suggestions about other ways that discussion group members can continue their involvement with NWEI or environmental issues following the end of the course.

In its first three years of existence, NWEI has been remarkably successful in reaching a sizable number of individuals throughout the region. By May 1997, approximately 7,000 people had participated in 700 discussion groups, with fifteen to twenty percent of these individuals having taken more than one class. The strength of local interest in these topics was evident from the beginning. Following an October 1993 article in the *Oregonian,* Portland's daily paper, the Roys received 600 letters or phone calls seeking more information about their activities. NWEI members in 1997 numbered approximately 800 people. A review of a sample of 150 evaluations of the Deep Ecology and Voluntary Simplicity courses during 1995 and 1996 suggested that for most people, the opportunity to consider these issues with others was positive.

For some people, the courses confirmed their own personal choices and values, encouraging them to continue on with a path that is not always widely supported in the broader society. As one person noted, the class ". . . has given me permission to live the way I wanted to but felt constricted and inhibited by societal norms." The courses also increased people's consciousness about the ways their own decisions affected the environment. It helped them to broaden and deepen their understanding of the environmental crisis and what will be required to address it. An employee of the Environmental Protection Agency said of the Deep Ecology course, "It provided a wider perspective than my own views. The readings also introduced me to books and other readings in an organized way and in a context. I plan to continue to read about the subject and become more active in accelerating wider acceptance of this view of humanity's relationship to the rest of the earth." In addition to personal changes, some participants spoke of how the course—especially in deep ecology—was leading them and their co-workers to think of workplace decisions from an environmental perspective. One person wrote: "It helps increase our confidence around the issues of environmental protection. You must be willing to speak up when people are planning to do things that damage the environment." Another observed, "Indirectly, it will add to our 'greening effort' in the way we will design our projects. It will increase our 'will' to be more 'focused' on our effort."

Perhaps most significantly, these courses brought together people who often felt that they were alone in their concerns and showed them the potential of working with others. A participant in the Voluntary Simplicity course wrote that such a group ". . . creates [an] awareness that we can make a difference—[it] helps me personally not to feel alone in my small ways of helping the environment—every little bit does help. The course gives a foundation to talk to others about a simpler lifestyle and how that will help the planet." After the Deep Ecology course a participant wrote that this experience "[gave] me hope in the world. Sometimes I feel pessimistic that the human race is headed in a path that [means] sure destruction of the earth, and when I hear the same concern from others, I see a light that we could reach if we really tried."

One of the most striking outcomes of the seminars is the way that they stimulate a proportion of their participants to become more actively engaged in the work of NWEI. This has accounted for the spread of NWEI courses throughout the Pacific Northwest. During the third year of the organization's existence, almost forty percent of the courses took place in communities outside the Portland metropolitan area, ranging from Southern Oregon to British Columbia. Beyond the Pacific Northwest, in six regions in the United States and in Scotland, groups are attempting to form sister earth institutes based upon the model established by NWEI. In February 1997, the Great Plains Earth Institute received a $55,000 grant and opened an office in Wichita, Kansas. In an interesting way, NWEI's vision of a more ecologically sound way of life is being spread in a manner similar to the dissemination of new religions, exemplars *par excellence* of shifts in worldview and cultural revolution. It is too early to say whether a worldview premised on voluntary simplicity and ecological balance will have the same compelling quality of religious systems that hold out the promise of eternal salvation or enlightenment, but if the cultural shift required to avert environmental disaster is to happen, the process that will support it may well need to resemble religious conversion.

Over and beyond becoming an active member of NWEI, people who are especially affected by the ideas and practices they encounter in the courses occasionally form support groups aimed at helping members find ways to realize environmental values in their own lives. Members of these groups encourage one another to reduce expenses and make purchases based on need rather than desire. Such groups may provide a necessary antidote to the all-encompassing messages of the market and the media which are dominated by a very different perspective. In some instances, these groups begin interacting socially, creating small communities of families who get together on a regular basis. In an effort to further reduce expenses, they work as well as play with one another, gathering to help each other with large projects such as house painting or building a fence. In this way, members get to know one another in a variety of capacities and begin to form the kinds of interpersonal relationships that were common in extended families and pre-modern communities but have become increasingly rare in the late twentieth century. Such groups bear a close resemblance to the "base communities" advocated by Gustav Landauer, a German social activist and political thinker whose writings spawned the efflorescence of these small organizations based on neighborliness and political activism (Buber 1950).

In addition to these informal support groups, NWEI has adopted a number of other activities that are related to the workplace seminars. In an effort to encourage people to reduce energy use and disposable wastes, NWEI urges people to sponsor what are called "Eco-parties." Organizers of an Eco-party invite friends, co-workers, or neighbors to their home and then NWEI provides a program. Before coming to the party, all guests are sent a checklist about energy and resource use as well as recycling in their own homes. They bring these lists to the party and then learn about ways their host or hostess could save more water and energy and reduce wastes and toxins. A similar audit is offered to people who want to apply some of what they have learned during one of the seminars at their place of employment. These "Workplace Green Teams" are helped to find ways to recycle more effectively, reduce paper or styrofoam use, replace incandescent lights with high-efficiency fluorescent fixtures, or encourage food vendors to reduce unnecessary packaging materials. To demonstrate other ways that professionals and business people can organize among themselves to address environmental concerns, NWEI organized Oregon Lawyers for Environmental Responsibility. One of their activities involved the preparation of a model petition to file with courts in Oregon aimed at reducing paper in the litigation process.

In addition to providing these vehicles for seminar participants interested in taking their experience one step further, NWEI sponsors events designed to attract members of the general public to its ideals. Vickie Robin, co-author of *Your Money or Your Life*, a best-selling book that describes ways to reduce expenses and achieve financial independence on a middle-class salary, offered well-attended workshops in 1995. Joanna Macy, religious scholar and social activist, facilitated sessions in 1996 on ways to confront and use despair in our efforts to deal with the twin threats of nuclear annihilation and environmental degradation. Gary Snyder, Pulitzer prize-winning poet and long-time environmental spokesman, came to Portland to read from his work, *Mountains and Rivers Without End*. In June of 1997, NWEI was the lead sponsor, along with Nike, Portland General Electric, Wacker Siltronic Corporation, and Bank of America, of a conference introducing The Natural Step to the Northwest. The Natural Step seeks to motivate private and governmental organizations to become leaders in the use of sustainable practices. Hosting these events brings additional public attention to the Northwest Earth Institute and facilitates ongoing interest in its activities.

NWEI has also sought to reach out to adolescents by supporting the development of high school Earth Clubs. Many secondary schools in the Portland area already have such clubs, and NWEI is not interested in usurping their place. Rather, it sponsors conferences that pull together students and teachers from throughout the region to discuss environmental concerns and different kinds of club activities and projects. During the organization's second year, grants from three foundations were assembled to create a specific position to coordinate these activities. The person hired to do this work acts as a consultant to different clubs, seeking to help them evolve in ways that will increase their scope, membership, and effectiveness.

Finally, *EarthMatters*, the newsletter of the organization, provides a forum for communication and ongoing education among NWEI members. Published quarterly, it is a rich source of philosophical insights, pragmatic suggestions, and news of the organization. As with the *Mattole Restoration Newsletter*, this publication offers access to information and ideas not easily available in the mainstream media. Regular encounters with such materials serve to reinforce understandings that emerge from workplace seminars and other events and to encourage continued efforts to modify one's lifestyle in an environmentally beneficial manner.

A recent survey by Gerald Celente (1997) indicated that one in twenty baby boomers is now reconsidering the blandishments of consumer society and is taking steps to simplify his or her life. A Merck Family Foundation (1995) study similarly points to a growing number of people who are deciding that the pressure to buy and have more is not leading to personal fulfillment. David Korten (1996), president of the New York-based People Centered Development Forum, recently reported that one-quarter of the population of the United States is ready to embrace a philosophy not predicated on economic expansion and material progress but on affirmation of the values of human community, diversity, and justice. The work of the Northwest Earth Institute furthers such trends and provides a forum within the context of peoples' workplaces or religious organizations where these issues can be explored. By reaching out to a diverse population, trusting in the ability of people to educate themselves and their fellows, and providing models of action and intellectual resources, NWEI serves as a tool to transform the understandings and lifestyles of people who take its message seriously. By encouraging individuals to come together around these issues, NWEI is laying a foundation upon which people will be able to begin making the difficult and risky decisions that will necessarily accompany movement to a low-growth, low-consumption society in which a much higher premium will be placed on mutual support and collaboration.

CONCLUSION

This chapter began with an acknowledgement of the difficulties involved in altering the way that adults think about the natural environment and their relationship to it within the context of a competitive market society. Only if a sizable constituency of voters evolves who support the premises of environmental education and ecological literacy will schools be able to create programs that focus on these issues. What kinds of practices have the Mattole Restoration Council and the Northwest Earth Institute adopted that might guide environmentalists and ecological educators in their own attempts to reach the broader public in a manner that leads to fundamental shifts in values and behavior?

First, both organizations provide ways for people to address their concerns about the environment in a practical manner. The Mattole

Restoration Council draws its members into activities that involve mapping, surveying, planning, tree planting, propagating salmon, monitoring hatchboxes, writing articles, and participating in educational plays. Members of the Northwest Earth Institute are encouraged to monitor their finances, reduce expenses, make their homes more energy efficient, recycle more consistently, form support groups, and reach out to their fellow workers, friends, and neighbors in an effort to spread the word about more environmentally beneficent ways of living. In each instance, the concrete activities supported by these organizations allow people to engage in work (and play) that clearly contributes to the restoration of damaged ecosystems and endangered species or the emergence of a lifestyle based on reduced resource consumption and community building. Although leaders of these efforts are quick to say that the verdict remains out as to whether or not their labors will avert environmental catastrophe, the steps taken by their members are leading them more in the direction of ecological sustainability than if they were to do nothing at all. From this standpoint, the Mattole Restoration Council and the Northwest Earth Institute serve as valuable antidotes to despair, apathy, and the sense of helplessness that can arise on the margins of consciousness when we are faced with a set of problems that seem so overwhelming and beyond the control of average people. Citizens drawn to these two organizations are enacting Margaret Mead's often quoted observation that small groups of people joining together to address common problems can be the source of important cultural change.

Second, by focusing on the potential of self-education in nonformal settings, the Mattole Restoration Council and the Northwest Earth Institute demonstrate a faith in the capacity of those who engage in their work to learn what they need to know to improve communities. Rather than assuming that the grave challenges faced by our society can only be solved by experts, members of these organizations believe they can develop the insights and skills required to address them. Their efforts are reminiscent of a process Myles Horton, the founder of the Highlander Research and Education Center (then the Highlander Folk School), utilized when he first went into Appalachian communities in the 1930s. Initially sent to work as a Bible teacher, Horton quickly realized that the people he had been sent to teach had more pressing concerns. He turned their Bible meetings into forums during which community members were encouraged to speak about the problems they were facing. As they did so, Horton would ask whether anyone in the room could help them address their difficulties, or if not, if they were acquainted with someone else who could. The community discovered that it possessed the skills and knowledge to solve many of its problems. To address those it could not solve, Horton later came back to create a center that provided training in union and community organizing (Adams 1975). The Mattole Restoration Council and the Northwest Earth Institute operate on a similar premise.

A third common characteristic of these organizations is that both strive to draw their members into the experience of a mutually supportive community. Given the degree to which individuals are isolated in contemporary society, this experience in itself can be an important attraction. Humans are social animals who thrive in conditions where they experience care and the gratification that is associated with successful group efforts. Our sense of meaning, identity, and power is closely linked to whether or not we have the opportunity to live and work with others willing to join with us to fulfill mutual needs and goals. If we are unable to contribute to the well-being of others, it is not uncommon for our sense of efficacy to plummet. Much of the depression that is becoming endemic in industrial societies can be attributed to the social isolation of their members and reduced opportunities for active care. The Mattole Restoration Council and the Northwest Earth Institute provide vehicles through which their members' need to care and be cared for can be expressed.

These organizations have also chosen a route to reach the public that is not overtly confrontational or political. They aim to bring together a diverse group of people, and the adoption at the outset of a more defined political agenda would likely turn people away. To be successful in its goals, the Mattole Restoration Council must affect the thinking and behavior of resource exploiters such as loggers, ranchers, and fishermen (and women). Without their willing assistance, the watershed will not be restored. Many of the behaviors that must be altered—such as salmon poaching, road building, and clearcutting—have not been well regulated by governmental policy. Although the state can influence such behaviors, interest group politics tend to make this process contentious and divisive. Rather than seek the imposition of law, the Mattole Restoration Council attempts to persuade the citizens of its region to act in ways that will benefit the common good. In this instance, that good is the revitalization of salmon runs that are valued by most people. By doing so, they are enacting some of the principles of negotiation and mutual respect that are described in Daniel Kemmis's volume, *Community and the Politics of Place* (1990).

Similarly, the Northwest Earth Institute generally avoids taking explicit positions with regard to public policy issues or the election of public officials. Unlike the Conservation League, it offers no suggestions regarding voting decisions prior to an election. Nor do its readings offer much analysis of the way geopolitical decisions and global economic forces are contributing to the environmental crisis. Colleagues with whom I discussed the readings in the Deep Ecology course felt that this was a serious weakness in NWEI's approach. At the same time, if the organization were to focus on this kind of analysis, its work would almost certainly become suspect in the eyes of the governmental agencies and businesses it is attempting to influence. If taken to heart, however, the values inherent in the philosophy of deep ecology or voluntary simplicity have profound political and economic implications. Acted upon by large numbers of people in the public domain—both in the market and in the voting booth—these perspectives could fundamentally alter the shape of political discourse and decision making.

Both the Mattole Restoration Council and the Northwest Earth Institute demonstrate educational practices that contribute to the shift in consciousness that is essential if we are to create an ecologically sustainable culture. By combining an exploration of ecosophical perspectives with practical action, relying upon the capacity of their members to educate themselves and create their own venues for continued learning, embedding their activities in the formation of supportive communities, and reaching out to a diverse population in a challenging but nonconfrontational manner, these organizations have been able to engage a growing number of people in their regions to their activities and draw to themselves state and national attention. Each provides a locus around which people who share elements of an ecological perspective can gather and find others who are interested in moving in a similar direction. A decade ago, I recall hearing a Filipino activist during the Marcos era speak of a candlelight march that was held in downtown Manila during the period before Corazon Aquino came to power. He was one of the first to arrive at a fountain that was the designated starting point for the march. For many minutes, it seemed as if only he and a few others were going to participate in this demonstration against the government. In the middle of a dark night and a repressive regime, the light from their candles and lives seemed feeble. At one point, however, people in small groups with their lit candles began to stream out of the side streets that surrounded the plaza. It was not long before the light they held in their hands transformed the darkness of their city into a wave of illumination that permanently altered the Philippines. The members of the Mattole Restoration Council and the Northwest Earth Institute may, figuratively speaking, be among the first people concerned about the creation of an ecologically informed society to hold up their candles and encourage others to walk with them toward its realization.

Notes

1. In his response to a draft of this chapter written in March 1997, Freeman House wrote: "Loggers and roadbuilders are developing similar kinds of understanding. This is an evolution of the Council which has grown out of the short-lived experiences of the Mattole Watershed Alliance, a truly cross-cultural group which met for a few years in the early nineties. . . . The most interesting outcome of the cooperative work is that we learned as much from the loggers and the roadbuilders as they did from us. When a particular piece of the landscape becomes the context for discourse, opportunities for mutual self-education arise. Ideological and economic differences can be set aside when the focus moves to the land itself and to the particulars of the work that has to be done there. Jay Fraenke . . . has become the premiere road removal artist in this region. He gained his primary heavy equipment skills *building* logging roads and learned the much more demanding skills involved in taking them out through contract work at Redwood National Park. This kind of on-the-job education has the potential for creating not so much an environmental public as an inhabitory culture that puts the learning to work in its day-to-day land use practices."

References

Adams, Frank. (1975). *Unearthing seeds of fire: The idea of Highlander.* Winston-Salem, North Carolina: John F. Blair.

Bateson, Gregory. (1972). *Steps to an ecology of mind.* New York: Ballantine.

Berg, Peter, and Raymond Dasmann. (1990). Reinhabiting California. In Van Andruss, Christopher Plant, Judith Plant, and Eleanor Wright (Eds.), *Home! A bioregional reader,* pp. 35–38. Philadelphia: New Society Publishers.

Bowers, C.A. (1987). *Elements of a post-liberal theory of education.* New York: Teachers College Press.

Brant, John. (1995). Down shifters. *Worth: Financial Intelligence* (September), pp. 98–107.

Brown, Lester, Christopher Flavin, and Sandra Postell. (1990). Earth Day 2030. *World Watch* (March/April), pp. 12–21.

Buber, Martin. (1950). *Paths in utopia.* Syracuse: Syracuse University Press.

Calente, Gerald. (1997). *Trends 2000: How to prepare for and profit from the changes of the 21st century.* New York: Warner Books.

Freire, Paulo. (1973). *Education for critical consciousness.* New York: Continuum.

Goldsmith, Edward. (1992). *The way: An ecological worldview.* Boston: Shambhala.

House, Freeman. (1995). Reinhabitation and ecological restoration: A marriage proposal. Talk delivered at the Society for Ecological Restoration's International Conference, Seattle, Washington, September 14–16.

———. (1994). Restoring relations: The vernacular approach to ecological restoration. Keynote address at the Third Annual Meeting of the Society for Ecological Restoration, California chapter, Nevada City, California, May.

———. (1990). To learn the things we need to know: Engaging the particulars of the planet's recovery. In Van Andruss, Christopher Plant, Judith Plant, and Eleanor Wright (Eds.), *Home! A bioregional reader,* pp. 111–120. Philadelphia: New Society Publishers.

Kemmis, Daniel. (1990). *Community and the politics of place.* Norman: University of Oklahoma Press.

Korten, David. (1996). Corporate America and individual rights. Address given to the Alliance Convention. Hunt, Texas, December.

Kuhn, Thomas. (1966). *The structure of scientific revolutions.* Chicago: University of Chicago Press.

Mattole Restoration Council. (1995). *Dynamics of recovery: A plan to enhance the Mattole Estuary*. Petrolia, California: Author.

Macy, Joanna. (1985). *Dharma and development: Religion as resource in the Sarvodaya self-help movement.* West Hartford, Connecticut: Kumarian Press.

Meadows, Donnella, Dennis Meadows, and Jurgen Randers. (1991). *Beyond the limits: Confronting global collapse, envisioning a sustainable future.* Post Mills, Vt.: Chelsea Green Publishing.

Merck Family Fund. (1995). *Yearning for balance—views of Americans on consumption, materialism, and the environment.* Takoma Park, Md.: Author.

Motavalli, Jim. (1996). Goodbye to all that. *E Magazine* (March/April), p. 31.

Smith, Gregory A. (1995). The Petrolia School: Learning to live in place. *Holistic Education Review* 8 *(1)*: 44–52.

Thomas, Sarah. (1996). Lessons from the earth: A Portland couple takes the environment to work. *Horizon Air Magazine* (January), p. 7.

12 Reassembling the Pieces

Ecological Design and the Liberal Arts

David W. Orr

The worst thing we can do to our children
is to convince them that ugliness is normal.
—Rene Dubos

As commonly practiced, education has little to do with its specific setting or locality. The typical campus is regarded mostly as a place where learning occurs, but is, itself, believed to be the source of no useful learning. It is intended, rather, to be convenient, efficient, or aesthetically pleasing, but not instructional. It neither requires nor facilitates competence or mindfulness. By that standard, the same education could happen as well in California or in Kazakhstan, or on Mars, for that matter. The same could be said of the buildings and landscape that make up a college campus (Orr 1993). The design of buildings and landscape is thought to have little or nothing to do with the process of learning or the quality of scholarship that occurs in a particular place. In fact buildings and landscape reflect a hidden curriculum that powerfully influences the learning process.

The curriculum embedded in any building instructs as fully and as powerfully as any course taught in it. Most of my classes, for example, are taught in a building that I think Descartes would have liked. It is a building with lots of squareness and straight lines. There is nothing whatsoever that reflects its locality in northeast Ohio in what had once been a vast forested wetland (Sherman 1996). How it is cooled, heated, and lighted and at what true cost to the world is an utter mystery to its occupants. It offers no clue about the origins of the materials used to build it. It tells no story. With only minor modifications it could be converted to a factory or prison. When classes are over, students seldom linger for long. The building resonates with no part of our biology, evolutionary experience, or esthetic sensibilities. It reflects no understanding of ecology or ecological processes. It is intended to be functional, efficient, minimally offensive, and little more. But what else does it do?

First, it tells its users that locality, knowing where you are, is unimportant. To be sure, this is not said in so many words anywhere in this or any other building. Second, because it uses energy wastefully, the building tells its users that energy is cheap and abundant and can be squandered with no thought for the morrow. Third, nowhere in the building do students learn about the materials used in its construction or who was downwind or downstream from the wells, mines, forests, and manufacturing facilities where those materials originated or where they eventually will be discarded. And the lesson learned is mindlessness, which is to say it teaches that disconnectedness is normal. And try as one might to teach that we are implicated in the larger enterprise of life, standard architectural design mostly conveys other lessons. There is often a miscalibration between the lesson of interconnectedness when it is taught in classes and the way buildings actually work. Buildings are provisioned with energy, materials, and water, and dispose of their waste in ways that say to students that the world is linear and that we are no part of the larger web of life. Finally, there is no apparent connection in this or any other building on campus to the larger set of issues having to do with climatic change, biotic impoverishment, and the unravelling of the fabric of life on earth. Students begin to suspect, I think, that those issues are unreal or that they are unsolvable in any practical way, or that they occur elsewhere.

Is it possible to design buildings and entire campuses in ways that promote ecological competence and mindfulness (Lyle 1994)? Through better design is it possible to teach our students that our problems are solvable and that we are connected to the larger community of life? Concerned for many years about patterns of resource use on college campuses, I organized, as an experiment, a class of students in 1992–1993 to develop what architects call a pre-program for an environmental studies center at Oberlin College. Twenty-five students and a dozen architects met over two semesters to develop the core ideas for the project. The first order of business was to question why we ought to do anything at all. Once the need for facilities was established, the participants questioned whether we ought to build new facilities or renovate an existing building. Students and faculty examined a dozen or so possibilities to renovate and for a variety of reasons decided that the best approach was new construction. The basic program that emerged from the year-long class called for a an approximately 14,000 square-foot building that:

- discharged no wastewater (i.e., drinking water in, drinking water out);
- generated more electricity than it used;
- used no materials known to be carcinogenic, mutagenic, or endocrine disrupters;
- used energy and materials with great efficiency;

- promoted competence with environmental technologies;
- used products and materials grown or manufactured sustainably;
- was landscaped to promote biological diversity;
- promoted analytical skill in assessing full costs over the lifetime of the building;
- became in its design and operations genuinely pedagogical; and
- met rigorous requirements for full-cost accounting.

We intended, in other words, a building that caused no ugliness, human or ecological, somewhere else or at some later time.

Given opposition of the president, the project sat on the shelf for nearly two years before being endorsed by a new president in the spring 1995. With the approval of the Trustees, the project went forward in June 1995. The terms of the approval required funding from "sources not otherwise likely to give to Oberlin College," and two years in which to do the design work and bring the project to groundbreaking. Both requirements influenced the pace and character of the project. The fact that we could not solicit funds from donors affiliated in one way or another with the College required that the building be designed to be as widely appealing as possible. But no other kind of building would be worth doing anyway. The two-year timetable required that we move quickly to select an architect and design team and get on with the job at hand.

As a first step, we hired two graduates from the Class of 1993 to help coordinate the design of the project and to engage students, faculty, and the wider community in the design process. We also engaged architect John Lyle to help conduct the major design charettes or planning sessions that began in the fall of 1995. Some 250 students, faculty, and community members participated in the thirteen charettes in which the goals for the Center were developed and refined. In the same period we advertised the project nationally and eventually received twenty-six applications from architectural firms with interests in the emerging field of "green architecture." We selected five for interview and in January 1996 selected William McDonough & Partners in Charlottesville, Virginia.

No architect alone, however talented, could design the building that we proposed. It was necessary, therefore, to assemble a design team that would meet throughout the process. To fulfill the requirement that the building generate more electricity than it used, we engaged Amory Lovins and Bill Browning from the Rocky Mountain Institute as well as scientists from NASA, Lewis Space Center. In order to meet the standard of zero discharge we hired John Todd and

Michael Shaw, the leading figures in the field of ecological engineering. For landscaping we brought in John Lyle and the firm of Andropogen, Inc. from Philadelphia. To this team we added structural and mechanical engineers (Lev Zetlin, Inc. New York City), and a contracting firm from Akron. During the programming and schematic design phase this team and representatives from the College met by conference call weekly and in regular working sessions.

The team approach to architectural design was a new process for the College. Typically, the architects do their work alone, passing finished blueprints along to the structural and mechanical engineers who do their thing and hand the project off to the landscape architects. By engaging the full design team from the beginning we intended to maximize the integration of building systems and technologies and the relationship between the building and its landscape. Early on, we decided that the standard for technology in the building was to be state-of-the-shelf, but the standard for the overall design of the building and its various systems was to be state-of-the-art. In other words, we did not want the risk of untried technologies, but we did want the overall product to be at the frontier of what it is now possible to do with ecologically smart design.

The building program called for major changes, not only in the design process but also in the selection of materials, relationship to manufacturers, and in the way we counted the costs of the project. We intended to use materials that did not compromise the dignity or health of people somewhere else. We also wanted to use materials that had as little embodied fossil energy as possible, hence giving preference to those locally manufactured or grown. In the process we discovered how little is generally known about the ecological and human effects of the materials system and how little the present tax and pricing system supports standards upholding ecological or human integrity. Unsurprisingly, we also discovered that the present system of building codes does little to encourage innovation leading to greater resource efficiency and environmental quality.

Typically, buildings are a kind of snapshot of the state of technology at a given time. In this case, however, we intended for the building to remain technologically dynamic over a long period of time. In effect we proposed that the building adapt or learn as the state of technology changed and as our understanding of design became more sophisticated. This meant that we did not necessarily want to own particular components of the building such as a photovoltaic electric system which would be rendered obsolete as the technology advanced. We are exploring other arrangements, including leasing materials and technologies that will change markedly over the lifetime of the building.

The same strategy applied to materials. McDonough and Partners regarded the building as a union of two different metabolisms, one industrial, the other ecological. Materials that might eventually decompose into soil were considered part of an ecological metabolism. Otherwise they were part of an industrial metabolism and might be leased from the manufacturer and eventually returned as a feedstock to be remanufactured into new product.

The manner in which we appraised the total cost of the project represented another departure from standard practice of design and construction. Costs are normally considered synonymous with those of design and construction. As a consequence, institutions tend to ignore the costs that buildings incur over expected lifetimes as well as of those other costs to environment and human health not included in the prices of energy, materials, and waste disposal. The costs of this project, accordingly, were higher because we included:

- students, faculty, and community members in the design;
- research into materials and technologies to meet program goals;
- higher performance standards, e.g., zero discharge and net energy export;
- more sophisticated technologies;
- greater efforts to integrate technologies and systems;
- a building maintenance fund in the project budget.

In addition, we expect to do a materials audit of the building, including an estimate of the amount of CO_2 released by the construction along with a menu of possibilities to offset these costs.

The project is on schedule for a 1998 groundbreaking with a tentative completion date of Spring 1999. The basic energy, lighting, and fluid dynamics models have been completed and we now know that the goals described in the building program can be met within reasonable costs. When completed the building will generate a substantial portion of the electricity it will use. It will purify wastewater on site. It will minimize or eliminate the use of toxic materials. It will be designed to remain technologically dynamic well into the future. It will be instrumented to display energy and significant ecological data in the atrium. The story of the building will be prominently displayed throughout the structure. It will be landscaped to include a small restored wetland and forest as well as gardens and orchards. In short, it is being designed and built to instruct its users in the arts of ecological competence and the possibilities of ecological design applied to buildings, energy systems, wastewater, landscapes, and technology.

As important as the building and its landscape, the more important effects of the project have been its impact on those who participated in the project. Some of the students who devoted time and energy to the project began to describe it as their "legacy" to the College. Because of their work on the project, many of them learned about ecological design and how to solve real problems by doing it with some of the best practitioners in the world. Some of the faculty who participated in the effort and who were skeptical about the possibility of changing the institution, came to see change as sometimes possible. And some of the Trustees and administrators who initially saw this as a risky project, perhaps came to regard risks incurred for the right goals as worthwhile.

The real test, however, lies ahead. It will be tempting for some, no doubt, to regard this as an interesting, but isolated experiment having no relation to other buildings now in the planning stage or for campus landscaping or resource management. The pedagogically challenged will see no further possibilities for rethinking the process, substance, and the goals of education. If so, the Center will exist as an island on a campus that mirrors the larger culture. On the other hand, the project offers a model that might inform:

- architectural standards for all new construction and renovation;
- decisions about landscape management;
- financial decisions about payback times and full-cost accounting;
- courses and projects around the solution to real problems;
- how we engage the wider community.

By some estimates, humankind is preparing to build more in the next half-century than it has built throughout all of recorded history. If we do this inefficiently and carelessly, we will cast a long ecological shadow on the human future. If we fail to pay the full environmental costs of development, the resulting ecological and human damage will be irreparable. To the extent that we do not aim for efficiency and the use of renewable energy sources, the energy and maintenance costs will unnecessarily divert capital from other and far better purposes. The dream of sustainability, however defined, would then prove to be only a fantasy. Ideas and ideals need to be rendered into models and examples that make them visible, comprehensible, and compelling. Who will decide?

More than any other institutions in modern society, colleges and universities have a moral stake in the health, beauty, and integrity of the world our students will inherit. We have an obligation to provide our students with tangible models that calibrate our values and capabilities, models that they can see, touch, and experience. We have an obligation to create grounds for hope in our students, who sometimes define themselves as the "X generation." But hope is different than wishful thinking so we have a corollary obligation to equip our students with analytical skills and practical competence necessary to act on high expectations. When the pedagogical abstractions, words, and whole courses do not fit the way the buildings and landscape constituting the academic campus in fact work, they learn that hope is just wishful thinking or worse, rank hypocrisy. In short, we have an obligation to equip our students to do the hard work ahead of:

- learning to power civilization by current sunlight;
- reducing the amount of materials, water, and land use per capita;
- growing their food and fiber sustainably;
- disinventing the concept of waste;
- preserving biological diversity;
- restoring ecologies ruined in the past century;
- rethinking the political basis of modern society;
- developing economies that can be sustained within the limits of nature;
- distributing wealth fairly within and between generations.

No generation ever faced a more daunting agenda. True. But none ever faced more exciting possibilities either. Do we now have or could we acquire the knowhow to power civilization by current sunlight or to reduce the size of the "human footprint" (Wackernagel and Rees 1996) or grow our food sustainably or prevent pollution or preserve biological diversity or restore degraded ecologies? In each case I believe that the answer is "yes." Whether we possess the will and moral energy to do so while rethinking political and economic systems and the distribution of wealth within and between generations remains to be seen.

Finally, the potential for ecologically smarter design in all of its manifestations in architecture, landscape design, community design, the management of agricultural and forest lands, manufacturing, and technology does not amount to a fix for all that ails us. Reducing the amount of damage we do to the world per capita will only buy us a few decades, perhaps a century if we are lucky. If we squander that reprieve, we will have succeeded only in delaying the eventual collision between unfettered human desires and the limits of the earth. The default setting of our civilization needs to be reset to ensure that we build a sustainable world that is also humanly sustaining. This is not a battle between left and right or haves and have-nots as it is often described. At a deeper level the issue has to with art and beauty. In the largest sense, what we must do to ensure human tenure on the earth is to cultivate a new standard that defines beauty as that which causes no ugliness somewhere else or at some later time.

References

Lyle, John. (1994). *Regenerative design for sustainable development.* New York: John Wiley.

Orr, David, W. (1993). Architecture as pedagogy. *Conservation Biology* 7*(1):* 10–12.

Sherman, Thomas. (1996). *A place on the Glacial Till.* New York: Oxford University Press.

Wackernagel, Mathis, and William Rees. (1996). *Our ecological footprint: Reducing human impact on the earth.* Gabriola Island, B.C.: New Society Publishers.

SELECTED PROGRAMS AND RESOURCES THAT ADDRESS ECOLOGICAL EDUCATION

Chrysalis: A Charter School
Attention: Paul Krapfel
18080 Brincat Manor
Cottonwood, CA 967022

Common Roots Program
Attention: Joseph Kiefer and Martin Kemple
Food Works
64 Main Street
Montpelier, VT 05602

Environmental Middle School: A Special Focus Public School
Attention: Sarah Taylor
2421 SE Orange Street
Portland, OR 97214

Institute of American Indian Arts
Attention: Gregory Cajete
P.O. Box 1167
Espanola, NM 87532

Mattole Restoration Council
Attention: Freeman House
P.O. Box 160
Petrolia, CA 95558

Northwest Earth Institute
Attention: Richard Roy
921 SW Morrison Street
Suite 532
Portland, OR 97205

Programs on Alternatives to Development
Attention: Gustavo Esteva, Opcion, S.C.
Cordobanes 24
San Jose Insurgentes, Mexico, D.F. C.P. 3900

Program for Cross-Cultural Education and Rural Development
Attention: Ray Barnhardt and Oscar Kawagley
School of Education
University of Alaska-Fairbanks
Fairbanks, AL 99775

Program in Education, Culture, and Ecology: Master's and Doctoral Specialization
Attention: Dilafruz Williams
School of Education
Curriculum and Instruction
Portland State University
Portland, OR 97207-0751

Program in Environmental Studies
Attention: David Orr
Oberlin College
Oberlin, OH 44074

Program in Environmental Studies
Attention: Stephanie Kaza
The University of Vermont, Environmental Program, The Bittersweet
153 South Prospect Street
Burlington, VT 05401-3595

Program in Environmental Studies and Environmental Education
Attention: Peter Corcoran
Florida Gulf Coast University
17595 South Tamiami Trail, 3200
Fort Meyers, FL 33908-4500

Program in Teacher Education
Attention: Gregory Smith
Lewis & Clark College
Campus Box 14
Portland, OR 97219

BIOGRAPHICAL SKETCHES

Ray Barnhardt is a professor of Cross-Cultural Education and Rural Development at the University of Alaska-Fairbanks, where he has been involved in teaching and research related to Native education issues since 1970. His research interests include Native teacher education, indigenous knowledge systems, institutional adaptations to rural and cross-cultural settings, and alternative approaches to management and organization. His experiences in education go beyond Alaska to Baltimore, Canada, Iceland, and New Zealand.

C. A. Bowers, professor of Education at Portland State University, has written extensively on education, modernity, and the ecological crisis. His most recent books include: *Elements of a Post-Liberal Theory of Education*; *Education, Cultural Myths, and the Ecological Crisis*; and *Responsive Teaching: An Ecological Approach to Classroom Patterns of Language, Culture, and Thought* (with David Flinders); and *Why the Environmental Movement Needs an Education Agenda*.

Gregory Cajete, associate professor at the University of New Mexico, is a Tewa Indian from Santa Clara Pueblo, New Mexico. He has taught at the Institute of American Indian Arts in Santa Fe, where he was the founding director of the Center for Research and Cultural Exchange. He is the author of *Look to the Mountain: An Ecology of Indigenous Education*.

Peter Blaze Corcoran, is a professor of Environmental Studies and Environmental Education at Florida Gulf Coast University, the newest campus of the Florida State University System that opened in Fall 1997. He has been a member of the faculty at College of the Atlantic, Swarthmore College, and Bates College. He is a past president of the North American Association of Environmental Education. His research interests include the significant life experiences that lead to environmental sensitivity, professional development in environmental education, and philosophy of the environment. He has been active in international environmental education and has worked on projects in Australia, Fiji, Canada, Sri Lanka, Russia, and Kazakhstan.

Angayuqaq Oscar Kawagley was born at Mamterilleq, now known as Bethel, Alaska, where he was raised by a grandmother who encouraged him to obtain a Western education, along with the education he received as a Yupiaq child in the camps along the rivers of Southwest Alaska. Although this created conflicting values, he feels he has come full circle and is now doing research to find ways in which his Yupiaq peoples' language and culture can be used in the classroom to meld the modern ways to the Yupiaq thought world. He is an associate professor of Education and co-director of the Alaska Rural Systemic Initiative, at the University of Alaska-Fairbanks.

Stephanie Kaza is an associate professor of Environmental Studies at the University of Vermont, where she teaches environmental ethics, international environmental studies, religion and ecology, radical environmentalism, and nature writing. She formerly directed the Education Programs at Point Reyes Bird Observatory and U.C. Berkeley Botanical Garden. Stephanie is the author of *The Attentive Heart*, a collection of meditation essays on West Coast trees.

Martin Kemple is co-founder and program director of *Food Works*. He has co-authored with *Food Works* staff *The In/door River Book: The Complete Guide of Integrated Activities for Building and Maintaining A Model Watershed in Your Classroom*; and forthcoming *The Giving Garden: A Step-by-Step Manual for Creating Youth Gardening Programs in Schools and Communities*. He has been adjunct professor at Burlington College and Norwich University teaching courses on underdevelopment from rural Africa to rural America.

Joseph Kiefer is co-founder and education director of *Food Works*, the educational nonprofit organization based in Montpelier, Vermont, which offers courses and workshops to teachers and community organizers for creating integrated programs in gardening and local natural and cultural history. He has taught in-residence at California Polytechnic University at Pomona, and through Goddard College, the College of St. Joseph and Trinity College in Burlington, Vermont.

Paul Krapfel is an educator for Carter House Natural Science Museum in Redding, California. With support from the Howard Hughes Medical Institute, he and his wife, Alysia Krapfel, have been developing for teachers in their region natural science investigations focused on local plants and animals. This work has led them to recently create *Chrysalis*, a museum-based charter school that emphasizes nature study.

David W. Orr is professor and chair of the Environmental Studies Program at Oberlin College, Ohio. He is author of *Ecological Literacy: Education and the Transition to a Postmodern World* and *Earth in Mind: On Education, Environment, and the Human Prospect.*

Madhu Suri Prakash is professor-in-charge of Education Theory and Policy at The Pennsylvania State University. Her study and teaching of ecological literacy has led her to engage in extensive academic and grassroots research in indigenous knowledge as well as the regeneration of cultural practices of peoples classified as "underdeveloped." She reports on these studies in "Grassroots Postmodernism," a special issue of *Interculture* (1996). With Gustavo Esteva, she has co-authored *Grassroots Postmodernism: Beyond Human Rights, the Individual Self, and the Global Economy*.

Hedy Richardson, a classroom teacher for many years, has travelled widely witnessing communal disintegration from modern development. In Guatemala as an in-country assistant to "Doctors without Borders" she worked part-time in the jungles offering medical and other support primarily to indigenous peoples. Disturbed by a perceived loss of meaning in her students' lives and by increasing global homogenization, she is writing: "Hope in an Age of Despair," a Ph.D. thesis on the social thoughts of Wendell Berry and Jacques Ellul.

Elaine G. Schwartz has a doctorate in Education from the University of Arizona, Tucson. She has written on multiculturalism, and also on ecological literacy, in the *Harvard Educational Review* and the *Journal of Children's Literature*.

Gregory A. Smith is an associate professor of Teacher Education at Lewis and Clark College. He has authored *Education and the Environment: Learning to Live with Limits*. He is coauthor of *Reducing the Risk: Schools as Communities of Support* and editor of *Public Schools That Work: Creating Community.*

Sarah Taylor is founder of and coordinator/teacher at the Environmental Middle School in the Portland Public School District, Portland, Oregon. She has served as a teacher and coordinator of support programs for disadvantaged children for more than twenty years. As a certified midwife she has helped deliver over 300 babies. Born a Quaker, gardening comes "naturally" to her.

Dilafruz R. Williams is a professor of Education at Portland State University. She has helped found the Environmental Middle School. She has written on community, environmental education, Gandhi's educational philosophy, and cooperative learning.

INDEX

Printed in the United States
28779LVS00003B/16-24